For Zion's Sake

Yehuda Z. Blum

A Herzl Press Publication
Cornwall Books
New York • London • Toronto

Cornwall Books
440 Forsgate Drive
Cranbury, NJ 08512

Cornwall Books
25 Sicilian Avenue
London WC1A 2QH, England

Cornwall Books
2133 Royal Windsor Drive
Unit 1
Mississauga, Ontario
Canada L5J 1K5

Herzl Press
515 Park Avenue
New York, New York 10022

The paper used in this publication meets the requirements
of the American National Standard for Permanence of Paper
for Printed Library Materials Z39.48-1984.

Library of Congress Cataloging-in-Publication Data

Blum, Yehuda Zvi, 1931–
  For Zion's sake.

  Speeches presented at the United Nations, 1978–1984.
    1. Israel—Foreign relations. 2. United Nations—
Israel. 3. Jewish-Arab relations—1973– .
I. Title.
DS119.6.B58   1987   327.5694   86-47797
ISBN 0-8453-4809-4 (alk. paper)

Printed in the United States of America

To my wife Moriah
and our children
Ariel, Efrat, and Binyamin

For Zion's sake I will not be silent,
For Jerusalem's sake I will not be still,
Till her victory emerge resplendent
And her triumph like a flaming torch.
                                    Isaiah 62:1

Contents

Preface

This book contains a selection of my statements, addresses, and communications made in the years 1978–84, during which I served as the Permanent Representative of Israel to the United Nations. It reflects the main Israel-related issues that arose in the course of my years of service as the head of Israel's Permanent Mission to the world organization. While the United Nations has been devoting for many years a grotesquely disproportionate amount of time to the Arab-Israel conflict, this phenomenon was perhaps most vividly demonstrated during the tumultuous years of my tenure when the Security Council, for example, devoted most of its time—and of its formal meetings—to one or another aspect of that conflict.

The topics discussed include such issues as the Camp David peace process and the Israel-Egypt peace treaty, the status of Jerusalem and of the Golan Heights, the destruction of the Iraqi nuclear reactor, the various aspects of the hostilities in Lebanon in 1982, as well as a presentation of Israel's basic position on such questions as the nature of the Arab-Israel conflict, Jewish settlements in Judea and Samaria, disarmament (including the establishment of a nuclear-weapon-free zone in the Middle East) and South Africa's *apartheid* policies. The introductory chapter deals with various aspects of the troubled relationship between Israel and the United Nations, while the concluding chapter presents a personal view of one Holocaust survivor of that tragic period of Jewish and world history. Special chapters are also devoted to the predicament of the Jewish communities in the Soviet Union and in Moslem countries and to an exposure of the hypocritical attitude of the Soviet Union, which has been a prime mover in the anti-Israel campaigns waged at the United Nations.

The proper presentation of these issues in book form required the editing, consolidation, and abbreviation of statements and communications with a view to avoiding repetition, and ensuring a systematic presentation of the topics discussed. I was determined, however, to retain the language and arguments of the original statements, for I believe that any subsequent changes based on the benefit of hindsight would not only have been misleading (and thus unwarranted) but also would have done injustice to the discussion of the issues treated in the book, which should be evaluated in the light of the situation that obtained at the time.

It is my belief that many—if not most—of the issues treated are basic problems confronting the State of Israel and that, consequently, the views expressed in the book are of more than ephemeral value.

I owe a special debt of gratitude to former Prime Minister Menachem Begin and to the late Moshe Dayan (Israel's Foreign Minister in the years 1977–79) for the confidence they placed in me by sponsoring my appointment as Israel's Ambassador to the United Nations, and to the Israel Cabinet, which confirmed their proposal and thus gave me the distinct privilege of representing my country and my people at the foremost international forum of our time.

Rabbi Dr. Israel Miller, vice-president of Yeshiva University, was the first to raise with me the idea of the publication of this book and devoted much time and energy to its realization. Mr. Kalman Sultanik, chairman of the Herzl Press, and Mr. Jack J. Spitzer, past president of B'nai B'rith, displayed unceasing interest in the book and their support was vital in ensuring its publication. Dr. Mordecai S. Chertoff, editor of the Herzl Press, brought his vast erudition and expert touch to the editing of the book. Mr. Sam E. Bloch, World Zionist Organization Director of Publications, expertly attended to its production. I am greatly indebted to them as well as to many other friends and colleagues too numerous to name.

I also wish to record my appreciation to the Herzl Press and to Cornwall Books for the smooth production of the book and for the many courtesies shown to me.

Virtually all the members of Israel's Permanent Mission to the United Nations contributed one way or another to the preparation of the texts included in the book. To all of them I wish to express my gratitude. In particular I should like to record my indebtedness to my former deputy, Mr. Aryeh Levin (currently head of the Israel Foreign Ministry's Research Department) and to Dr. Joseph Neville Lamdan (currently Counsellor at the Israel Embassy in Washington) for their considerable contribution in the preparation of many of the statements, as well as to Dr. Avi Beker and Miss Ruth Blaukopf, who did most of the research work. My loyal and efficient assistant, Miss Leah Berkovits, not only typed the many drafts of virtually all my statements but also made valuable suggestions as to substance and form. Credit for photographs is due to Alexander Archer, Isaac Berez, Robert A. Cumins, Richard Lobell, Arturo Mari *(L'Osservatore Romano)*, David Rubinger, Yaakov Saad (Israel Government Press Office), Michele

Singer, UN photographers Yutaka Nagata, Milton Grant, and Saw Lwin, and Yeshiva University.

The representation of a state at the United Nations is not confined to regular office hours. It totally absorbs the person holding the office, at the expense of evenings, weekends, holidays and vacations. My family endured the many inconveniences and dislocations arising from this situation with patience and understanding. To my wife Moriah and to our children Ariel David, Efrat, and Binyamin, this book is dedicated with love and affection.

Y.Z.B.

The Hebrew University
Mount Scopus, Jerusalem
Festival of Chanukah 5747/December 1986

For Zion's Sake

1

Israel and the United Nations

A

The Basic Position

I

Statement made on the presentation of credentials to the Secretary-General of the UN on 5 September 1978, and excerpt from statement of 23 July 1980 in the UN General Assembly.

It is an honor to serve my country and my people in this Organization, the Charter of which espouses those universal principles which were first proclaimed in Jerusalem almost three thousand years ago by the prophets of Israel: the equality and brotherhood of man, the intrinsic dignity and value of the human being, and the ideals of social justice and eternal peace among nations.

It is thus fitting that the words of Isaiah proclaiming the ideal of beating swords into plowshares—the idea of total and general disarmament in United Nations parlance—grace the Isaiah Wall across the street, so as to serve as a kind of motto for this Organization.

It is a privilege to serve as the representative of Israel in this world body for yet another reason. It is all too often forgotten that the United Nations is the product of the great war-time coalition that came into being to fight the forces of nazism and fascism, the enemies of mankind, of human progress and decency. Those forces of evil and hatred singled out the Jewish people as their prime target, just as the forces of hatred have done throughout history.

While they inflicted untold misery and destruction upon the whole world, there can be little doubt that the main victim of their genocidal practices was the Jewish people. It was thus only natural that Jews the world over rallied to the cause of the United Nations which fought the Nazi-Fascist scourge. More than one and one-half million of them fought in the ranks of the Allied forces that eventually crushed the Axis powers and brought this Organization into being. These facts appear now to be forgotten in the United Nations.

Unfortunately, in recent years the United Nations has departed very considerably from its goals and principles. No doubt there are many reasons for this development, but the one that probably stands out most clearly is the fact that the United Nations is now dominated by a coalition of dictatorships and totalitarian regimes that have suppressed human rights and the rule of law in their own countries, while at the same time pretending to champion those very causes in the international arena. We are thus being treated in the United Nations to the preposterous spectacle of states who have made a mockery of parliamentary democracy at home, professing their devotion to its principles internationally. As long as this situation persists, it is difficult to see how the steady decline in the standing and prestige of the United Nations can be checked.

It is my distinct privilege to represent in this Organization one of the oldest nations on earth. In our long history, we have repeatedly been assailed by those who are opposed to the ideals and values which the Jewish people has bequeathed to mankind and which we have epitomized in our very being. Never in our long history have we been confounded by the overwhelming odds confronting us. Never in our long history have we been intimidated into forsaking the values that we stand for or into compromising our national integrity.

We will not be in any way deterred by the cacophonous chorus of our detractors or by the forest of arms raised in support of immoral and unfair resolutions flying in the face of truth and justice. It surely would be absurd to think that a people with the past and depth of experience of my people can be browbeaten by the howls of cynics, bigots, hypocrites and opportunists. Israel will not be deflected. Irsael will not give up its resolve.

II

Excerpts from address at the sixty-fifth National Commission meeting of the Anti-Defamation League of B'nai B'rith, at the Hilton Hotel, New York, on 17 November 1978.

Why is it that the United Nations has strayed so far from its own Charter and principles? And what attitude should Israel adopt toward the world organization? It is my contention that we must make a crucial distinction here. Israel fully supports and endorses the philosophy of the United Nations and the principles enunciated in its Charter. It could not be otherwise. For the world organization was created, in the aftermath of the greatest holocaust ever to afflict mankind, in order to translate into practice the universal principles of peace and justice first proclaimed in Jerusalem by the prophets of Israel nearly three thousand years ago. Israel and the Jewish people unreservedly support all these principles proclaimed by the UN Charter, for they are all deeply ingrained in our faith, beliefs and tradition. Indeed, it is precisely *because* we identify so strongly with those ideals that we have been and will continue to be the most vigorous critics of any attempt to subvert the United Nations Charter and to turn the world organization away from its principles and purposes.

When the king of Thebes in Sophocles' *Antigone* accuses his own son of turning against him and taking Antigone's side against his own autocratic authority, the son replies: "Nay Sire, It is for *you* that I am fighting." The tragedy of the play is not so much the fate of the righteous and pious Antigone as the self-destruction of the king who has abused and misused his authority.

What we oppose is precisely the departure by the United Nations from its Charter and ideals, a departure that has so severely eroded the standing of the world organization in recent years.

The list of deliberate violations and abuses of both the letter and spirit of the UN Charter is long, and I will not burden you with a long recitation. What is clear, however, is that the automatic majority which has slowly but surely gnawed away at the ideals and principles of the world organization, pays not the slightest attention to the legality of its actions. These actions have undermined not only the standing and prestige of the United Nations, but that of international law itself.

What can one say about an organization whose Commission on Human Rights annually condemns Israel for every crime in the book, and refuses to denounce the massacres in Uganda and Cambodia? What can we say about such a body when Uganda itself is a full-fledged member of the thirty-two-member UN Commission on Human Rights along with such other stalwart defenders of human rights as the Soviet Union, Libya, Syria, Cuba and Pakistan? What can we say of a body charged with investigating violations of human rights throughout the world, when, according to *The Washington Post*, three-quarters of its own members are guilty of massive violations of human rights? What is damaged by such an abuse is not only the United Nations, but the very concept of a universal monitoring of human rights violations. If the Commission on Human Rights' main function is to cover up rather than expose such violations, tyrants and dictators throughout the world will sleep easier, their barbarism in a sense legitimized by the United Nations itself.

Here we come to the greatest and most flagrant abuse of all. The United Nations Charter forthrightly and unambiguously proclaims the principle of universality. In articles 55 and 56 of the Charter of the United Nations, "all members pledge themselves to take joint and separate action" to promote "*universal* respect for, and observance of, human rights and fundamental freedoms for all." Indeed, the document in which these freedoms are defined is called the "*Universal* Declaration of Human Rights," and every one of the thirty articles which make up that declaration begins with an affirmation of the principle of *universality.*

The meaning is clear and unambiguous—the application of one universal standard whenever and wherever human rights are violated in any part of the world. By converting universality in principle to selectiveness in practice, the automatic majority has perverted both the letter and the spirit of the United Nations Charter and disqualified itself from making judgments on questions of human rights. Those members who persist in singling out Israel for condemnation while ignoring the massacres in Cambodia and Lebanon, the persecution of dissidents in Soviet-bloc countries, the elimination of minorities in Uganda and Iraq and other grave violations of human rights throughout the world, have done a grave disservice to the noble principles on which the world organization rests. Those who annually attack Israel for trading with South Africa while their own trade with that country dwarfs that of Israel, have similarly violated the principle of universality and under-mined the entire campaign against *apartheid*. Israel is not afraid of being judged. But let the same standard apply to all, including those who sit in judgment on us.

Constitutions are generally adopted with a view to safeguarding the interests of the weak, and any tampering with such basic instruments ad-versely affects those interests. Since the United Nations consists over-whelmingly of small states, it would be in the best interests of that majority to insist on the preservation of the Charter and of the rule of law, rather than on their subversion. Any illusory short-term benefits gained from disregard of the Charter are more than offset by the long-term damage caused to the interests of the violators themselves. The big powers have other means of safeguarding their rights and interests. It is precisely the small countries who depend most on the sanctity of law in international relations to preserve their national interests and who would have most to gain by a return to constitu-tional legality and a consequent strengthening of the United Nations.

Can the decline be reversed? Can the increasingly alarming discrepancy between United Nations principles and practice be narrowed? I am afraid the prognosis is not encouraging. We are being treated in the United Nations to the preposterous spectacle of a majority which has made a mockery of the principles of parliamentary democracy at home, professing its devotion to those principles internationally. As long as this standard persists, it is diffi-cult to see how the steady decline in the standing and prestige of the United Nations can be checked.

B

The Double Standard Practiced against Israel at the United Nations

I

Excerpts from statement made in the UN General Assembly on 23 July 1980.

There is the world of reality—and there is the world of the United Nations.

There is the UN Charter—and there is its persistent violation by the majority within this Organization.

There are the rules of procedure of the General Assembly—and there are the arbitrary procedures applied to every aspect of the Arab-Israel conflict.

There are the indisputable facts of that conflict—and there is the complete distortion of those facts in the documents, deliberations and resolutions of the United Nations.

There is a balanced and practical approach to peace-making in the Middle East—and there is a concerted campaign to frustrate the peace process through the United Nations and thus prolong the conflict in the Middle East.

Anyone reviewing the business of the United Nations in recent years would be bound to conclude that there are hardly any international crises or threats to peace and security in the world other than the Arab-Israel conflict. The Soviet Union has withdrawn from Afghanistan. Its troops have stopped slaughtering thousands of ordinary Afghanis. Sweetness and light radiate from Southeast Asia. There are no threats to the sovereignty, national independence and territorial integrity of states in that region. The huge flow of refugees from Vietnam and Cambodia has ceased. A hundred and twenty thousand individuals were not driven out recently from Cuba and turned into refugees. All has been and remains quiet in Africa, from the top to the bottom of that continent, including the Sahara, the Maghreb and the Horn of Africa. In the Middle East, there are no tensions between Iran and Iraq. The two Yemens have been acting as model neighbors. The Syrian army of occupation has pulled back from Lebanon. Stability and tranquility reign in the north of that war-torn country. International terrorism, with its concomitant features of indiscriminate murder and the taking of hostages, has been brought under control. Apparently, were it not for Israel, international harmony would reign over all, and it is only Israel that prevents the advent of the Messianic era.

Indeed, from the apparent dearth of emergencies throughout the world, the outside observer might even conclude that the human condition is a happy one. But as we all know, nothing could be further from the truth. When one looks at the vast assemblage of nations gathered here and tries to compute the sum total of human misery that most of them represent one is forced to a quite different conclusion. Indeed, as one contemplates the very real threats to the existence of literally hundreds of millions of human beings, the wars, the lack of freedom, the brutal suppression of minorities, the mass death sentences, the persecution and torture of dissidents, the cruelty and the degradation, the disease, the malnutrition and the poverty in the world today, one can only conclude that the lawless majority of this Assembly shamelessly turns its back on the real problems facing mankind by indulging so much of its time in barren, anti-Israel exercises.

The fact is that many of the states represented here regularly violate every human standard and international norm in the conduct of their affairs, both domestic and external. They regularly practice every crime that they mendaciously attribute to Israel. The international crimes and the threats to peace persistently perpetrated by totalitarian and dictatorial regimes which rush to harass Israel are legion, yet the General Assembly passes over them in silence.

The reason for this hypocrisy, cynicism and bias is not hard to explain. In everything to do with the Arab-Israel conflict, a majority of this Assembly lets itself be led—in some cases willingly, in others under duress—by a coalition of extreme Arab states, in conjunction with the Soviet Union, its satellites and the radicals in the Non-Aligned Group of countries.

Virtually all the Arab states are still obsessed with Israel. Most of them still refuse to recognize Israel and its right to exist. Most of them are still committed to the destruction of Israel, and to the use of "all means" to achieve that objective. Among these "means" are the manipulation of this Organization, the monopolization of its time, the abuse of its means and machinery, and even the harnessing of the Secretariat, so that the whole UN system can be exploited in the relentless Arab campaign of political warfare against Israel.

Those who seem to think that an orgy of special reports, special committees, special missions, special sessions, special units, special forces and special agencies can resolve anything, have lost touch with reality. There is nothing special or magical about any of these. In the final analysis, they will not change anything on the ground. They will not bring peace in the Middle East any closer.

II

Letter dated 25 August 1983, addressed to the Secretary-General of the United Nations concerning the alleged "poisoning" by Israel of Arab high-school girls in Judea and Samaria.

At the meeting of the Security Council on 28 July 1983, the Permanent Representative of Jordan referred to what he called "cases of mass poisoning which mysteriously occurred among schoolgirls in the West Bank last February . . ."

At the same meeting of the Security Council, the Permanent Representative of Democratic Yemen, addressing the same issue, stated that "students in cities of the West Bank have been poisoned."

As Your Excellency will recall, towards the end of March 1983, a series of false reports and accusations began to circulate concerning an outbreak of headaches, dizziness and nausea among female high school students in various localities in Judea and Samaria. The Israel medical authorities, who immediately instituted an inquiry into the matter, could not establish the existence of any organic cause.

This fact notwithstanding, various Arab Governments and media, as well as Arab representatives to the United Nations, used that occasion to mount a renewed attack in their relentless campaign of vilification against Israel.

Thus, the representative of Iraq, in his capacity as Chairman of the Arab Group for the month of March, in a letter to the President of the Security Council dated 29 March 1983, stated that "Israeli terrorism has reached the point of the implementation of schemes for the collective poisoning of students and inhabitants."

Not content with this misstatement of the facts, the representative of Iraq, in a further letter dated 31 March 1983, asserted that "these poisoning cases were not coincidental. They were caused by a yellow substance containing sulphur concentrates which emitted poisonous gases with dangerous physical and psychological consequences as well as other possible consequences."

Similarly, the representative of Jordan in his letter to the President of the Security Council dated 29 March 1983 referred to "collective poisoning to which more than 1,000 Palestinian schoolgirls were exposed."

The Permanent Representative of the Syrian Arab Republic, speaking in the Security Council on 29 March 1983, in the debate on the situation in Nicaragua, compounded the above-mentioned allegations when he told the Council that Israel "exercises genocide against the Arabs . . . and even poisons their schoolchildren. . . . Poisonous gases are used on Arab schools in the West Bank. . . . What is the use of murdering and poisoning our schoolchildren? . . ."

The representative of Senegal, as Chairman of the Committee on the Exercise of the Inalienable Rights of the Palestinian People, saw fit to follow suit, and in a letter addressed to Your Excellency dated 30 March 1983, alluded to the "reported illness among Arab schoolgirls. . . . Local residents believe the illness to have been induced by some kind of poison, perhaps even gas poisoning."

Against this background of ongoing false allegations, I sent a letter to the President of the Security Council on 3 April 1983, in which I stated that the Israel medical authorities were undertaking a comprehensive examination of the causes of the above-mentioned symptoms. I also emphasized that the Israel Ministry of Health had decided to request an independent assessment of the causes of the above-mentioned phenomenon, to be undertaken by international health authorities, and that Israel had approached the International Committee of the Red Cross in this regard.

I also pointed out in the same letter that, reporting on that organization's findings on 3 April 1983, Dr. Franz Altherr, representative of the International Committee of the Red Cross, had stated that it was his impression that there was no indication of the existence of poisonous agents. It was Dr. Altherr's feeling that this was a mass phenomenon without any organic basis.

In the same letter, I also informed the President of the Security Council that, in further efforts to obtain impartial and internationally-recognized medical opinion, Israel had approached the United States Centers for Disease Control, at Atlanta, Georgia, and the World Health Organization and that experts of both bodies were then due to arrive in Israel.

Even before the arrival in Israel of the representatives of the World Health Organization and the Centers for Disease Control, the Security Council authorized its President to issue a statement dated 4 April 1983, expressing the Council's "great concern" regarding "cases of mass poisoning in the occupied Arab territory of the West Bank as referred to in document S/15673," and requested Your Excellency "to conduct independent inquiries concerning the causes and effects of the serious problem of the reported cases of poisoning. . . ."

At the end of April 1983, the Atlanta Centers for Disease Control published the results of their investigations, asserting, in summary, that "this epidemic of acute illness was induced by anxiety . . . . Its subsequent spread was mediated by psychogenic factors. Newspaper and radio reports may have contributed to this spread. The epidemic ended after West Bank schools were closed . . .We observed no evidence of reproductive impairment in affected patients."

On 10 May 1983, Your Excellency transmitted to the Security Council the "Report by the Director-General of the World Health Organization on a health emergency of an ill-defined nature on the West Bank," stating, *inter alia*, that "the WHO inquiry has not been able to indicate any specific cause or causes of this ill-defined health emergency." In regard to the clinical findings submitted by the Israel health authorities to WHO, that organization's report stated that it "found no reason whatsoever to challenge the findings reported to it."

These findings of the various medical authorities are fully corroborated by the conclusions reached in the medical literature on similar phenomena in other countries which, incidentally, did not merit any correspondence on the part of various permanent representatives, let alone consideration by, and a statement on behalf of, the Security Council.

In this connection, I have the honor to draw Your Excellency's attention to an article entitled "An Epidemic of Overbreathing among Schoolgirls" by Peter D. Moss and Colin P. McEvedy, published on 26 November 1966, in the *British Medical Journal* for that year, pp. 1295–1300.

I should also like to draw your attention to an article by Gary W. Small and Jonathan F. Borus entitled "Outbreak of Illness in a School Chorus," published on 17 March 1983, in *The New England Journal of Medicine* for that year, pp. 632–35.

In the light of the great concern displayed by the Security Council last April regarding the phenomenon in question, it was to be expected that the Council would see fit to take note of the fact that the allegations against Israel proved to be without foundation, even though, given the prevailing constellation in the United Nations, it was not to be expected that the Council would go so far as to redress the wrong done to Israel. Similarly, while it was perhaps too much to expect that Arab representatives would want to apologize for having levelled wild and completely unfounded charges of "poisoning" against my country, one would have expected that, at the very least, they would have the decency to refrain from repeating those accusations.

I therefore note with regret the Security Council's total silence on the matter since the publication of the above-mentioned reports. Likewise, the silence observed now on this matter by some of the permanent representatives who irresponsibly and shamelessly hurled their unfounded charges against Israel and, even more so, the repetition at this stage of those charges by other representatives, fully attest to the moral and intellectual standards of the representatives concerned, as well as to their inability or unwillingness to come to terms with reality.

I have the honor to request that this letter be circulated as a document of the General Assembly and of the Security Council.

C

Zionism at the United Nations

I. The Aim of the Detractors

Excerpt from address to the 81st National Convention of the Zionist Organization of America, Shoreham Hotel, Washington, D.C., 8 September 1978.

As the memory of the Second World War and of the genocide perpetrated against the Jewish people through acts of commission and omission steadily dims, attempts are being made to relegate the facts of Jewish martyrdom to the realm of oblivion. The endeavors to reduce the figures of the Jewish victims of the Holocaust, to question the very existence of extermination camps, etc., cannot be divorced from the emergence of a new brand of anti-Semitism. In the years immediately following the Second World War, the universal abhorrence and revulsion at the crimes committed against the Jewish people were of such magnitude that even the most inveterate anti-Semites were forced into ideological hiding.

Thirty years later, the anti-Semitic international was allowed to resurface, this time on the rostrum of the United Nations General Assembly. The anti-Semitic international looked for a suitable code-word that would identify the Jew, without calling him by his name, in a manner that would be instantly understood by all neo-anti-Semites the world over. Zionism became the code-word that met the requirements of the anti-Semitic international and it was thus that the onslaught against the national liberation movement of the Jewish people was launched in the United Nations.

For years Israel has been subjected in the United Nations to an outpouring of invective unprecedented in the annals of international organizations and to a barrage of hostile resolutions which culminated in the infamous resolution of 1975 that equated Zionism with racism.

The onslaught on Zionism did have one salutary effect which its enemies did not anticipate: it has done more for Zionism than scores of Zionist speeches and pamphlets might have achieved. It has intensified Zionist consciousness among countless Jews who in the past probably would not have identified themselves as Zionists in the organizational sense of this term. Suddenly, you could see in the streets of New York and elsewhere, thousands of Jews proudly displaying the "I am a Zionist" button. This reaction naturally stemmed from the instinctive feeling of Jews throughout the world that the foul attack on Zionism was in effect a calculated assault on their Jewishness.

This instinctive reaction is of course fully justified. For Zionism is nothing other than the modern manifestation of the Jewish people's age-old yearning to return to its ancient homeland.

In a religious sense, one cannot divorce Zionism from Judaism, for the yearning for Zion is a central component of the Jewish faith. In a purely secular vein, Zionism recognizes the inseparable bond between the people of Israel and the Land of Israel, and has as its goal the national liberation of the Jewish people through their return to Eretz Israel. Zionism is, in fact, the most ancient national liberation movement in history, one which has been preserved by Jews since biblical times and which in, turn, has sustained us as a people despite the many years of exile. Zionism is of the essence of Jewish existence; the consummation of Jewish history. Just as Zionism cannot be separated from Judaism, anti-Zionism cannot be divorced from anti-Semitism. Just as classical anti-Semitism denies the equal rights of Jews as citizens within society, anti-Zionism denies the right of the Jewish people to equality within the international community. The principle of anti-Jewish discrimination has simply been transferred from the realm of the individual to the domain of collective identities. The fact remains: to say one is anti-Zionist but not anti-Semitic, is to say one believes Jews have a right to live in their houses but not in their homes.

Zionism is the product of the free will of the Jewish people, exercised despite overwhelming adversity. As Israel's philosophical lifeblood, Zionism is predicated on the mutually dependent relationship between the Diaspora and the Jewish state, a fluid exchange of people and ideas throughout the Jewish world. Today, Zionism continues to be an imperative for Jewish existence.

For the Jews of Israel, threatened with physical aggression, for the Jews of communist and Arab lands, faced with spiritual and numerical extinction, and for the Jews of the West, who must contend with the erosive power of assimilation, Zionism remains the national liberation movement of the Jewish people.

II. Zionism and "Hegemonism"

Statement made in the United Nations General Assembly on 14 December 1979, in connection with the adoption of a resolution that declared that Zionism was a form of "hegemonism."

The draft resolution before us is about to spawn yet another monstrous perversion. It could have seen the light of day only in the surrealistic world of this Assembly.

The word "hegemonism" was coined as part of the shadow-boxing between the world's heavyweights. It has a certain use as a code-word in international politics today and entered the shadow world of the Assembly agenda. Certain delegations, however, whose opposition to the peaceful settlement of disputes is well known and who prefer to flex their muscles rather than curb their appetites for power and influence, are clearly unhappy with mere shadow-boxing.

Those delegations have thus selected as their target the national liberation movement of the Jewish people, a people that has suffered intolerably at the hands of almost all of the imperial and hegemonistic powers the world has ever seen. This bloc of Arab petro-colonialists and Arab petro-hegemonists has sought to conceal its own attitudes of exclusivism, by including Zionism in the draft resolution dealing with hegemonism.

Zionism and hegemonism are a contradiction in terms, if ever there was such a contradiction. Zionism is the Jewish people's national liberation movement, the expression of its quest for freedom and for equality with other nations. But in this Organization, the Jewish people's national liberation movement, one of the most ancient of its kind in existence, is maligned and slandered in an endless spate of malice and venom.

In their drive to annihilate the Jewish people, its enemies throughout history began by distorting the image of the Jew, by rewriting Jewish history, by fabricating some of the most odious historic and racial theories and libels. The Arab states, in their campaign to destroy the Jewish state, have adopted the same method of falsifying Jewish history and, in particular, the meaning of the Zionist movement. Zionism was the struggle of the Jewish people against the mighty imperial forces of the ancient world. Zionism was the dream of the Jewish people, uprooted from its Land and dispersed all over the world, to strive to return to the Land of Israel. Zionism was the participation of the Jewish people in Jewish brigades that fought with the Allies against Hitler while Arab leaders collaborated with him. Zionism aims at restoring to the Jewish people the rights possessed by other nations.

As a former Foreign Minister of Israel, Abba Eban has written:

> Zionism is nothing more—but also nothing less—than the Jewish people's sense of origin and destination in the land linked eternally with its name. It is also the instrument whereby the Jewish nation seeks an authentic fulfillment of itself. And the drama is enacted in the region in which the Arab nation has realized its sovereignty in twenty States comprising a hundred million people in 4½ million square miles, with vast resources. The issue therefore is not whether the world will come to terms with Arab nationalism. The question is at what point Arab nationalism, with its prodigious glut of advantage, wealth and opportunity, will come to terms with the modest but equal rights of another Middle Eastern nation to pursue its life in security and peace.

The Arab states will come to terms with Israel's right to exist only when they renounce their exclusivist and hegemonistic attitude toward the presence of a non-Arab and non-Muslim state in the Middle East.

Many Members must be aware that the absurdity of including Zionism in the draft resolution before us is made possible only by the fact that individual delegations do not vote in such cases according to the dictates of conscience. On the contrary, outrageous resolutions of this type have to be steamrollered through the Assembly by the hegemonistic bloc of Arab petro-colonialists. Is it not hegemonism of the purest kind when the Arab states reserve for themselves the exclusive right to define the national movement of another people? A group of countries, intoxicated with the power inherent in the automatic majority, has for years subjected the United Nations to an outpouring of invective against Israel unprecedented in the annals of international organizations, and to a barrage of hostile resolutions which culminated in the infamous and abominable resolution of 1975 purporting to equate Zionism with racism. The aim of these Arab states has been to lend a semblance of respectability to anti-Semitism disguised as opposition to Zionism.

It was during that paroxysm of insanity and orgy of hate in 1975, that the then permanent representative of the United States to the United Nations, Ambassador Moynihan, warned that a terrible lie had been unleashed in this Organization, a lie that would have terrible consequences:

> People will begin to say, as indeed they have already begun to say, that the United Nations is a place where lies are told. . . .

The fact is that the lies told in the United Nations have turned this forum into the laughing-stock of international society. Informed opinion no longer takes seriously the deliberations here. What is more, it is no longer even outraged by a perverse mentality that, having purported to equate Zionism with racism and hegemonism, could equate it with similar justification with vegetarianism, rheumatism, philatelism or any other "ism."

About two hours ago, the people of Israel lit the first candle ushering in the eight-day festival of Chanukah. Within the next few hours, the Jewish people throughout the world will also light the first candle of the festival.

Chanukah commemorates the victory of the Maccabees twenty-two centuries ago over a hegemonistic empire of another age. Had the Maccabees lived today, they no doubt would be condemned by the numerical majority in this Assembly as Zionists because they took a stand against imperialism. But for over two thousand years the Jewish people have been commemorating the victory of the Maccabees, the defenders of their rights and avengers of their wrongs, and celebrating the victory of the weak over the strong and of the few over the many.

This is the strength of the Jewish people, deriving from its unswerving attachment to its land—the Land of Israel. Many foreign empires have ruled over that land. They have come and gone, they have been vanquished and they have vanished from the face of the earth. But one small nation, more ancient still, has outlived them all, and today enjoys again national sovereignty in its patrimony. That nation will not waver or falter in the face of obscenities, rhetorical abuse and condemnation in this hall.

The anti-Semitic outbursts of the Arab petro-hegemonists and their ilk cannot and will not hurt the Jewish people. But they will further erode whatever little respect, resonance and prestige the United Nations still enjoys.

D

Anti-Semitism at the United Nations*

I

Excerpted from letters dated 16 August 1982 and 12 October 1982, addressed to the Secretary-General of the UN.

Recent weeks have witnessed an ominous upsurge in anti-Jewish acts of violence in various countries in Europe and elsewhere. These acts of violence culminated in the criminal attacks against Jewish and Israel targets in Paris, most notably the dastardly terrorist attack on 9 August 1982 against a Jewish restaurant and the ensuing rampage in neighboring streets which caused the deaths of six persons and the wounding of twenty-two. These events have once again highlighted the well-known links that exist between international anti-Semitism and international terrorism and its linchpin, the PLO.

Despite attempts that have been made in recent years to obscure these ties (by resorting to various devices, including the use of all kinds of aliases) it has become evident that virtually every anti-Jewish excess in various parts of the world, even if carried out in some cases by local terrorists (such as the French "Action Directe"), could be traced to the PLO or to one of the groups associated with it.

The intensification of these anti-Jewish excesses and the general resurgence of anti-Semitism, in particular of its more violent manifestations, is unquestionably related to the anti-Israel hysteria fostered in recent weeks in many countries through official pronouncements and distortions of the media. The climate thus created has been considered by many hitherto clandestine anti-Semites as propitious for a return to open anti-Jewish activities and violence.

Responsibility for the ominous and sinister developments of recent years—culminating in numerous acts of anti-Jewish violence—rests heavily with the United Nations. In a barrage of "anti-Zionist" and "anti-Israel" resolutions (most notably the infamous General Assembly resolution of 10 November 1975 which contained the obscene proposition that Zionism is a

---

*The terms "anti-Semitism", "anti-Semite" and "anti-Semitic" are used throughout within their commonly accepted meaning, denoting hostility to Jews (cf., *The Concise Oxford Dictionary of Current English*).

form of racism), accompanied by "anti-Zionist" rhetoric and activities of various kinds it has been converted into a major forum of contemporary international anti-Semites.

On numerous occasions in recent years, I took the opportunity to warn against this degradation of the United Nations and of the ideals it stands for. Thus, for example, in my letter of 21 December 1978 addressed to the Secretary General, I strongly protested the misuse of United Nations facilities to house an exhibition mounted by the terrorist PLO, which constituted not only a vulgar attack on a member state but also "vilified the Bible, Judaism and values which have contributed so much to world civilization as a whole." In the same letter, I also pointed out that "while it is outrageous that the Headquarters of the Organization should have been exploited for this purpose, it is not surprising that the PLO should have produced an exhibit which would have been worthy of the anti-Semitic Nazi publication, *Der Stürmer.*" I further stated that "it is absolutely unacceptable that little more than three decades after the victory of the United Nations over the Nazis, an exhibition reminiscent of the worst kind of Nazi incitement against the Jewish people should have been entertained in the Headquarters of the United Nations."

Less than three months later, on 16 March 1979, the Permanent Representative of Jordan, Mr. Hazem Nuseibeh, told the Security Council:

> Has the world been polarized into an omnipotent race and subservient Gentiles born into this world to serve the aims of the 'master race'? We, the Gentiles, are several billion human souls, and yet how much weight, I wonder, do we carry in the councils of some of the mighty?

Speaking in the General Assembly on 8 December 1980, the same speaker claimed that there is a Jewish cabal "which controls, manipulates and exploits the rest of humanity by controlling the money and wealth of the world."

In the same diatribe, Mr. Nuseibeh stated:

> People like Lord Rothschild every day, in iron-clad secrecy, decide and flash round the world how high the price of gold should be on each particular day. . . .The United States. . .has a national income of upwards of $ 2,000 billion per annum, and, while millions of hardworking, God-fearing Americans are unemployed, the Zionists own a lion's share of that great abundance.

These utterances by Mr. Nuseibeh prompted me to exercise my right of reply in the plenary of the General Assembly, on 10 December 1980, when I stated, *inter alia:*

There is . . . one aspect of this debate that I must address myself to, and that is the crudely anti-Semitic tone which pervaded a number of the statements made. The crudest anti-Semitic slanders were uttered by the representative. . .of Jordan. This, of course, is by no means the first time that Mr. Nuseibeh has . . . embarrassed this Assembly by drawing almost word for word from such notoriously anti-Semitic works as the so-called *Protocols of the Elders of Zion*, a scurrilous fabrication published in Tsarist Russia at the turn of the century.

These odious charges are nothing but out-and-out anti-Semitism of the worst and most virulent kind. If this Assembly were to stop playing at being a mock parliament and were to introduce some real parliamentary rules and ethics, such calumnies would have long been ruled out of order. But by a curious paradox, representatives in this Organization enjoy an immunity to spread anti-Semitic invective with an openness and in a way which would not be tolerated in any decent society.

I have warned of the danger of this Organization's becoming a world center for anti-Semitism . . .

Nowadays, it is fashionable to avoid direct attacks on Jews and the Jewish people. Instead, anti-Semites now attack Zionism and Zionists. In this Organization, a new code word—anti-Zionism—has gained currency. But anti-Semites throughout the world understand its meaning full well, and the attempt in this Organization to bestow respectability upon 'anti-Zionism' has in practice only encouraged anti-Semitism in various parts of the world, including the so-called enlightened countries, as the events of the last few years—indeed, months—have clearly shown.

There used to be a time when some delegates here claimed that they were not anti-Jewish, but merely anti-Zionist. That cover has long been blown . . . to the lasting shame of this Organization.

In fairness to Mr. Nuseibeh, it should be pointed out that he has not been alone at the United Nations in his anti-Semitic outbursts; he has been joined by many of his Arab and other colleagues, including Soviet and other Eastern-bloc representatives. In fact, the Soviet Union has become one of the major purveyors of contemporary anti-Semitism, both domestically and internationally, and the statements of its representatives, as well as of those of many other Eastern-bloc countries, clearly bear out this appalling fact.

In this connection I should also like to draw Your Excellency's attention to my statement in the plenary of the General Assembly on 10 October 1980, following the despicable attack in Paris, on 3 October, on the Jewish synagogue of rue Copernic, during the Friday night service, resulting in the deaths of three persons and the wounding of twenty. On that occasion, I told the General Assembly:

> Throughout our long history, the Jewish people has all too often been the unfortunate victim of every form of intolerance, hatred and oppression. Indeed, within the living memory of many of those here today, we have been the victims of the most senseless, ruthless and vile application of persecution ever conceived and perpetrated by man. It is a chilling irony of fate that as the rostrum of this Assembly was being abused for a call for holy war against my country, a Jewish house of worship was made the target of a vicious bomb attack. That outrage in the heart of Europe must serve as a reminder of how a campaign of hatred, launched by rabble-rousers and bigots, can so easily lead to conflagration and massacre.

> If member states are unable to put a stop to this ominous development, the United Nations will be used for the perpetration of the very evil it was designed to combat. It will have irreparably betrayed its own *raison d'être*. We therefore voice these concerns now in the hope that there is still time to arrest this dangerous trend.

At the same time, it is impossible to absolve from shared responsibility for the recrudescence of this ugly phenomenon all those public personalities, including world leaders who, over the years, through irresponsible and loose statements as well as frivolous gestures, have given encouragement to this age-old scourge of civilization. The inescapable connection between the sad and degrading deterioration of the United Nations into a cover for the call to terror, and the acts of world leaders who have endeavored to cast a cloak of legitimacy upon the terrorist PLO must, and should, stand at the forefront of our most immediate concerns. Indeed, it must be clear that governments and others who in recent months have tried to enhance the standing of the terrorist PLO cannot now wash their hands of these recent eruptions of anti-Jewish violence.

I take this opportunity to appeal to Your Excellency to use your best endeavors, with a view to combating within the United Nations this most vile form of racism and racial and religious discrimination.

I also appeal to Your Excellency to exert your influence with the member states of this Organization to ensure that the plague-carriers of international terrorism (led by its flag-bearer, the terrorist PLO) and of international anti-Semitism be prevented from continuing to operate freely in an atmosphere of benevolent consent, formal protestations notwithstanding.

I have the honor to request that this letter be circulated as an official document of the General Assembly.

II

Letter dated 16 January 1984, addressed to the Secretary General of the United Nations.

In my letters dated 16 August 1982 and 12 October 1982 I drew Your Excellency's urgent attention to the ominous upsurge of anti-Semitism at the United Nations in recent years.

Regrettably, the thirty-eighth session of the General Assembly (1983) was characterized by a further intensification of this sinister phenomenon, thus converting the United Nations into one of the foremost arenas for the operation of international anti-Semitism.

In my letter of 8 December 1983 I drew Your Excellency's attention to the racist and religious incitement contained in the statement of the same day of the Permanent Representative of Libya, Mr. Treiki. In that statement, the representative of Libya said, in reference to Israel and the Jewish people:

> The time has come for the United Nations to strive to save the peoples of the world from this racist entity. It is high time for the United Nations and the United States, in particular, to realize that the Jewish Zionists here in the United States attempt to destroy Americans. Look around New York. Who are the owners of pornographic film operations and houses? Is it not the Jews who are exploiting the American people and trying to debase them? If we succeed in eliminating that entity, we shall by the same token save the American and European peoples.

> We hope that the day will soon come when we can eradicate this affront, this aberration of history which we committed when we accepted within our Organization this band of criminals, mercenaries and terrorists.

On the same occasion, the representative of Libya also referred to the people of Israel as "the most vile people upon this earth."

Unfortunately, the representative of Libya was not alone in such a display of rabid anti-Semitism. The Permanent Representative of Iran, Mr. Rajaie-Khorassani, had already expressed, on 2 November 1983, with reference to Israel, his hope "that the Moslem countries in the area will soon consider the final solution." As is well known, "the final solution" was the Nazi code-name for the genocide perpetrated against the Jews of Europe during the Second World War.

Iranian representatives have also repeatedly referred to Israel as a "cancerous growth" (see, for example, the statement by the foreign minister of Iran, Mr. Velayati, of 30 September 1983: "There is no cure for the cancerous growth of Zionism but surgery") or "cancerous tumor" (see, for example, the statement of Mr. Hosein Latify of 19 December 1983: "The Zionist entity . . . should be removed like a cancerous tumor").

When the representative of Iran, at the plenary meeting of the General Assembly, on 19 December 1983, also used obscene language with regard to the representative of Israel ("the Zionist entity agent with the retarded mind and archaic logic and with a polluted reasoning . . .") without being called to order by the chair for this intolerable behavior, the representative of the United States, Congressman Solarz, protested the use of this kind of abusive language. Thereupon, the Permanent Representative of Syria, Mr. El-Fattal, interjected that: "We have a limited amount of time. There are attempts in this hall on the part of the United States representative to gain the Jewish vote. . . ."

Assaults on the Jewish people in an ostensibly more sophisticated but equally vicious form were also made in the course of the recent session of the General Assembly by certain Soviet-bloc representatives. Thus, for example, the representative of the Byelorussian Soviet Socialist Republic, Mr. Ogurtsov, on 29 November 1983, at the fifty-fifth meeting of the Third Committee, referred in a derisive manner to the Bible, just as Soviet-bloc representatives routinely deride the Jewish people as "the chosen people."

These motifs, so characteristic of the notorious Tsarist anti-Semitic forgery known as the *Protocols of the Elders of Zion* and subsequently of the Nazi and Fascist propaganda of the 1930s and 1940s—and which feature prominently also in the contemporary anti-Semitic literature in the Soviet Union and elsewhere—found their echo and reflection also in some statements of Arab representatives. Thus, for example, the representative of Iraq, Mr. Haddawi, told the Third Committee, on 26 October 1983, that "the Jewish people . . . called itself the chosen people and sometimes called others 'enemies'."

In the same vein of deriding the Jewish people, the representative of Syria, Mr. Adhami, told the Fourth Committee, at its meeting of 14 October 1981, what he called a "Jewish story" of a man who went to his rabbi to enter the birthdate of his son. The man asked which date he should give, last year or this year. "Why not give the true date?" the rabbi asked the man. "I didn't think of that," the father answered. The Syrian delegate said the story portrayed the "Jewish mentality of the Zionist delegate." (United Nations Press Release of 14 October 1981: the passage does not appear in the summary record of the meeting in question.)

Throughout all these years, the State of Israel and the Jewish people have been under no illusions with regard to the true intent and purpose of the "anti-Zionist" and "anti-Israel" outbursts at the United Nations and elsewhere. It has been well understood by decent people everywhere that behind the "anti-Zionist" and "anti-Israel" tirades there lurks anti-Semitism, pure and simple, and that "anti-Israel" and "anti-Zionist" slogans are being used by closet and crypto-anti-Semites to disguise their true intentions. As the various samples referred to above, as well as others, abundantly demonstrate, the mask has now finally fallen and the ugly face of anti-Semitism—one of the oldest and vilest manifestations of racism and religious intolerance—has been clearly revealed. It has thus become evident again that the alleged distinction between "anti-Zionism" (and "anti-Israelism") on the one hand, and anti-Semitism, on the other, has no basis in reality. Israel has repeatedly warned that this distinction—which has been asserted by Israel's enemies at the United Nations—is in fact merely a crude attempt to disguise their enmity against the Jewish people behind a smokescreen of antagonism to Zionism, which is the national liberation movement of the Jewish people.

That the phenomenon of open anti-Semitism has reached such alarming proportions at the United Nations has to be ascribed to a large degree to the shocking complacency displayed in this regard in recent years. The absence of reaction to the numerous anti-Semitic outbursts at the United Nations has been construed by many an anti-Semite as indifference, amounting to acquiescence.

In my letter of 21 December 1978 to the Secretary-General I had already warned against this degradation of the United Nations and of the ideals for which it stands.

We have also repeatedly stated that by a curious paradox, representatives at the United Nations enjoy an immunity to spread anti-Semitic invective with an openness and in a way which would not be tolerated in any decent society.

Regrettably, Israel's repeated warnings, both from the rostrum of the General Assembly and through a series of letters addressed to the Secretary-General in recent years, have gone unheeded.

As already indicated, no less serious than these anti-Semitic outbursts in themselves has been the absence of any reaction to them on the part of the presiding officers and of virtually the entire membership of the Organization. In particular, it is difficult to refrain from giving expression to a sense of profound dismay at the studious silence observed at the United Nations by those representatives whose countries in the 1930s and 1940s were directly involved in the anti-Jewish persecutions of the Nazi-Fascist era. Similarly, it is difficult to comprehend the silence of those representatives whose countries during that period either directly experienced or otherwise witnessed the pernicious effects of such anti-Semitic behavior and who surely must know the terrible dangers to the very fabric of civilized society inherent in a permissive attitude toward such manifestations of racism and religious intolerance.

There can be little doubt that the escalation at the United Nations of anti-Semitic rhetoric in recent years—whether direct or in the form of "anti-Zionist" and "anti-Israel" campaigns and resolutions—has been largely responsible for the recrudescence of anti-Semitism worldwide and for the resulting numerous acts of anti-Jewish violence in recent years. Indeed, through the barrage of "anti-Israel" and "anti-Zionist" resolutions adopted at the United Nations in recent years—culminating in the obscene proposition contained in the infamous General Assembly resolution of 10 November 1975 that Zionism was a form of racism—the United Nations, to its lasting shame, has been converted into one of the foremost contemporary forums of international anti-Semitism. The endless broadsides of hate and vituperation launched against Israel and the Jewish people from platforms of the United Nations, or under its aegis, have found their echo and their mainstay in the official pronouncements of governments and in the distortions of the media in many countries.

The grotesque character of this situation surely cannot escape the attention of those who still remember that this Organization is the product of the great wartime coalition that came into being to fight the forces of nazism and fascism. Those forces of evil and hatred had singled out the Jewish people as their prime target. It is a cruel and chilling irony of fate that less than four decades after nazism and fascism were defeated—with the participation of more than one and a half million Jews who fought in the ranks of the Allied forces to eradicate this scourge of mankind—the United Nations should have become the favorite arena for airing with impunity one of the main tenets of the genocidal Nazi-Fascist legacy.

What is at stake is the very ability of the United Nations to survive as the organization envisaged by its founders and by the Charter of the United Nations. If anti-Semitism is permitted to continue to rear its ugly head at the United Nations, this certainly cannot augur well for the Organization. Countenancing by the United Nations of such behavior and rhetoric must unavoidably expose the United Nations to the well-justified contempt and revulsion of decent people and civilized public opinion everywhere. If the United Nations is unable to put a stop to the spread of this vicious phenomenon, it will be used for the perpetration of the very evil it was designed to combat. It will then have irreparably betrayed its own *raison d'être*.

As the representative of Israel—the state in which the Jewish people has restored its sovereignty after eighteen centuries of exile, persecution and martyrdom unparalleled in the annals of mankind—I earnestly urge Your Excellency, in the year after we marked the thirty-fifth anniversary of the adoption of the Universal Declaration of Human Rights and of the Convention on the Prevention and Punishment of the Crime of Genocide, to condemn unequivocally these vile manifestations of anti-Semitic racism and religious intolerance, alongside all manifestations of racism and religious discrimination and prejudice. I also emphatically appeal to Your Excellency to take all the necessary steps to ensure that such manifestations of bigotry do not recur at the United Nations and that, in its activities, the Organization ceases to violate the principles and ideals enshrined in its own Charter.

As the constitution of the United Nations Educational, Scientific and Cultural Organization states in its preamble, "wars begin in the minds of men." By the same token, racism, racial discrimination, religious intolerance, prejudice and bigotry also start in the minds of men. Consequently, racist verbal violence cannot and should not be dismissed as inconsequential; racist physical violence has invariably been preceded by racist verbal violence. It has been rightly observed that the terrible calamity that befell the Jewish people within the living memory of many of us had begun with defamation. It is therefore essential that the ugly and vicious anti-Semitic rhetoric at the United Nations be confronted without delay, in a firm and unambiguous manner. For, as we have all been admonished by Edmund Burke some two centuries ago: "The only thing necessary for the triumph of evil is for good men to do nothing."

I have the honor to request that this letter be circulated as a document of the General Assembly.

E

The Degeneration of the United Nations

On 5 February 1982, the UN General Assembly by a vote of 86 to 21, with 34 abstentions, declared that Israel was not "a peace-loving State." This was repeated on 28 April 1982 by a similar majority. The following is a consolidated version of statements before the vote made in the General Assembly on those two occasions.

We are celebrating these days throughout the world the centennial of the birth of an illustrious son of the Jewish people—Franz Kafka. With uncanny clairvoyance, Kafka identified the malaise of the twentieth century, so much so that his name is even used as an adjective to describe what we now term Kafkaesque situations. And nowhere have his predictions become more relevant than in this building which reeks of a Kafkaesque atmosphere *par excellence*. Indeed, such works of Kafka as *The Castle* and *The Trial* should be made compulsory reading for representatives here so as to better enable them to understand the workings of this Organization.

The United Nations of 1982 has become a workshop for the semanticist and simultaneously his despair. In this building words have either lost any meaning or been assigned one diametrically opposed to the regular meaning given them in the real world. In this building, Southern Yemen, East Germany and Afghanistan are democracies. In this building, Libya, Cuba, Vietnam and Iraq are peace-loving states. In this building, Cuba is a non-aligned country. In this building the Soviet Union is the leader of an alleged peace camp and any challenge in this regard is always readily refuted by the representatives of Budapest, Prague, Kabul and Warsaw who can well testify to the Soviet Union's peaceful intentions. In this building the Arab aggressors who have been ganging up on my country since its establishment as an independent state, and who openly profess their desire to see it disappear from the face of the earth, are proclaimed the victims of aggression while Israel, the target of their sinister designs, is branded as an aggressor. In short, in this building, the warmongers are declared the aggressed upon and the victims become the aggressors.

Small wonder that, as a result, the outside world is no longer even amused by what is going on here and watches these proceedings with the contempt and disgust they justly deserve.

In this Organization, like so often throughout history, the treatment of my people has become the litmus test with which to ascertain the moral and intellectual standards of the time. Throughout its long and tortuous history, the Jewish people has always been the target of hatred, harassment and persecution by all those who have been opposed to the values which my people first proclaimed and then bequeathed to the world and which are inextricably associated with it; namely, the equality and brotherhood of man, the intrinsic value and dignity of the human being, social justice, the abolition of war among nations, and universal peace. It is thus not surprising that my country has become in this Organization the target of all those who, while paying lip service to the Charter, are actively at work to destroy these principles as well as the Organization based on it. Ever since this Organization has been taken hostage by the anti-democratic and totalitarian forces of the world, they have turned their fury against my people which represents in their eyes, and rightly so, the ideals of freedom and equality which they detest and which they seek to destroy.

The shameless document before us—and I will not dignify it by calling it a draft resolution—does not reflect on Israel's love of peace, which is ingrained in our very existence. Rather it does reflect the moral degeneration and intellectual decay of all those who have participated in the preparation of this despicable concoction. They are the same countries who in recent years have been modeling this Organization in their own shape by gradually converting it into an anti-peace and anti-human rights organization, their hypocritical pontifications notwithstanding.

The accomplices to the drafting of this shameless document—and I will not dignify them by calling them sponsors—seek to isolate my people. Many tyrants throughout history have tried to do this before them. They are all gone and forgotten, while my people has returned to its land and restored its sovereignty there after eighteen centuries of exile and dispersion. This Organization cannot and will not isolate the people of Israel. But it can and does increasingly isolate itself from enlightened mankind which will not countenance endlessly the paroxysms of collective frenzy being exhibited here at regular intervals and with increasing frequency.

Stripped of all bigoted rhetoric and artificial encumbrances, the cause of the Arab-Israel conflict is a simple one: our Arab enemies begrudge our very existence, despite the fact that we are one of the smallest countries on earth. In fact, Israel's size is considerably smaller than that of such small states as Switzerland, Belgium or Denmark. If this Organization were less topsy-turvy than it is—if it were truly dedicated to the purposes and principles enshrined in the Charter—it would have long ago condemned the criminal design of Israel's enemies to destroy it—designs which are fueled by outsiders who are feeding on Arab obsessions in order to exploit them for their own selfish purposes. The shameless document before us does not contain any reference to the ongoing aggression of Syria and other Arab states against my country. It does not enjoin them to refrain from the use or threat of force against Israel. It does not call on them to resolve their dispute with Israel in a peaceful manner, as is required by the Charter. It ignores the repeated expressions of Israel's willingness to negotiate without any prior conditions with Syria, as well as with other Arab states, in conformity with Security Council resolutions 242 and 338 and the persistent rejection of our offer by Syria and other Arab states.

In view of the degeneration of this Organization and its perversion by the forces of international lawlessness, it is an affront to common decency that the words of a great visionary of peace—Isaiah the prophet of Israel—should be permitted to continue gracing the wall across the street from this building. In order to avoid further insult to the memory of this great son of the Jewish people, we appeal to the city of New York to consider removing the Isaiah inscription and thus to give expression to the abhorrence of civilized mankind at the systematic debasement of this Organization by the bigots, hypocrites and liars who now manipulate the United Nations.

The enemies of Israel have already been successful in transforming this Organization into an anti-peace organization where relations between states are being polarized and exacerbated instead of being harmonized, as we are enjoined by the Charter.

The draft resolution before us repeats the obscene libel that Israel is not a peace-loving state. Let me address myself very briefly to this abomination: the free and democratic state of Israel and the Jewish people are in no need of certification of their love of peace by the tropical gulags of Hanoi and Havana, by the Iraqi aggressors and oppressors of the Kurdish people, by the quislings of Kabul, by the genocidal criminals of the Pol Pot clique, by the oppressive régime of Zia ul-Hak of Pakistan, by the Syrian butchers of Hama and Beirut, by the level-headed ruler of Libya—that well-known paymaster of international terrorism—or by the medieval and backward régime of Saudi Arabia, the willing hosts of Idi Amin, that former respected member of the United Nations Commission on Human Rights. Israel is in no need of certification of its love of peace by the Soviet Union whose peaceful intentions have been so vividly demonstrated in the streets of Budapest, Prague, East Berlin, Warsaw and Kabul. Israel is in no need of certification of its love of peace by the Soviet Union's miserable lackeys in those and other capitals, in particular by the arrogant neo-Nazi bullyboys of East Berlin. This is a representative sample of the forces of international lawlessness that are about to condemn my country. A condemnation by them is indeed a badge of honor. To them, to all the moral perverts, the intellectual dwarfs, the unprincipled cynics and the bigots fanning the flames of religious hatred in this building, I wish to convey the sentiments of contempt not only of my own people but indeed of all free people around the world. In token whereof, I request that a roll-call be taken so that the list of those voting for the despicable concoction can stand as a roll of dishonor and as a lasting monument to the shamelessness of the moral perverts as well as of the cynics who use them to divert attention away from such embarrassing trouble spots as Kampuchea, Afghanistan, Poland, Lebanon and Iraq. It will also attest to the spinelessness of many of those who, while fully realizing the real intentions of this draft, will still not vote against the mendacious concoction for reasons of expediency, selfishness, greed, or sheer moral cowardice.

As is common after votings of this kind, I might be approached again by many delegates to express to me their regrets for their vote. In addition to government instructions, they usually invoke on such occasions bloc solidarity, Arab blackmail and similar worthy considerations. I wish to tell them publicly that I release them in advance from the need to go through this sickening and dishonest ritual.

The shameless document will not contribute to the advancement of peace in the Middle East. Nor is this its intention. Similarly, it will not deter Israel from doing everything necessary to ensure its existence and security. If the shameless document will be remembered at all, it will stand as a monument to the moral degeneration and intellectual corruption of its authors as well as to the moral bankruptcy to which they and their like have subjected this Organization.

There are moments when there is no room for equivocation or evasion or for considerations of expediency. This is such a moment for states to stand up and be counted.

F

Tendentious Anti-Israel Publications under United Nations Auspices

Letter dated 5 November 1982, addressed to the Secretary-General of the United Nations.

On several occasions in recent months I have registered with Your Excellency my Government's strong objections to publication in the *U.N. Chronicle* of material marked by declining professional standards and characterized by blatant bias on various issues relating to the Arab-Israel conflict.

Of late this publication has begun to display an even more tendentious and one-sided approach to Middle East matters, with a marked leaning to the use of pejorative and misleading phraseology in references to my country. The deterioration in the professional standards of this journal has been particularly marked since the June issue of this year.

In September the *U.N. Chronicle* reported a situation, clearly the fruit of a feverish editorial imagination, in which much of Southern Lebanon "lay in ruins." A month later, moreover, at a time when the real extent of the hostilities had become clear to the world, the October issue of the *U.N. Chronicle* reached yet new heights of editorial licence. In its efforts to impugn the reputation of my Government, to present a tendentious, distorted and highly exaggerated picture of events, and to vilify Israel's war against the scourge of PLO terror, the *U.N. Chronicle's* editors exceeded all bounds of fair reporting, thus seriously impairing the standing of the United Nations Secretariat as an impartial organ of the Organization.

Of the numerous objectionable points in the twelve pages devoted, in the October issue of the *U.N. Chronicle,* to recent events in Lebanon, I shall limit myself to only a few of the more glaring but typical examples.

The summary story commencing on page 3 of the October issue presents a picture of recent events in which all action from the Israel side is painted in graphically pejorative terms, whereas all action initiated by the terrorists is reported in studiously neutral terms. From page 4 to the top of page 7 alone Israel is reported as committing a "ferocious breach of the cease fire"; as "closing doors" to options; as turning "indiscriminate violence" on the civilian population; and as "trying to burn out Beirut and massacre its civilian population." Terrorist actions, however, are not credited to any body and are reported as "continuous outbreaks of firing and shelling in and around Beirut."

A transparent editorial device is used to devote exaggerated space to summaries from anti-Israel diatribes and communications. Prior to this summer the *U.N. Chronicle* reported the words of the speakers themselves, with attribution which enabled the reader to assess the relative merit of what was said. This apparently is no longer the editorial policy of the *U.N. Chronicle*. Now a new Orwellian régime of "newspeak" and "doublethink" is in force, namely, a new technique of presenting biased, tendentious and self-serving information, without indicating the identity of the speakers.

A further and most reprehensible example of bias is sadly apparent in the caption to the uncredited photograph on page 18, which presents an utterly erroneous picture of the story of Damour. The truth, as is well known, is very different from that suggested by the caption. This town of 15,000 Christians was attacked and destroyed by the terrorist PLO in mid-January 1976. On 21 January 1976 *The New York Times* correspondent reported that "this once proud town" was "a smoking ruin." On 29 July 1976 the *Washington Post* reported that Damour had been "gutted" and 500 of its inhabitants massacred.

On 21 June 1982 *The New York Times* correspondent once again visited Damour and reported that:

> For nearly seven years. . .the town was inaccessible to its own people; the PLO made it a stronghold, using the churches as firing ranges and armories.

It is thus a deliberate distortion of historical truth to suggest, even by implication, that the town of Damour was destroyed in the course of the hostilities of 1982, or that the town had a population of 16,000 in early June 1982. Those few hundreds of persons who were in the town at that time were, in fact, members of the various PLO terrorist factions billeted in the town for training purposes.

Since the story of Damour is too well known world-wide for the editors of the *U.N. Chronicle* to plead ignorance and good faith, one is led to the inescapable conclusion that they are guilty of deliberate misinformation and "newspeak."

A similar example of misinformation is contained in the again uncredited caption to the photograph on page 16 which describes the city of Beirut in allegedly "happier days." The reader cannot but presume that those "happier days" were enjoyed by the city prior to June 1982. Again, the truth is well known. By June 1982 Beirut had already endured seven years of bloody civil war, division into confessional strongholds and domination and occupation by the PLO and the Syrian army. During those seven years Beirut was, it may be remembered, the capital of international terrorism. These presumably were the "happier days" to which the caption writer refers.

Clearly the editors of the *U.N. Chronicle* have once again arrogated to themselves the right to pass value judgments not within their purview. The *U.N. Chronicle*, it should be reiterated, is published by the Department of Public *Information*—not by a department of public relations.

In this connection it is worth noting that no single picture has been used, despite the plethora of material, to depict the fear and destruction brought upon South Lebanon by the terrorist occupation, to describe the death and suffering inflicted upon the Christian and Moslem populations alike by the PLO, and, not least, to present to the reader some idea of the death, damage and anguish visited upon northern Israel by the bombardments and terror raids of the PLO.

No less conspicuous by their absence are pictures from Damour and from Chekka, scene of yet another of the many massacres perpetrated by the PLO, as well as pictures of the UNRWA (United Nations Relief and Works Agency for Palestine Refugees in the Near East) training school in Siblin abused by the PLO. (See the Report by the Legal Adviser of UNRWA of 18 October 1982, reported in the press release of the Department of Public Information contained in Doc. PAL/1502 of 27 October 1982.)

Regrettably, the *U.N. Chronicle* is not the only case of a decline in professional standards within the Department of Public Information. I would therefore also draw your attention to one other glaring example of the trends noted above which appears in the same Department's booklet *The U.N. Today—1982 (Suggestions for Speakers)*. Here also the catalogue of abuses is long and I will content myself with but a few illustrations.

On general political questions more pages are devoted to the Middle East than to any other subject. International crises, such as that in Poland, or the war between Ethiopia and Somalia are not mentioned at all. My country is consistently referred to in disparaging and insulting terms and there is no mention of that crowning achievement of Middle Eastern diplomacy, the Peace Treaty between Israel and Egypt.

On the other hand, in an exceedingly brief reference to the Soviet invasion of Afghanistan, it is reported that "the Assembly called for the withdrawal of foreign troops" from that country. Curiously, there is no mention of the country of origin of those "foreign troops." As indeed UPI noted in a report of 18 October 1982 on the said booklet, "the invasion might have been carried out by Martians." Moreover, whilst Israel "attacked" Iraq in the misterminology of the editors, the Soviet "Martians" were only a "party concerned" in Afghanistan.

In a further comment on the booklet in question, the said UPI report notes that:

> Dealing with the invasion of Cambodia—known as Kampuchea at the United Nations—almost four years ago, the booklet describes the

thrust into that country by several divisions of Vietnamese troops as "the outbreak of hostilities between Vietnam and Democratic Kampuchea." Vietnam is championed by the Soviet Union.

By comparison, the move into Lebanon by 20,000 Israeli troops in 1978 is described as "a massive invasion."

Moreover, within the context of human rights violations in the world dealt with in the booklet, there is no mention of countries such as the U.S.S.R. and radical Arab countries which are regularly named by respected international monitoring bodies like Amnesty International as major violators of human rights.

Clearly, then, the Department of Public Information has recently taken on the task of misinformation and has become a pliant tool in the hands of those practitioners of that art who would exploit the United Nations for their own nefarious ends. Selective and biased editing of publications does not serve either the cause of objectivity in reporting, or the promotion of world peace, of which this Organization should be the watchdog. One can only presume that these and similar instances are intended as samples of the "new world information order" contemplated by the Department of Public Information, according to recent press reports (see e.g. *The New York Times* of 15 October 1982).

In the process, the Department of Public Information, an integral part of the United Nations Secretariat, has once again misused international funds, gravely compromised the integrity of the Secretariat and exposed the Organization as a whole to further criticism and contempt, and to a further erosion of its already shaken reputation.

Whilst emphatically protesting these new and dangerous trends within the United Nations Secretariat and its publishing channels, I have the honor to request Your Excellency to instruct the Department of Public Information to cease forthwith these dubious practices. Furthermore, I must also request that Your Excellency issue the necessary instructions to ensure that the October 1982 issue of the *U.N. Chronicle* be withdrawn from circulation and that a revised issue conforming to acceptable professional standards of fairness and honesty in reporting be prepared and distributed.

I have the honor to request that this letter be circulated as an official document of the General Assembly.

2

The Question of Palestine

A

History of the Conflict

Consolidated and abbreviated version of statements made in the UN General Assembly and Security Council in the years 1978–1982.

The United Nations has been discussing the Arab-Israel conflict for over thirty years. Had this Organization encouraged the Arab states to live up to their commitments under the United Nations Charter, this conflict could have been resolved peacefully long ago through dialogue and negotiation. The Organization, however, has long permitted itself to be exploited by those opposed to peace in the Middle East. These forces set out not only to block any progress on this issue, but have sought also to inflate the conflict, by adding an ever-increasing number of features to their Middle East repertoire.

We know that almost every item on the General Assembly's agenda is being distorted and abused by Arab delegations and their supporters in their campaign against Israel. We know, too, that some of those sitting through this charade have been overwhelmed by the endless repetition of untruths, half-truths and myths with which this item has become encrusted.

In stark contrast to the realities of the situation in the Middle East, this Assembly has been harnessed to a systematic campaign that has learned much from the advertising industry. Here in this hall, year after year, we have been subjected to an unending tirade of invective, to an endless stream of repetitive speeches and to an ever-growing accumulation of equally repetitive resolutions, passed from one international conference to another, from one committee to another, from one year to the next. All of this has its purposes: to dull the mind, to numb the participants until they obediently, and out of pure exhaustion, repeat the prescribed slogans at the prescribed time.

That these slogans are totally detached from reality, that they are in flagrant violation of the United Nations Charter, which instructs the Organization to promote international peace and security, not to obstruct it—all of this is irrelevant to the sloganeers. And the outside world, at first offended by this distortion of Charter ideals, is now simply bored and no longer regards the proceedings of this body seriously. Surely, many representatives must have noticed the declining resonance of the General Assembly in recent years.

That said, I have no illusions that anything which I may say will influence those who, for whatever reason, have been harnessed to the campaign of hatred against Israel in recent years in this hall. My statement is therefore directed specifically to those who are open to an objective study of the situation in the Middle East and who are prepared to listen to both sides of the conflict.

The Jewish People and the Land of Israel

The UN's approach to the issue now before us is very different from what it was when first brought before this Organization in 1947. When it was first discussed then, virtually everybody recognized the right of the Jewish people to self-determination and its right to sovereignty in its homeland. It was also evident at that time that the core of the Arab-Israel conflict was the unwillingness of the Arab world to come to terms with the rights of the Jewish people. Nowadays, those rights are scarcely, if ever, mentioned. Today, all the emphasis is put on the claims of the Palestinian Arabs, and the empty charge is trotted out by speaker after speaker from various quarters that the Palestinian Arabs are, as it were, a people uprooted from its land, a nation denied its rights.

The crude repetition of these falsities does not make them any truer—or more accurately—any less false.

The first myth which has to be dispelled is that at any time prior to the British Mandate there was an Arab political entity called Palestine. Throughout history there has never been a kingdom, a principality, let alone a state, called Palestine. The term "Palestine" was given currency by the Romans in an attempt to obliterate the Jewish character of the Land of Israel. Until this century, it was purely a geographical concept referring to an area of undefined expanse. Indeed, throughout the centuries that area was governed in the main from distant capitals of successive empires.

Only after World War I was Palestine created as a separate political entity, for the specific purpose of reconstituting therein a national home for the Jewish people. In so doing, the League of Nations recognized that only one people in history has, for three-thousand years and more, preserved and maintained its unbroken links with the Holy Land. That people is the Jewish people. For that reason it has been known throughout the annals of mankind as the Land of Israel, which is the translation of its name in Hebrew—Eretz Yisrael.

The association of the Jewish people with the Land of Israel, unique in its circumstances, has become part and parcel of the history of mankind, inextricably entwined in the fabric and texture of world culture. Here at the United Nations, constant attempts have been made over the past thirty years to obscure the inseparable bond between the Jewish people and the Jewish homeland. But no amount of distortion and fabrication in this building can undo so central a fact of the political, spiritual, cultural and religious history of the world.

In witness of the profound historical and national ties between the Jewish people and its land, there has been an uninterrupted Jewish presence in the land from ancient times to the present day. Although Jewish sovereignty was crushed under Roman imperial might, the physical and spiritual nexus between the Jewish people and the Land of Israel was not broken. Throughout the succeeding centuries, even if a large part of the nation was driven from one exile to another, many stayed on, reinforced time after time by returning exiles, maintaining their communities in the face of all manner of persecution, natural disaster and alien conquest. For nearly two thousand years they provided the nucleus around which the aspirations of the dispersed and persecuted nation were galvanized, and through them, the nation clung to the dream of returning to its land. Throughout all these centuries, the Jewish people prayed daily for its return to Jerusalem, the center and the sole focus of its national and spiritual life. The Jewish people has the longest unbroken historical association with the Holy City, and for the last century-and-a-half, Jews have uninterruptedly been the majority of its population.

The passionate yearnings of return finally gave birth to the practical ideas and political organizations which, amid the storms of the nineteenth and twentieth centuries, launched the mass movement for the return to Zion and for restored Jewish national independence. Upheld and fortified in dispersion and adversity by the vision of an ultimate return, the Jewish people did not forsake its homeland or forgo its links with it.

The Jews were never a people without a homeland. Having been robbed of their land, Jews never ceased to give expression to their anguish at their deprivation and to pray for and demand its return. Throughout the nearly two millennia of dispersion, the Land of Israel remained the focus of the Jewish national culture. Every single day, in all those seventy generations, Jews gave voice to their attachment to Zion.

In their daily prayers they turned toward Jerusalem, the heart and soul of the Jewish people, the one and only eternal capital of Israel. Every year, on the ninth day of Av, according to the Hebrew calendar the anniversary of the destruction of Jerusalem by Rome and of the resulting loss of Jewish national independence and sovereignty in the Land of Israel, the Jewish people has marked that calamitous event as a day of fast and mourning devoted to spiritual reflection and national rededication.

The consciousness of the Jew that the Land of Israel was his country was not a theoretical exercise or an article of theology or a sophisticated political outlook. It was in a sense all of these—and it was also a pervasive and inextricable element in the very warp and woof of his daily life. Jewish prayers, Jewish literature are saturated with the love and the longing for and the sense of belonging to the Land of Israel. For every Jew, in his home on family occasions, in his daily customs on weekdays and the Sabbath, when he said grace over meals, when he married, when he built his house, when he said his words of comfort to mourners, the context was always his exile, his hope and belief in the return to Zion, and the reconstruction of his homeland. He carried Eretz Israel with him wherever he went. Jewish festivals attuned to the circumstances and conditions of the Jewish homeland. Whether Jews remained in warm Italy or Spain, whether they found homes in cold Eastern Europe, whether they found their way to North America or came to live in the Southern Hemisphere where the seasons are reversed, they always celebrated the spring and autumn and winter of the Land of Israel. They prayed for dew in May and for rain in October.

The Jewish people has kept faith with its land, and the land in turn has kept faith with the Jewish people.

There was a time when this fundamental truth was acknowledged also by the Arabs themselves. Thus for example, on 23 March 1918, there appeared in the Mecca newspaper *Al-Qibla* an article written or inspired by Sherif Hussein, the leader of the Arab national movement at that time, the great-grandfather of the present King of Jordan. The article was written two months after Hussein had been officially informed of the British Government's Balfour Declaration, promising the Jewish people a national home in Palestine. The article notes:

> The resources of the country (Palestine) are still virgin soil and will be developed by the Jewish immigrants. One of the most amazing things until recent times was that the Palestinian used to leave his country, wandering over the high seas in every direction. His native soil could not retain its hold on him. . . . At the same time we have seen the Jews from foreign countries streaming to Palestine from Russia, Germany, Austria, Spain, America. The cause of causes could not escape those who had the gift of a deeper insight. They knew that the country was for its original sons, for all their differences, a sacred and beloved homeland. The return of these exiles to their homeland will prove

materially and spiritually an experimental school for their brethren who are with them in the fields, factories, trades, and in all things connected with toil and labor.

After World War I, this same self-evident truth was recognized at the Paris Peace Conference by the Emir Faisal, leader of the Arab delegation representing Arab national aspirations at the conference, who stated that his delegation was fully acquainted with the proposals submitted by the Zionist Organization to the peace conference, and went on to say:

> We will do our best, in so far as we are concerned, to help them through. We will wish the Jews a most hearty welcome home.

Moreover, Faisal signed an Agreement of Understanding and Co-operation with Dr. Chaim Weizmann, then representing the Zionist Movement and later the first president of Israel. The first article of that agreement stated:

> The Arab State and Palestine in all their relations and undertakings shall be controlled by the most cordial goodwill and understanding, and to this end Arab and Jewish duly accredited agents shall be established and maintained in the respective territories.

In other words, Faisal spoke of an Arab State on the one hand, and of a Jewish State—called Palestine—on the other.
Times may have changed but historic truth is immutable.

The Mandate Period

The bond between the Jewish people and the Land of Israel also found expression as a matter of course in the League of Nations mandate for Palestine. The preamble to the Mandate referred to "the establishment in Palestine of a national home for the Jewish people."

In 1921, the mandatory power decided to establish on the area of the Palestine Mandate, east of the River Jordan, an emirate under Abdullah ibn Hussein of the Hashemite family of Mecca. In 1922, the "Jewish national home" Articles of the Mandate for Palestine were declared inapplicable to that area—Transjordan—which nonetheless remained an integral part of Mandated Palestine. At the same time, "close settlement by Jews on the land"—as provided for in the Palestine mandate—was thereafter arbitrarily restricted to the area west of the River Jordan—or to about 20 percent of the original area of Mandated Palestine. In simple terms, that meant that the Jewish national home was to be established thenceforth in an area which was no more than a tiny fraction—less than ⅕ of one percent—of the total area of the twenty-one Arab states.

In 1946 the Kingdom of Transjordan was established. The Arabs of Palestine thus achieved their statehood in 80 percent of Mandated Palestine. In this way, they preceded by two years the establishment of an independent Jewish state in Palestine. It also is significant that the monarch of Transjordan had to be dissuaded from calling it the "Kingdom of Palestine."

The Arab Rejection of Second Partition of Palestine

In February 1947, nine months after the establishment of that Arab state in Palestine, the question of what remained of Mandated Palestine was brought before the United Nations. In an attempt to resolve the claims of the Jewish and Arab communities living in what can only be called the rump of Mandated Palestine, the General Assembly adopted the partition resolution 181 (II) of 29 November 1947 that recommended a further truncation of the area west of the River Jordan. In its desire to achieve a peaceful solution, the Jewish people expressed its readiness to make this concession and to reconcile itself to the painful sacrifice involved, despite the fact that the projected Jewish state would have extended over only one eighth of the Palestine Mandate originally designated for a Jewish national home. That acceptance, however, was contingent on reciprocity, that is, a similar acceptance also by the Arab side.

No such readiness was forthcoming from the Arab side. The Arabs in Palestine and all the states members of the Arab League categorically rejected the resolution. At the United Nations, the Arab states formally announced on the record that they reserved to themselves complete freedom of action, and then set out to thwart the resolution of the General Assembly by the illegal use of force from the moment of its adoption.*

With the termination of the mandate over Palestine on 14 May 1948, the armies of the seven Arab states illegally crossed the international boundaries, in clear violation of the Charter of the United Nations. Their armed aggression was aimed at crushing the newly established State of Israel.

Notwithstanding the progressive realization of the national rights of the Arabs, the Arab states were and have been unable to reconcile themselves to the existence of one sovereign Jewish state in the Middle East. They begrudged and still begrudge its very presence on a miniscule sliver of land associated with the Jewish people throughout the millennia, and recognized also by the international community as the national home for the Jewish people.

---

*See Chapter 3 on the UN Partition Resolution of 29 November 1947.

The Core of the Problem: Arab Refusal to Recognize Israel's Right to Exist

Everything that we have witnessed in the Middle East since 1947 flows from this fundamental fact—the unwillingness of Arab governments to accept, and co-exist with, a sovereign Jewish state. This is the core of the Arab-Israel conflict, and everything else is pretext or subterfuge. This is the reason why the Arab states have launched four major wars against Israel, with the express purpose of destroying it. This is the reason why they have developed a ramified series of battlefronts and a variety of weapons against Israel.

These weapons have involved, for example, an economic boycott against Israel, which has been extended into a secondary boycott on third parties trading with Israel. Various countries have been blackmailed into joining this campaign against Israel. A propaganda war of major proportions, using the techniques developed by Goebbels and his gang, has been directed for years against Israel. Children in Arab schools have been exposed to hate literature reminiscent of the Nazi gutter press. The culture and heritage of the Jewish people have been vilified. Not even the Bible, this great gift of the Jewish people to humanity, was spared. And the United Nations has been seized upon, in all its various organs and agencies, as an instrument readily at the disposal of the Arab states, in their relentless political warfare against Israel.

The PLO's True Character and Aims

Within this context, but with even uglier intent, the Arab states also created the terrorist organization which came to be known as the PLO. This murder organization was founded in 1964, three years before the Six Day War of 1967, at a time when Judea, Samaria and the Gaza District were under Jordanian and Egyptian occupation, respectively. In other words, it is evident that the PLO was created by the Arab states merely as another weapon in their serried arsenal for the destruction of Israel, even within the 1949 Armistice Lines.

The PLO operative in Saudi Arabia, Rafiq Natshe, confirmed this on 13 November 1979, in the Saudi newspaper *al-Riad,* when he explained that:

> The Palestinian revolution was born in 1965 from a strategic concept of liberating all Palestine, and the revolution will not change this, whatever the pressures put on it. The best solution is for the Palestinians to return to their homeland and the Jewish foreigner to the country of his birth. . . . Any Palestinian entity to be established on any part of the Palestinian territories will be a starting-point for the liberation of the Palestinian territories in all of Palestine.

One has not had to wait for such fortuitous reaffirmations of faith as this. The PLO's so-called covenant is permeated with the criminal concept of the elimination of the State of Israel. This document was originally written in 1964, and subsequently amended in 1968. It has been reaffirmed since, year after year, by all the central institutions of the terrorist PLO.

Nonetheless, when Yasir Arafat, the head of that murder organization, was interviewed on the ABC television program "Issues and Answers" on 10 September 1979, he pretended that he had forgotten what was written in his organization's covenant. In reply to the question, "Will the PLO ever disavow its stated objective of destroying the State of Israel?" Arafat retorted with mock naiveté: "Where did you ever read such a thing? I do not remember such a thing written in our documents. . . ."

Yasir Arafat seems to have a highly selective memory. But members of this Assembly are aware that almost every article in the PLO covenant calls for or implies the dissolution of the State of Israel. Article 19 declares that "the establishment of the State of Israel is fundamentally null and void, whatever time has elapsed"; Article 20 asserts that "the claim of historical or spiritual ties between Jews and Palestine does not tally with historical realities." With the stroke of a pen, the PLO has sought to deny more than three thousand years of Jewish and world history. Article 15 grotesquely sets out the "purging of the Zionist presence from Palestine" as a "national duty."

These are not abstract declarations, but operational principles. Most specifically, Articles 9 and 10 of the covenant declare that "armed struggle is the only way to liberate Palestine"; and that "fedayeen action"—the PLO euphemism for indiscriminate terror—forms "the nucleus of the popular Palestinian war of liberation."

The PLO has not hesitated to translate words into deeds. Attempts at mass murder of innocent men, women, and children, in Israel and throughout the world, have characterized the PLO and its activities since its creation in 1964. Indeed, since then it has attempted thousands of individual acts of terror. Over one thousand men, women, and children—not only Jews, but also Arabs and others—have been murdered, and more than five thousand people have been maimed and wounded.

These grim statistics do not reflect the agony of each man, woman, and child murdered or maimed by the PLO. Their gangs have cut down pregnant women in cold blood, have shot Olympic athletes bound hand and foot, slaughtered peaceful pilgrims and tourists. They have specialized in holding defenseless children hostage in their schools and have brutally blown them up in their schoolbuses. The PLO has planted bombs in crowded marketplaces and teeming public squares and has caused death and injury to innocent passers-by. The common denominator in all these atrocities is that the PLO, in its cowardly way, chooses only to attack civilian targets, with the aim of mass murder. And to cap it all, the PLO has openly boasted of its responsibility for virtually every one of these outrages.

As we all know, the PLO has had no inhibitions about violating the sovereignty and territorial integrity of many states members of the United Nations, and has shown little respect for the niceties of law, order and public security in those countries. Because of the active support it receives from certain Arab governments, the PLO has become the linchpin of the "terrorist international," which is plaguing society throughout the world today. It services and supplies the needs of other terrorist groups in Europe, Latin America, Asia and Africa, all of which, for example, train openly on PLO bases and plan and practice terrorist attacks without let or hindrance.

Civil aviation has been disrupted to the extent that every traveler today is thoroughly inconvenienced every time he passes through a major airport. International sports events, once a symbol of fraternity of men meeting in friendly competition, have not been spared. The immunity of diplomats, once the very basis of international communication between nations, both friendly and in conflict, has been willfully flouted, with the seizure, taking hostage and even murder of diplomats and representatives from many countries.

The grave threat to international security which is created in this way is further exacerbated by the encouragement which the PLO derives from the favorable attitudes here at the United Nations, in violation of the United Nations Charter and the rules of procedure of the various organs.

The Arab Strategy after 1967: Demand for a Second Arab State in Palestine

Until 1967 the problem of the Palestinian Arabs had been viewed by all as a refugee problem, as it essentially was and is. Before 1967 Israel did not control Judea, Samaria and the Gaza District. Yet there was no demand then for the establishment of a so-called Palestinian state in those areas. The explanation for this is very simple: the entire world knew that the Kingdom of Jordan—on the territory of 80 percent of the Palestine Mandate—is the Palestinian Arab state, just as the State of Israel is the Palestinian Jewish state. The entire world also knew that the vast majority of Palestinian Arabs are Jordanian citizens and that the majority of Jordanian citizens are Palestinian Arabs.

These basic facts also explain, for example, why the Security Council, in adopting resolution 242 on 22 November 1967, which lays down the guidelines for peace in the Middle East, makes no reference to an allegedly homeless Palestinian Arab people. This is surely significant, particularly when one bears in mind that the resolution was adopted unanimously. Members of the Council did not know in 1967 of the existence of a "homeless" Palestinian Arab people. Instead, the Council resolution, reflecting accurately the realities of the situation, spoke of the necessity for "achieving a just settlement of the refugee problem."

However, from that point on, Arab strategists appreciated that, given the general political climate which had developed in the world by the late 1960s, they stood more to gain by promoting the alleged existence of a *second* Palestinian Arab people, entitled to a *second* Arab state in the area of the former Palestine Mandate. The advantages of that tactical sleight-of-hand were obvious: it would enable the Arab states to claim that there was still a Palestinian Arab people deprived of the rights to self-determination and independence. The implementation of those claims would clearly be at the expense of Israel.

Leading spokesmen of the PLO admit that this bogus thesis was invented to work toward the destruction of the State of Israel. For instance, Zuhair Muhsin, the head of the PLO's so-called "military department" until his death in 1979, was quoted in the Dutch daily newspaper *Trouw*, on 31 March 1977:

> There are no differences between Jordanians, Palestinians, Syrians and Lebanese . . . We are one people.
>
> It is only for political reasons that we carefully stress our Palestinian identity, for it is in the national interest of the Arabs to encourage a separate Palestinian identity to counter Zionism. Yes, the existence of a separate Palestinian identity serves only tactical purposes.
>
> The founding of a Palestinian state is a new tool in the continuing battle against Israel and for Arab unity.
>
> Jordan is a state with defined borders. It cannot claim Haifa or Jaffa, whereas I have a right to Haifa, Jaffa, Jerusalem or Beersheba. After we have attained all our rights in the whole of Palestine, we must not postpone, even for a single moment, the reunification of Jordan and Palestine.

The meaning could not be clearer. The assertion of a second Palestinian Arab identity is merely one more subterfuge designed to bring about the destruction of the State of Israel.

The Arab states, which continue to oppose both Israel's existence and its right to exist, have been exploiting every international forum available to them. In recent years they have had no difficulty in pushing through the Assembly and every international organization available to them, political or otherwise, a series of resolutions purporting to accord to Palestinian Arabs, for a second time, the national rights which have, for all practical purposes, been realized through the establishment of Jordan on almost 80 percent of the territory of what was historical and Mandated Palestine.

The purpose has been twofold. They have set out to delegitimize the State of Israel, and this, for example, was the aim of the nefarious resolution pushed through the 1975 Assembly describing Zionism, the national liberation movement of the Jewish people, as a form of racism.

In parallel, they have sought to legitimize the second set of national rights which they claim for the Palestinian Arabs, ostensibly under the leadership of the terrorist group which those same Arab states created as a weapon to destroy Israel.

It was in conformity with this strategy that they took advantage of the numerical majority at their disposal in this Organization to set up the so-called "Palestine Committee" in 1975. That committee is made up of twenty-three members, of whom nineteen do not have diplomatic relations with Israel and, not by coincidence, many of whom even deny Israel's right to exist to this very day.

The Arab strategists, not content with having abused the General Assembly, have proceeded systematically to subvert every organ and body of this Organization for their destructive purposes. In the wake of the Palestine Committee, they even established a so-called Special Unit on Palestinian Rights within the Secretariat itself, thus compromising the Secretariat's integrity and misappropriating international funds as part of their design. Over the years this unit, under the close guidance of the Palestine Committee, has produced a series of pseudo-scientific studies bearing the emblem of the United Nations, replete with deliberate distortions and conscious falsifications of well-known historical facts.

From its outset, the Palestine Committee has been a pliant tool in the hands of the PLO, and hence it comes as no surprise that its recommendations, first formulated in 1976, are nothing but a prescription for the dismantlement of Israel in stages.

This approach is in conformity with the tactics which the PLO had worked out for itself some years ago. Once again one must refer to the historical record. In 1974, the PLO's so-called National Council, meeting in Cairo, adopted a ten-point platform which incorporated a phased political program for the eventual take-over of the entire territory of the former Palestine Mandate on both sides—let me stress—on both sides of the River Jordan. This program is sometimes described by the PLO spokesmen as a two- or three-stage policy. In essence, it aims in its first stage at the establishment of a second Palestinian Arab State anywhere in the territories administered by Israel since 1967. The second stage is to use this proposed state as a launching pad for the ultimate overthrow of Israel.

This program was described with complete candor by Farouk Kaddoumi, one of Yasir Arafat's henchmen, in *Newsweek* magazine on 14 March 1977:

There are two (initial) phases to our return: the first phase to the 1967 lines, and the second to the 1948 lines. The third stage is the democratic State of Palestine. So we are fighting for these three stages.

Asked if the PLO has become more moderate, Kaddoumi replied:

By moderation we mean we are ready . . . to establish a state on a part of our territory. In the past we said no, on all of it, immediately, a democratic State of Palestine. Now we say, no, this can be implemented in three stages. That is moderation.

This is the harsh truth, notwithstanding the wishful thinking and illusions of certain international figures, in Europe and elsewhere.

The brutal fact is, and remains, that the PLO's real aim and character, as an instrument in the hands of the Arab rejectionist states, is proven day by day by its criminal acts of terror and barbarism against the citizens of Israel and against its representatives abroad. The Government of Israel, as a responsible, self-respecting government, cannot take a superficial or simplistic view of the evidence readily available to all of us.

Here, at the United Nations, the PLO does not reveal its true colors. Intent on cultivating a false image of moderation, it has mastered the art of double-talk in order to maintain an aura of respectability. But we in the Middle East hear the radio broadcasts that emanate daily from Damascus, Beirut and Baghdad. On the PLO broadcasting station which calls itseslf the *Voice of Palestine* we have heard Yasir Arafat, in passing out a new class from a terrorist training course, declare that "these fighters are the people who will reach Jerusalem and Jaffa" (19 September 1978). For those who are perhaps unfamiliar with the geography of the region, the *Palestine Corner* on Damascus Radio recently explained:

Israel does not exist in the Arab nation, and there is no Zionist state in the Arab homeland. Only the Arabs have Palestine from Nazareth to Rafah and from the Mediterranean Sea to the Jordan River.

This is our formula for peace. I am going to repeat it on your station so that everyone listening knows exactly what the PLO wants. . . .

Our goal is to establish an independent, sovereign Palestinian state on every inch of Palestinian territory evacuated by Israeli forces. I repeat: on every inch of Palestinian soil evacuated by Israeli forces. . . .

This means that the PLO will acknowledge or accept the establishment of a Palestinian state in the West Bank and Gaza as *one of the stages* towards an envisaged independent Palestinian state in *all* of Palestine.

(18 September 1978)

We who live in the Middle East, who hear and read the PLO's own statements there and who have witnessed the mangled bodies of women and children being pulled from buses and stores bombed by the PLO, cannot be misled.

When I say "we in the Middle East," I am referring not only to Israel. Indeed, the damage which the terrorists have inflicted on us is dwarfed by the havoc they have wrought in the territories of our neighbors. Jordan is certainly aware of Arafat's declaration in 1974 that:

> Jordan is ours, Palestine is ours, and we shall build our national entity on the whole of this land after having freed it of both the Zionist presence and the reactionary traitor presence [King Hussein].
> (Arafat in letter to Jordanian Students' Congress in Baghdad, reported in *The Washington Post* of 12 November 1974

Indeed, point five of the Ten Points approved by the PLO Council in June 1974 calls, in effect, for a struggle against the Jordanian regime. That this was not idle rhetoric had already been demonstrated in the assassination of Jordanian Prime Minister Wasfi Tal in Cairo in November 1971. King Hussein did not hesitate to call the PLO "criminals" when they threatened to tear his country apart. Nor has he forgotten the PLO's attempt to subvert his regime in 1970. The King said about the PLO:

> The PLO as the sole representative of the people of Palestine? Ridiculous! How can half a dozen splintered organizations—partly ruled by criminals who quarrel among themselves about radical ideologies—make such a claim? What they call representation, or war of liberation, is nothing but terror."
> (*Muenchner Merkur*, 28–29 October 1978)

But the General Assembly's memory is selective. Now that Syria once again patronizes the PLO this forum can conveniently forget Tel al-Zatar and the pitched battles between the Syrians and the PLO during the Lebanese civil war. It can forget President Assad's statement on Damascus Radio, when PLO terrorists attacked the Semiramis Hotel in Damascus:

> We condemn this act of terror, committed by a gang of traitors and criminals. We refuse to bargain with them.
> (Radio Damascus, 27 September 1976)

And the Assembly can forget the article by Syria's Defense Minister, General Mustafa T'lass, in *Tishrin*, the official Syrian Army newspaper, where he bitterly attacked the PLO:

> My Palestinian comrades, the Moslems of Lebanon have begun to hate you because you are interfering in their daily life and their personal

liberty. What, then, is the aim of your liberation? Is your sublime target the massacre of Lebanon? Or perhaps your grand design was to slaughter the residents of the Semiramis Hotel in Damascus? You are mistaken, Palestinian comrades, because you arouse nothing but disgust among all honest Arab citizens.

(10 September 1976)

But perhaps the greatest tragedy of all caused by the PLO is that which befell the people of Lebanon. Whatever the current political accommodations of Jordan and Syria, the Lebanese are still today suffering from the havoc wrought by the PLO.*

One of the tragedies of the Palestinian Arabs has been that for over fifty years they have been dominated by an extremist leadership. Starting with the notorious Mufti of Jerusalem, who was wanted by the Allies as a war criminal for his complicity in the Nazi genocide of European Jewry, that leadership had no compunction about terrorizing and assassinating its political rivals. It was totally lacking in political realism and obstinately opposed to compromise. It led those whom it claimed to represent from one disaster to another. The Palestinian Arabs in Judea, Samaria and the Gaza District, who are prepared to live in peace with Israel, have been steadily terrorized and intimidated by the PLO, which has been conducting without let-up a campaign of political assassination against them. To quote from *The Times* of London of 27 November 1981:

. . . the Palestinian people . . . ever since the birth of Israel have paid dearly for the extremism and intrigue of the Arab radicals who destroyed the Lebanon, nearly destroyed Jordan and will not rest, they say, until they have destroyed Israel. The Arab radicals . . . cannot deliver anything except what they have delivered in the past: bloodshed and futility.

PLO terrorism has been used to intimidate Palestinian Arabs willing to coexist peacefully with Israel. After President Sadat's visit to Jerusalem the so-called "Democratic Front for the Liberation of Palestine," one of the constituent members under the PLO umbrella, swore to assassinate any Palestinian Arab who accepted President Sadat's invitation to the Cairo Conference. The PLO made good its threat. Its information agency, WAFA, announced that orders had been issued "to liquidate a number of agents" and boasted that it had already killed Hamdi Kadi, in charge of education in Ramallah. The same day, the PLO observer at the United Nations publicly justified the murder, telling NBC news:

"The collaborators with the forces of occupation are executed. They are not assassinated. So this man must have been executed because of his collaboration with the forces of occupation."

---

*On the PLO role in Lebanon, see Chapter 8, Section E.

Asked by the disbelieving NBC interviewer whether he actually condoned what had been done, Mr. Terzi replied: "Those who collaborate with the enemy should be executed, yes."

In its desperate attempt to sabotage any peace agreement, the PLO has escalated its campaign of intimidation. Other Palestinian Arabs have been assassinated, like Abdel-Nur Janho, a Christian Arab merchant in Ramallah who rejected the PLO because, in his words, "We must live together. Hatred helps no one." He and others like him have been the victims of PLO hatred. The PLO's message to the residents of the territories is clear. Kadi, Janho and others have become symbols of fear, so that the PLO may try to claim that Palestinian Arabs reject any settlement with Israel. Sometimes, however, even PLO terror cannot quell a silent protest. As Janho's son, Khalil, reported to *New York Times* correspondent Flora Lewis:

> "When my father was killed, Khalaf (the mayor of Ramallah) told me there wouldn't be three people at his funeral. Well, it was the biggest funeral ever seen on the West Bank. There were cars halfway to Jerusalem."
>
> (*New York Times* News Service, 21 August 1978)

In the summer of 1979, the PLO assassinated the Imam of Gaza, a prominent religious leader who was prepared to work for peace. In parallel, the PLO has stepped up its anti-peace campaign, taking advantage, for example, of the academic freedom prevailing in the universities established by Israel in the areas concerned as well as exploiting the democratic institutions also encouraged by the Israel administration.

If I have dwelt at length on the policy and program of the PLO, it is because *that* is the policy and program which the General Assembly is once again being asked to endorse and accept.

The Two Refugee Problems in the Middle East

In the light of all that I have said, let me try to define the true nature and scope of the problem today. For this we have to return again to 1947. Immediately after the adoption of General Assembly resolution 181(II), the Arabs resorted to the illegal use of force, with a view to destroying that resolution. Subsequently the armies of seven Arab states marched against the fledgling State of Israel on the day it was established, on 14 May 1948.

As a result of those acts of aggression in 1948, the Arab states created two refugee problems—not just one, as is commonly supposed.

By the time Arab aggression against Israel was successfully thwarted in 1949, some six hundred thousand Palestinian Arabs had become refugees and found themselves in areas—including Judea, Samaria and the Gaza

District—controlled by Arab governments. Instead of absorbing and integrating their Palestinian brethren, who speak the same language, share the same cultural, historical and religious heritage and frequently even have family relations in the Arab host countries, those countries forced them to remain in camps and exploited them callously as a political weapon against Israel.

A much larger refugee problem was caused by Arab hostility toward the ancient Jewish communities in Arab lands. From 1948 to the present day more than eight hundred thousand Jews have been forced to leave Arab countries. About six hundred fifty thousand of them came to Israel—in most cases with only their clothes on their backs. Hence, in effect, a *de facto* exchange of populations has taken place between the Arab states and Israel, triggered by Arab aggression in 1947–1948.

These Jewish refugees integrated themselves into Israel's society, and today Jews from Arab lands and from other Muslim countries, as well as their offspring born in Israel, form the majority of the Jewish population of Israel.

On the other hand, the world continues to hear much clamor about the Arab refugees, who are still at the center of the Palestinian problem as we know it today. But when one takes a closer look at that group of refugees, it can readily be seen that it is not a problem of major dimensions. According to United Nations figures, there have been anything between 60 million and 100 million refugees and displaced persons since the end of World War II. Even if one accepts the more conservative figure, the Arab refugees in 1948 constituted no more than 1 percent of the total. The vast majority of the other refugee problems in the world, including that of the Jewish refugees, has been solved by their absorption and rehabilitation into their new countries or places of residence. To be sure, this has already been done as regards most of the Arab refugees and their offspring, at least two-thirds of whom continue to live in the territory of the former Palestine Mandate and are nationals of Jordan, the Palestinian Arab state created on the bulk of that territory.*

B

Is Peace Attainable?

Consolidated and abbreviated version of statements made in the UN General Assembly in the years 1978–1982.

At a time when restraint, sensitivity and quiet consultation are of the utmost importance, the current proceedings of the General Assembly are

---

*For full discussion of "The Two Refugee Problems," see Section C in this chapter.

particularly inappropriate. In Cairo, Jerusalem, and Washington real issues are being addressed with earnestness and in good faith in a genuine attempt to reach agreement. Here at the United Nations, the stale, extremist and unproductive formulae of former years are being rehashed in a form of ritualistic incantation, divorced from reality.

There is a sharp difference between condemnation and negotiation. It is no exaggeration to say that the proceedings in this hall in recent years constitute a negation of the negotiating process. "To negotiate" is defined by Webster's dictionary as follows: "To confer with another so as to arrive at the settlement of some matter; . . . to arrange for or bring about through conference, discussion and compromise." That process presupposes mutual recognition and respect by each side for the other. Compromise is impossible when one side refuses to recognize the existence of the other. This Assembly's recourse to condemnation therefore not only negates the very principle of negotiations and compromise, but constitutes an implicit acknowledgement and acceptance of the absolute refusal of the hard-line Arab states to recognize the existence of the State of Israel.

That refusal and that rejection, as embodied in the very name "rejectionist," forms the heart and core of the Arab-Israel conflict. That rejection predated the rebirth of the State of Israel. It results directly from the Arab refusal to come to terms with the revival of Jewish independence and national sovereignty in the Jewish homeland and the creation of a Jewish state in the Middle East alongside the Arab states of the region. All subsequent problems, including the refugee problems (both Jewish and Arab) and that of borders, are the *result* of the ongoing conflict, *not* its cause.

There is no better evidence of this fact than the events since President Sadat's visit to Jerusalem. The moment the president of the Arab Republic of Egypt recognized the need for a new departure in the Middle East, negotiations began. There arose difficulties and snags and problems, as there will inevitably be when real national interests are involved. But by *any* standards the progress toward peace has been remarkable. When compared with the length of time taken to negotiate the Panama Canal Treaty, or a German-Polish Treaty, or with the fluctuating hopes for further progress in the SALT negotiations, it must be admitted that the breakthroughs achieved by Israel and Egypt are remarkable. With patience, the remaining difficulties can and will be solved as well.

Pointing equally to the core of the Middle East conflict has been the hysterical reaction of the hard-line Arab states to Egypt's readiness to negotiate with Israel. It is not this or that provision in the Camp David Accords to which the rejectionists object but to the very fact of the recognition of Israel's existence that is signaled by the signing of a peace treaty. Therefore, from the outset of the current peace process, the Libyan-Syrian-Iraqi Axis, at the head of the Arab rejectionist camp, has left no stone unturned in its efforts to undermine the prospects of peace. This rejectionist troika has tried to raise barriers at every phase of the peace process.

Immediately after the historic talks between President Sadat and Prime Minister Begin in Jerusalem they convened in Tripoli what was proclaimed as the "Summit of Resistance and Confrontation." There they decided, as reported in *The New York Times* of 6 December 1977:

> To work for the elimination of the results of President Sadat's visit to the Zionist entity and his negotiations with the leaders of the Zionist enemy.

Immediately after the achievement of the Camp David Accords, they hastened to Damascus and established what they called the "Steadfastness Front," whose aims, as reported in *The Washington Post* on 22 September 1978 were:

> to set up functioning machinery for military, political and economic cooperation . . . seeking to frustrate the Camp David agreements.

Paralleling the peace negotiations in Washington, they met again in Baghdad in November 1978 and resolved, in article six of their concluding statement:

> to invite the Government of the Arab Republic of Egypt to renounce the two agreements and not to sign the peace treaty with the enemy.

And now, in the General Assembly, the representatives of the rejectionist troika and their supporters have given ample voice to their belligerent intentions and their uncompromising unwillingness to negotiate and come to terms with Israel.

In other words, every constructive step toward peace has been countered by a step in the opposite direction by those who still refuse to recognize reality. And as Egypt and Israel have broken new ground and reached agreements almost unthinkable before, the rejectionist states have remained mired in the same bellicose rhetoric in which they indulged thirty years ago when they made no secret of their intention to eliminate Israel from the map. Indeed, for those who harbor any doubts as to the roots and origins of the Arab-Israel conflict, I can only refer to the United Nations records themselves, and draw attention to the striking parallels between the statements of 1947 and those issued by the Baghdad Summit.*

The basic fact often deliberately ignored or glossed over in the deliberations taking place here is that the Arab-Israel conflict flows from the Arab

---

*See Chapter 3 below.

refusal to accept the existence of a Jewish state and the consequent attempt to destroy Israel. That has been the core of the conflict since 1948 and that is what it remains today in the eyes of the "rejectionist" camp. The territorial situation, which many speakers here seem to regard as the root cause of all the problems, is a direct function of four wars of aggression launched by the Arab states against Israel. Indeed, distinguished delegates would do well to refer to the declaration of the Baghdad Conference itself which states unambiguously:

> The conflict with the Zionist enemy goes beyond the struggle of the countries whose territories were occupied in 1967 and involves the entire Arab nation in view of the military, political, economic and *cultural* danger which the Zionist enemy represents to the entire Arab nation, its fundamental nationalist interests, its civilization and destiny.

In conjunction with the avowed aims of the Baghdad Summit to eliminate the State of Israel goes the anti-historical attempt to project backwards the existence of a Palestinian Arab people. In 1919 and 1920 the Arabs objected to the Palestine Mandate, partly on the grounds that they should not be separated from their brethren outside the area of the mandate. They claimed that they were not Palestinians but part of the Syrian people and of the greater Arab nation.

On 31 May 1956, Ahmed Shukairy, then Saudi Arabian delegate to the UN and later founder of the so-called PLO, told the Security Council: "It is common knowledge that Palestine is nothing but southern Syria."

President Assad of Syria expressed the same sentiment in March of 1974 when he said that: "Palestine is a basic part of southern Syria." (*The New York Times*, 9 March 1974).

In fact, the Baghdad decisions themselves refer continuously to the "Arab-Zionist conflict" and state their concern with the effects of the Camp David accords:

> On the *Arab* struggle against the Zionist aggression on the *Arab* nation. . . .

> All sons of the Arab nation and all Arab countries are concerned with this issue and committed to struggle for its cause and offer all material and moral sacrifices for its sake. . . .

> This fact dictates to all countries of the Arab nation the need to shoulder the responsibility of participating in this struggle with all potentials at their disposal. . . .

> The Conference resolved that Arab states should co-ordinate efforts of those Arab states capable of effective participation.

For the rejectionists, therefore, the heart and core of the Arab-Israel conflict remains what it was in 1947—their refusal to recognize or come to terms with the national liberation movement of the Jewish people and with the very existence of a Jewish state in the Middle East.

I have labored this point because it is a crucial one. As soon as the rejectionists come to terms with the reality of a Jewish state in the Middle East, negotiations can begin toward a rapid solution of all outstanding issues. The question of the Palestinian Arabs, while complex and difficult, *can* be solved. Contrary to the claims of the propagandists who have been trumpeting the slogan of an "uprooted people," the fact remains that 80 percent of the Palestinian Arabs today live in the territory of mandated Palestine. In fact, Jordan is itself a Palestinian Arab state, constituting as it does nearly three-quarters of the territory of the Palestine Mandate. With goodwill on both sides and with the resources available, the problem is not insoluble.

To the Camp David framework envisaging a self-governing authority for the Palestinian Arab inhabitants of Judea, Samaria and the Gaza District the PLO, backed by the hard-line rejectionists, has replied with terror. Three leading Arab citizens in those areas have been assassinated by PLO terrorists. Hundreds of local Arab leaders have received threatening letters warning them not to cooperate in the implementation of the Camp David accords. For the PLO and its supporters the slogan of Palestinian rights has become a code-word aimed at subverting every constructive solution to the conflict by threats and terror.

On the basic question before us today, the choice before the General Assembly is clear. It can regurgitate the sterile and time-worn slogans of the rejectionists who still seek a solution without Israel. Or it can lend its support to the path of peace through negotiations that has already yielded more than thirty years of war and conflict. Israel, the Jewish people and the Hebrew culture and heritage have been an integral part of Middle Eastern history, from the dawn of civilization; they will continue to be so in the future. Alongside the twenty-one Arab states with their immense territories stretching from the Atlantic Ocean to the Persian Gulf, their vast manpower, natural resources and oil, there is also ample room for a Jewish state in the region to which it historically and spiritually belongs. If this body is to make any contribution toward a peaceful settlement in the Middle East, it must remind the Arab rejectionists of the Jewish people's inalienable right to the Land of Israel and its right to self-determination, national independence and sovereignty. If the General Assembly is unable to lend this modicum of support to the peace process, I appeal to it at least not to obstruct that process by giving encouragement to the forces of war.

Four wars and a history of uninterrupted provocations aimed at destroying Israel have shown that military force cannot solve the Arab-Israel conflict. Most recently the Yom Kippur War of 1973, with its great destruction and loss of life, again showed the impossibility of achieving a solution by war. The time has long come to abandon the bankrupt slogans of the Khartoum conference which proclaimed: "No peace, no negotiations and no recognition of Israel." For those negative concepts—reaffirmed in essence at the Baghdad Summit—are intimately linked; there can be no peace without recognition and negotiations.

Israel firmly believes that a new reality has been created in the Middle East precisely because the negotiating process, for the first time, has taken the rights and interests of both sides into account. Direct negotiations between Egypt and Israel on issues which seemed intractable have now produced the first Arab-Israel peace treaty. Israel is willing to enter also into negotiations on the second agreement reached at Camp David—the framework for peace in the Middle East. We have stated before, and I take this opportunity to state again, that Israel seeks the full implementation of both Camp David accords—in letter and in spirit. We view the peace treaty with the Arab Republic of Egypt as the first step in the search for a peace settlement in the entire Middle East.

The Camp David frameworks have proved to be the only constructive way toward the achievement of peace in our region to have emerged in over thirty years.

With regard to the Palestinian Arab residents of Judea, Samaria and the Gaza District, the Camp David framework sees the solution in terms of their full autonomy, for a transitional period of five years, before reaching an agreement on the final status of the areas concerned. To that end, it was agreed to negotiate on a principle of self-government—to be exercised through an administrative council—for the Arab inhabitants of the areas in question.

The Camp David framework invites the Palestinian Arab residents of Judea, Samaria and the Gaza District to play an active role in shaping their future, by calling on them to participate not only in current negotiations to set up a self-governing administrative council, but also in the negotiations which will determine the final status of the areas they live in as well as in the eventual negotiations on a peace treaty between Israel and Jordan, in which the delimitation of boundaries between the two countries will be agreed.

This solution offers the Palestinian Arabs concerned greater opportunities than anything they have ever experienced in their history. It offers them the prospect of governing themselves, of prosperity and of peaceful co-existence alongside their neighbors. It offers them a secure future, free from terror.

A framework for peaceful co-existence between Jew and Arab is thus clearly emerging now; the PLO, Jordan, Syria and their ilk are conspiring to destroy it. The greater the promise for Jewish-Arab understanding and co-operation, the greater the combined rejectionist effort to see it terminated.

The terrorist chiefs as well as the leaders of Jordan, Syria and their rejectionist friends are obviously gnawed by the fear that the Palestinian Arabs might strike out in a different direction, aimed at peaceful co-existence and mutual accommodation with Israel in a spirit of reconciliation between the two fraternal Semitic peoples.

It must surely be recognized by now that the pattern adopted by this Organization in its deliberations on the Arab-Israel conflict has proved sterile and has indeed become an obstacle to a peaceful settlement. Yet, that conflict is clearly amenable to solution, given a political will to effect a solution. Moreover, it is a conflict for which a framework for a solution exists, and indeed, one which has over the last few years been moving toward a solution within that framework.

Hence we do not need alternative frameworks, we do not need alternative plans. The Camp David framework for peace in the Middle East is based on and anchored in Security Council resolution 242 (1967).

As sight is often lost of this fundamental fact, let me quote from the first paragraph of the framework:

> The agreed basis for a peaceful settlement of the conflict between Israel and its neighbors is UN Security Council Resolution 242 in all its parts.

It must be understood that any tampering with Security Council resolution 242 can only jeopardize the ongoing peace process. Any General Assembly document which makes partial and selective reference to Security Council resolution 242 is incompatible with the letter and spirit of that resolution. Similarly, any General Assembly resolution which ignores the rights of Israel, while persistently favoring and serving the interests of its adversaries, will be totally unproductive. For that is essentially the approach of the rejectionist Arabs who still deny the inalienable rights of the Jewish people to self-determination, national independence and sovereignty in its homeland.

An Arab state which was at war with Israel for three decades has now concluded a peace treaty with Israel and at the same time undertaken with Israel to work toward a comprehensive solution of other aspects of the Arab-Israel conflict.

By all precepts of international law and criteria of progress, the conclusion of a peace treaty and a determination to continue the peace process is surely not only a legitimate but also a desirable and commendable position for two sovereign states to take. No third party or parties have the legal or moral authority to question, let alone deny the validity of the accords attained.

Why is it then that the historic breakthrough to peace, embodied in the Camp David frameworks and the Egyptian-Israeli peace treaty, encounters so much hostility, prejudice and ill will?

The answer is clear. These agreements are incompatible with the avowed desire of the rejectionist Arab states and of their instrument, the terrorist PLO, to destroy Israel, if not at one stroke, then by stages. They disrupt the belligerent schemes of the rejectionists. They do not suit the interests of their allies, some close and some more distant, who are eager to continue and profit by fishing in the troubled waters of the Middle East.

What then are the conditions for a balanced UN approach to the solution of the Arab-Israel conflict?

First, the UN must return to the world of reality. In the process, it must also give up its hypocritical stand and stop applying double standards on everything to do with this conflict.

Second, the facts, the real facts, of the conflict in all its aspects must be admitted. It must be recognized that the Palestinian Arabs have long enjoyed self-determination and that an Arab state exists in Palestine—the Palestinian Arab state of Jordan—alongside the Palestinian Jewish state of Israel.

Third, it must be recognized that the core of the problem has always been and remains the denial of the right of the Jewish people to self-determination and national sovereignty in its ancestral homeland.

Fourth, and finally, the General Assembly must recognize that one-sided and biased resolutions, designed to bypass Security Council resolution 242, will not bring peace any closer. Resolutions and declarations bulldozed through the General Assembly solve nothing.

This simple truth was stated clearly by Andrei Vyshinsky, the distinguished representative of the U.S.S.R. in the Security Council, on 29 March 1954, when he observed:

> You can submit whatever resolutions you like. But life does not call for resolutions; it calls for decision which can promote the settlement of important international questions which are still outstanding.
>
> What is the proper method for this? The method is that of direct negotiation between the interested parties.

This option is open to all of Israel's neighbors. Indeed, it is the only constructive option open to them. The Arab States and their supporters can engage as much as they like in verbal warfare here at the United Nations. Given the parliamentary situation in the Assembly, they may even be able to push through whatever resolutions they like.

But these can only be Pyrrhic victories. Those who seem to think that an excess of repetitive Assembly resolutions adopted by large, automatic majorities, create "rights" or make "binding obligations" or even international law are deluding themselves.

Only when the Arabs exhibit a genuine willingness to make peace, or rather a willingness to make genuine peace; only when they sit down and negotiate with Israel on the basis of recognition and mutual respect, will a comprehensive solution to the Arab-Israel conflict in all its aspects be achieved.

Israel has shown its willingness and ability to make peace with its largest Arab neighbor. It is now up to the rest of the Arab world to show that it is willing to make peace with Israel. This Organization under its Charter is dedicated to the promotion of international peace and security and of peaceful relations among nations. Instead, it has grotesquely condemned a peace treaty of epoch-making proportions, while at the same time lending its support and granting irregular privileges to a group of international terrorists. If the United Nations has a contribution to make, it is to encourage the Arab states to come to terms with Israel and to negotiate with us directly, without preconditions, seriously and in mutual respect.

C

The Two Refugee Problems

Letter dated 27 June 1979, addressed to the Secretary-General of the UN, and circulated as a document of the General Assembly.

I have the honor to refer to the letter of 31 May 1979, addressed to you by the Permanent Representative of the United Arab Emirates in his capacity as chairman of the Arab group with regard to the budgetary problems of the United Nations Relief and Works Agency for Palestine Refugees in the Near East (UNRWA).

Support for the continued functioning of UNRWA and concern for its budgetary problems are shared by many members of the United Nations and particularly by those, like Israel, which give expression to their concern through financial contributions to the agency. However, the cause of UNRWA can surely not be helped by misrepresenting the origins of the refugee problem, and by the continued manipulation of the Palestinian Arab refugees and of the General Assembly resolutions relating to them for purposes of political propaganda.

The above-mentioned letter is unhelpful precisely because it is yet another attempt to exploit for political purposes the refugee problem, which is essentially a humanitarian question. The hypocrisy of countries such as the United Arab Emirates, in focusing narrowly on the issue of Palestinian Arab refugees, is highlighted when contrasted with their attitude to the desperate plight of non-Arab refugees, Asian and African.

In appraising the letter in question, the following facts should be borne in mind:

1. The refugee problem in the Middle East—in both its aspects involving Arab and Jewish refugees—was created by the Arabs, who resorted to the illegal use of force against the Jewish community in Palestine immediately after the adoption of the General Assembly Partition Resolution of 29 November 1947 and by the armies of seven Arab states which launched a war of aggression against the fledgling State of Israel on the day of its establishment. Had the Arabs recognized the inalienable rights of the Jewish people to self-determination and sovereignty in its homeland, and had they not set out to destroy by force of arms that General Assembly resolution there would have been no refugees, Arab or Jewish. Thus, responsibility for the refugee problem in the Middle East lies entirely with the Arabs.

2. Early in 1948, local Arab leaders and neighboring Arab governments began exhorting Palestinian Arabs to leave their homes in order to clear the way for the Arab irregular forces and later for the invading Arab armies, promising those who departed that they would soon return in the wake of a crushing Arab victory.

3. By the time Arab aggression against Israel was successfully thwarted in 1949, some 600,000 Palestinian Arabs had become refugees and found themselves in areas—including Judea, Samaria and the Gaza District—controlled by Arab governments. Instead of absorbing and integrating their Palestinian brethren, the Arab host countries forced them to remain in camps and exploited them callously as a political weapon against Israel. They continue to do so to the present day.

4. The thousands of Jews who lived in Judea, Samaria and the Gaza District until 1948 could not resist for long the invading Arab armies. Those of them who had survived the invasion and prison camps sought and found refuge in the State of Israel. These Jewish refugees remained for a short time recipients of aid from UNRWA, but soon they were fully rehabilitated and integrated into the society and economy of Israel.

5. A much larger problem of Jewish refugees was caused by Arab hostility toward the ancient Jewish communities in Arab lands. Those Jews, who at the time numbered nearly one million, had for centuries been treated as second-class citizens, subject to various forms of discrimination and persecution. Even before the defeat of the Arab armies in 1948–1949, they fell victim to violence and further persecution at the hands of Arabs thirsting for revenge. Many of them were murdered. Others were thrown into prison and tortured. Hundreds of thousands were forced to flee, leaving behind considerable property and material assets. Homes and businesses were looted. Bank accounts were frozen. Communal property and priceless cultural assets were expropriated, the bulk of them by Arab

governments. Thus, 3,000 years of organized Jewish life throughout the Middle East and North Africa came to an end.

6. From 1948 to the present day—and this process is still continuing—more than 800,000 Jews have been forced to leave Arab countries. About 650,000 of them have come to Israel—in most cases with only the clothes on their backs. Hence, in effect, an exchange of populations has taken place between the Arab states and Israel, triggered by Arab aggression in 1947–1948.

7. Little is heard about these Jewish refugees because they did not remain refugees for long. In contrast to the Arab governments' treatment of the Palestinian Arab refugees, the Government of Israel, with the financial assistance of the Jewish people, made strenuous efforts to rehabilitate the Jewish refugees. They integrated themselves into Israel society. They found shelter, new lives and dignity. Today, Jews from Moslem countries and their offspring form the majority of the Jewish population in Israel.

It is Israel's position that the problem of Arab refugees in the Middle East can only find a practical solution within a framework of resettlement following the *de facto* population exchange that has already taken place. They should be absorbed and rehabilitated in Arab countries in the same way as the Jewish refugees have been integrated into Israel.

This has been understood even by certain Palestinian Arab observers. Speaking about the plight of Jews in Arab countries, Sabri Jiryis wrote in the Lebanese daily *Al Nahar* on 15 May 1975:

> There is no need now to recount the circumstances which brought about the dislodgement of the Jews from Arab states from their countries, where they lived for centuries, expelling them in the most ugly manner, after confiscating their property or seizing control of it at the cheapest price. It is impossible to justify the matter by saying that it was the past régimes in the Arab world, aided by the imperialist power which worked in co-ordination with Zionism who did it. . . . The historical results ensuing from such an operation cannot be wiped out by such simple pretexts. . . . There is no need to say that the problem of those Jews and their transfer to Israel is not merely theoretical, at least as far as the Palestinians are concerned. It has a very practical repercussion on the future of the Palestinian problem.

Security Council resolution 242 (1967) of 22 November 1967 refers to the necessity "for achieving a just solution of the refugee problem." That formulation applies equally to Jewish refugees. As is well known, attempts in the Security Council to restrict it to Arab refugees failed. Israel reserves for redress within the framework of a comprehensive peace between itself and the Arab states the settlement of all claims of Jewish refugees from Arab lands.

Since the Second World War some 60 million persons have been displaced and have become refugees. Virtually all of these have found new homes and have been integrated into the host societies. The only significant exception to this almost general rule are the Arab refugees, a relatively small number by world standards, who have been forced by their brethren to live on international charity. Illustrative of the Arab states' callous approach toward the plight of these refugees is also the fact that of the $US 1.4 billion contributed since 1950 by the world community to UNRWA for the benefit of the Arab refugees only 5 percent has been provided by Arab states—the solicitousness of the representative of the United Arab Emirates notwithstanding.

The above-mentioned letter from the chairman of the Arab group, representing a country with one of the highest *per capita* incomes in the world, is surely an unconscionable piece of special pleading. It comes at a time when Arab states are amassing staggering oil wealth (primarily harming the developing countries in the process), when masses of other refugees throughout the world are in desperate straits, and when new and pressing refugee problems are being created day by day. It in no way furthers the cause of UNRWA and the tasks entrusted to it.

D

The Myth of Moslem Benevolence toward Jews in Arab Lands

Statements made in the UN General Assembly on 29 November 1979 and 4 December 1979.

Arab states, in refusing to reconcile themselves to the inalienable rights of the Jewish people, including its right to an independent and sovereign state, are reflecting a much broader approach of exclusivity, an attitude of racism, *vis-à-vis* minorities in their midst, that has characterized Arab political activity since the end of the First World War.

This form of exclusivism and perverted political mentality leaves no room for non-Arab and non-Muslim states in the region. It is for this reason that the Arabs have consistently suppressed the rights of all national, religious and ethnic minorities in the area. Hence, for example, in the 1930s Iraq suppressed with great brutality calls for a measure of autonomy made by the Assyrians—an ancient Christian group. It is for the same reason that, in the 1950s and 1960s, Syria worked systematically to break up and disperse the concentrations of the Kurds, an ethnic minority within its borders. It is for the same reason that, in the 1960s and 1970s, Iraq has put down harshly and tried to stamp out any moves for autonomy by the Kurds. And even more recently, this is one of the reasons why Syria was so swift to join the civil war in Lebanon, so that an end would be put, probably once and for all, to the only multi-denominational state in the Arab League.

One could in fact expand, to very great length, on the catalogue of intolerance toward religious and ethnic minorities in the area. This exclusivist attitude explains many of the phenomena in the recent history of the Middle East, including the total negativism in the formula adopted at Khartoum shortly after the Six Day War in 1967, which mandated "no recognition" of Israel, "no negotiations" with Israel, and "no peace" with Israel.

This attitude also explains the perverted psychology of the representative of the Palestinian Arab state of Jordan, who permits himself, in different UN organs and committees, to refer to Israel as "a cancercus growth," as "a bubonic plague," as "a blood-sucking vampire," and so on. It is not that Mr. Nuseibeh has perhaps been seeing too many Count Dracula films recently— it is that he is giving unrestrained expression to a fundamental attitude which refuses to admit the rights of the Jewish people to sovereignty in any part of the original area of Mandated Palestine.

All of this points to a sad conclusion, of wider implication, with regard to the entire Middle East. It is that peace will only come to the area, not only *vis-à-vis* the Arab-Israel conflict, but also *vis-à-vis* other conflicts in the region as a whole, when full recognition is given to the rights of all the national, religious and ethnic minorities which, it should be remembered, make up a very large part of the region's total population.

Despite all this, it has been alleged that before the establishment of Israel the condition of Jews in Arab lands was idyllic. It has also been alleged that were it not for the creation of the State of Israel, Jews and Arabs would, to this day, be living in amity and equality throughout the Arab world. There have been those who have invited the "Arab Jews" to return to their former homes.

The idyll of Arab-Jewish co-existence in Arab lands is a canard, if ever there was one. For centuries, Jews were barely tolerated as second-class citizens in Arab society.

But why should the Assembly take my word for it? Let me quote from a work by the well-known French author, Albert Memmi. I choose Albert Memmi advisedly, because he was born in Tunis in 1920. In the second chapter of his book, *Juifs et Arabes* published in Paris in 1974, entitled "Who is an Arab Jew?" he writes:

> The much vaunted idyllic life of the Jews in Arab lands is a myth! The
> truth . . . is that from the outset we were a minority in a hostile

environment; as such, we underwent all the fears, the agonies, and the
constant sense of frailty of the underdog. As far back as my childhood
memories go—in the tales of my father, my grandparents, my aunts and
uncles—coexistence with the Arabs was not just uncomfortable, it was
marked by threats periodically carried out.

The Jewish communities lived in the shadow of history, under arbitrary
rule and the fear of all-powerful monarchs whose decisions could not be
rescinded or even questioned. . . . But the Jews were at the mercy not
only of the monarch but also of the man in the street. My grandfather
still wore the obligatory and discriminatory Jewish garb, and in his time
every Jew might expect to be hit on the head by any Moslem whom he
happened to pass.

I have lived through the alarms of the ghetto; the rapidly barred doors
and windows, my father running home after hastily shutting his shop,
because of rumors of an impending pogrom. My parents stocked food
in expectation of a siege, which did not always materialize, but this
gives the measure of our anguish, our permanent insecurity.

· The rest of Memmi's description is extraordinarly painful. It explodes the
myth that Jews and Arabs lived together happily before the establishment of
Israel.

In fact, Jews have been persecuted and discriminated against by the Arabs
for many centuries. The medieval degradations suffered by the Jews in Arab
lands continued unabated, in varying degrees of intensity, down to our own
times.

Jews, like Christians, were a "tolerated people" *(dhimmi)* in the Arab
domain, but this does not mean tolerance in the modern sense of the word.
It means bare acceptance and the right to practice their religion as mono-
theists as against other idolators and non-believers.

Thus, in the early part of this century, Vambéry, one of many renowned
travelers who recorded the situation of the Jews in Arab lands, was moved
to reflect:

I do not know any more miserable, hapless, and pitiful individual on
God's earth than the Jahudi in those countries.

"Jahudi" is of course the Arabic term for Jew. When the Arabs talk glibly
of Jews and Arabs living in blissful harmony throughout the centuries, the
meaning is clear: the abasement and harassment of Jews in previous centuries
was indeed idyllic by comparison with the savage treatment meted out to
Jews in Arab lands in the past fifty years.

In the wake of political developments in the twentieth century, the persecution of Jews was intensified. Jews in Arab states were deprived of their most elementary human rights, their property was confiscated, their citizenship revoked and pogroms were organized against them with the tacit, or not so tacit, consent of the authorities.

Rabble-rousers could always be found to incite mobs for religious or any other reason, and the frenzied populace would fall upon the Jewish citizens and butcher them.

Since achieving independence in 1932, Iraq, for example, has subjected Jews to an incessant regime of terror. Official state policy toward the Jews has meant secret trials, torture and public executions.

I need hardly elaborate on what would have befallen the ancient Jewish community in Iraq during World War II, had the attempt of Rashid Ali al-Keilani to install a pro-Nazi regime there succeeded. While the revolution of the pro-Nazi officers was short-lived, several of them managed to reach Berlin, where they remained until the end of the war. A number of them were eventually arrested, tried and sentenced to death. Today, the officers connected with the pro-Nazi coup are hailed as national heroes in Iraq.

Only a month after the attempted Nazi coup in Iraq, a savage, but typical, pogrom took place in Baghdad. On the Jewish festival of Shavuot, Jews were murdered on their way to synagogue, many were dragged off buses and slaughtered, and their corpses run over by passing cars. Soldiers, policemen and members of youth groups massacred, raped, wounded and robbed, and burned down houses and shops. After three days of this anti-Semitic orgy, a hundred and eighty Jews were dead, hundreds more maimed and wounded, and over a million pounds sterling worth of property had been looted.

This scene repeated itself on a scale previously unknown even in Iraq, when the Arab states sought to take revenge in their frustration at their thwarted attempt to destroy the fledgling Jewish state of Israel. As a result of ever-increasing persecution, almost the entire Jewish community of Iraq fled, in total destitution, between 1948 and 1951.

The small remnant that was left behind lives on in squalid conditions, in constant fear for their lives. The Iraqi Government and particularly the secret police, threaten them even with murder. The authorities cut telephone lines to Jewish homes. Many have been arrested and released only after paying a high ransom for their lives. Jewish students have been expelled from universities and schools. Jews have been dismissed from their jobs.

During 1968, chanting mobs in the streets of Baghdad acclaimed the stringing-up in public of the bodies of nine Jews falsely accused of espionage.

In Libya, too, the Arabs seethed with vengeance when yet another attempt to destroy Israel was thwarted in 1967. Mobs ransacked and set fire to all Jewish shops in Tripoli and then began seeking out Jewish apartments to burn. The panic-stricken Jews barricaded themselves in their homes while the attacks continued. After the riots, refugees from Libya related how they were subsequently expelled from the country with only the clothes on their backs.

The simple and unadorned facts speak more eloquently of the long history of Jewish suffering and persecution in Arab lands than all the idyllic romances and fictional histories that we have heard in the speeches of some Arab representatives.

3

The United Nations Partition Resolution of 29 November 1947

I

Consolidated version of letters dated 22 November 1978 and 12 December 1978, addressed to the Secretary-General of the UN.

In his letter dated 8 September 1978, the Permanent Representative of Jordan again reverted to the time-worn clichés of Arab propaganda in his attempt to rewrite the history of the Arab-Israel conflict, and to distort both the facts and the applicable law.

The letter boldly invokes the General Assembly partition resolution of 29 November 1947, willfully ignoring the fact that all of the states that were members of the Arab League (including his own country, which in those days called itself Transjordan) categorically rejected that resolution. The Arab states formally announced, on the record, that they reserved to themselves complete freedom of action to thwart the resolution of the General Assembly by the illegal use of force, from the moment of its adoption.

Among the comments made that very same day were the following:

Saudi Arabia
    . . . the Government of Saudi Arabia registers, on this historic occasion, the fact that it does not consider itself bound by the resolution adopted today by the General Assembly. Furthermore, it reserves to itself the full right to act freely in whatever way it deems fit, in accordance with the principles of right and justice.

Iraq
. . . in the name of my Government, I wish to put on record that Iraq does not recognize the validity of this decision, will reserve freedom of action towards its implementation, and holds those who were influential in passing it against the free conscience of mankind responsible for the consequences.

Syria
My country will never recognize such a decision. It will never agree to be responsible for it. Let the consequences be on the heads of others, not on ours.

Yemen
. . . the Government of Yemen does not consider itself bound by such a decision for it is contrary to the letter and spirit of the Charter. The Government of Yemen will reserve its freedom of action towards the implementation of this decision.

At a meeting of the premiers and foreign ministers of Arab League states held at Cairo between 8 and 17 December 1947, it was decided that the Arabs were "determined to enter battle against the United Nations decision" and to take "decisive measures" to prevent the implementation of the General Assembly's resolution.

On 25 February 1948, the Egyptian representative stated very simply: "We do not choose to comply with the General Assembly's resolution on Palestine," and in mid-April the spokesman for the Palestine Arab Higher Committee added:

The representative of the Jewish Agency told us yesterday that they were not attackers, not aggressors; that the Arabs had begun the fight and that once the Arabs stopped shooting, they would stop shooting also. As a matter of fact, we do not deny this fact.

The acts of violence perpetrated in Palestine with the active assistance of the neighboring Arab states reached such proportions that on 16 February 1948, the United Nations Commission on Palestine, in its first special report to the Security Council, bluntly notified the Council that:

Powerful Arab interests, both inside and outside Palestine, are defying the resolution of the General Assembly and are engaged in a deliberate effort to alter by force the settlement envisaged there.

Similarly, in its report dated 10 April 1948 to the General Assembly at its second special session, the same Commission advised the Assembly that:

Arab opposition to the Plan of the Assembly has taken the form of organized efforts by strong Arab elements, both inside and outside of Palestine, to prevent its implementation and to thwart its objectives by threats and acts of violence, including repeated armed incursions into Palestinian territory.

With the termination of the Mandate over Palestine on 14 May 1948, the armies of seven Arab states, including the Transjordan Arab Legion, illegally crossed the international boundaries in clear violation of the Charter of the United Nations. The Arab governments which dispatched them had the effrontery to make formal announcements of their illegal action to the Security Council. Their armed aggression was aimed at crushing the newly established State of Israel. The fact that they failed in their armed aggression does not legitimize their violation of international law. At the same time, that armed aggression also precludes them from invoking in any form the benefits of a General Assembly resolution which they both rejected and set out to destroy.

When, in a letter dated 20 May 1948 addressed to the Security Council, Transjordan sought to evade a discussion of the illegal military intervention of its army beyond its borders, the representative of the United States stated that the position of the King of Transjordan was characterized

by a certain contumacy towards the United Nations and the Security Council. He has sent us an answer to our questions. These were questions addressed to him, as a ruler who is occupying land outside his domain, by the Security Council, a body which is organized in the world to ask these questions of him. . . .

The contumacy of that reply to the Security Council is the very best evidence of the illegal purpose of this Government in invading Palestine with armed forces and conducting the war which it is waging there. It is against the peace; it is not on behalf of the peace. It is an invasion with a definite purpose. . . .

Therefore, here we have the highest type of evidence of the international violation of the law: the admission by those who are committing this violation.

This view was also supported by the majority of the members of the Security Council:

Mr. Parodi (France)
. . . the moment the regular forces of several countries crossed their frontiers and entered a territory which, whatever its status, was not their own, the moment fighting continued in these conditions and

became more serious, we clearly had to deal with the question of international peace within the meaning of the Charter.

Mr. Gromyko (Union of Soviet Socialist Republics)

The USSR delegation cannot but express surprise at the position adopted by the Arab States in the Palestine question, and particularly at the fact that those States—or some of them, at least—have resorted to such action as sending their troops into Palestine and carrying out military operations aimed at the suppression of the national liberation movement in Palestine.

Incidentally, the national liberation movement Mr. Gromyko was referring to is none other than Zionism, the national liberation movement of the Jewish people.

Mr. Tarasenko (Ukrainian Soviet Socialist Republic)

We are concerned with the plain fact that a number of Palestine's neighbor States have sent their troops into Palestine. Our knowledge of that fact is not based on rumours, or on newspaper reports, but on official documents signed by the Governments of those States informing the Security Council that their troops have entered Palestine. I refer, in particular, to the documents signed and sent by the Governments of Egypt and Trans-Jordan.

Nor can there be any doubt of the purpose for which those forces have entered Palestine. We may be sure they have not gone there for a summer camp vacation or for exercises. Those forces have a definite military and political purpose.

In these circumstances it is difficult to deny that we are faced with a situation involving a breach of the peace.

. . . We have recently heard one of the parties state repeatedly that it considers it has an imprescriptible right to carry out armed intervention in the internal affairs of Palestine, to destroy the State of Israel by force of arms and to bombard the peaceful cities of Israel under the pretext of restoring order.

Mr. López (Colombia)

. . . We have now what seems to me a rather extraordinary case. For some time past, nations have gone to war without previous notification to the other party. It has been claimed that it was not in conformity with international law to do so, but nevertheless that is the way it has been done. If previous notice was given, it was given at such a time and in such a way as not to give the other party time to make any preparations to protect itself.

But in this case we are returning to the old practice. When Egypt decided to intervene actively in Palestine, it duly notified the Security Council. It cabled directly to the President of the Security Council, saying: 'We are going into Palestine with our army.' When King Abdullah decided to go into Palestine, he duly notified the Security Council that he was moving his army into Palestine. That has all been done in accordance with the best etiquette of war. There has been no sin of omission, nothing that is not in conformity with the niceties of international practice.

The violation of the international boundaries of Palestine by the Arab armies constituted an act of aggression in breach of the Charter of the United Nations and of general international law. The consequent illegal occupation of any territory previously forming part of the mandated territory of Palestine by any of the invading Arab armies, including that of Transjordan, cannot give rise to any legitimate claim. The purported "annexation" of Judea and Samaria by Jordan in 1950 was in violation both of general international law and of the Israel-Jordan General Armistice Agreement of 1949. It is therefore not surprising that the outside world refused to recognize the validity of this illegal act based exclusively on Jordan's unlawful invasion of Judea and Samaria, and that even the Arab League threatened Jordan with expulsion from its ranks because of it.

The Jordanian representative attempted in his letter to conceal these fundamental flaws inherent in the Jordanian claims by relying on the "unopposed" admission of Jordan to the United Nations in 1955, despite the fact that Jordan at that time illegally occupied territories beyond its borders. As is well known, the admission of a state into the United Nations does not in itself imply a recognition of its boundaries. In fact, there exist numerous instances of territorial disputes in which both parties to the dispute are Members of the United Nations.

At best, the Jordanian representative's reliance on the circumstances of his country's admission to the United Nations would seem to be a rather belated and oblique acknowledgement of the fact that Israel did not vote against it, notwithstanding the fact that Jordan was occupying territories beyond its boundaries.

II

Excerpts from address delivered at the annual "Torch of Learning Award" luncheon of the American Friends of the Hebrew University, held at the Pierre Hotel in New York on 4 November 1982.

It is indeed an awkward feeling for me to address a friendly audience for a change. I understand we are running late. I shall be as brief as possible, lest I experience something I have been experiencing at the United Nations—people walking out on me.

You have very correctly introduced me, Madam Chairperson, as the Permanent Representative of Israel to the United Nations, but you should know that I have been preceded by five equally permanent representatives.

I come from the world of the Hebrew University to the world of the United Nations. Incidentally, a number of my colleagues from the Hebrew University Law School are currently also in the service of the State of Israel: We have provided two of the Supreme Court Justices of the State of Israel, Justice Elon and Justice Barak, who, as you know, is one of the members of the Commission of Inquiry on the Sabra/Shatila events. The chairman of Israel's Broadcasting Authority, my colleague Reuven Yaron, is our Professor of Roman Law at the Hebrew University, and the Attorney-General of the State of Israel, Yitzhak Zamir, is our Professor of Administrative law. So I am only one of a band of five of a small faculty who are currently in the service of the State of Israel.

But while all the others have more or less remained within the world of law, I have had to make this transition into the world of lawlessness. There is no greater distance anywhere in the world than the distance that exists between a school of law and the United Nations. It is true that most of the statements and virtually all of the resolutions at the United Nations are couched in legal terms, but all this is done only to cover up the utter lawlessness that has prevailed at the United Nations in recent years.

It could not be otherwise, for this Organization is now totally dominated by a lawless majority; by a group of states who have trampled underfoot domestically every conceivable human right and every respect for legal considerations, and who have then come before the United Nations to blast those few remaining democracies—a small beleaguered minority at the United Nations—who *are* committed to the principles and the ideals of the United Nations. It is against this background that we must view the assaults on Israel's standing, status, and legitimacy at the United Nations.

The 1975 resolution equating Zionism with racism was only the culmination of a process that had started a decade before. All the other numerous anti-Israel resolutions that have been accusing us of crimes against mankind, of all conceivable violations of international law, of being an outlaw among nations, have only one real objective—to create an international climate in which Israel would be delegitimized and considered really a pariah among nations—an outcast, an outlaw—so as to enable our enemies eventually to proceed to the physical annihilation of the State of Israel.

This ideological stage, as it were, is only the preliminary to what has been and remains the true and real objective of our enemies: the physical liquidation of Israel as a sovereign and independent Jewish state.

In this regard, I must tell you in all candor that we are not at all pleased with the kind of response that is being given to these and similar assaults by our friends, with or without quotation marks. We are being very often told by "real friends" of Israel, and they believe that they are doing us a great favor by saying so, that they fully support Israel's right to exist. When I heard that in one of the Security Council debates last June or July coming from the British representative, I asked for the floor and told him that the people of Israel greatly appreciate his statement and I wish to assure him that we in Israel, for our part, fully support the right of Great Britain to exist in peace and security. We regard it as an insult to the State of Israel even to talk of Israel's right to exist. It is axiomatic. Nobody in this world raises any question with regard to the right of the Maldive Islands, the Comoro Islands, the Seychelles and similar major powers to exist and live in peace and security. It is only with regard to Israel that this has become an issue at all. The real answer should have been: nobody has the right to challenge, or even to raise the question of Israel's right to exist! We condemn the very notion that Israel's right to exist can be questioned.

But let us face it. To some extent we Israelis, and even more so Jews around the world, also have to share some of the blame for this development in recent years. Has it not been the Jewish people that for so many years has been trying to justify Israel's right to exist by virtue of the fact that the United Nations passed a certain resolution in 1947? The result is there for everybody to see. We are being told at the United Nations and elsewhere that Israel is the only country in the world that was created by the United Nations, and now this country which owes its very existence to the United Nations is flouting United Nations resolutions.

Let me make it very clear: Israel does *not* owe its existence to the United Nations. There was a certain resolution adopted in 1947 by the General Assembly which, like every General Assembly resolution, was in the nature of a recommendation. It is true that the Jewish side in 1947 accepted that recommendation on condition of reciprocity, which in the event was not forthcoming because the Arabs rejected that recommendation and set out to destroy it by force of arms. Had it been for the United Nations, I would not be standing here today in front of you as Israel's representative to the United Nations because there would not have been a State of Israel. Israel exists because in 1948, despite the fact that we were abandoned by the United Nations, which did nothing to implement its own resolution, the people of Israel and the Jewish people stood up and did everything they could, in order to bring the State of Israel into being, to defend it and to protect it and to ensure its existence and survival.

So it is the other way around. It is not the United Nations that saved Israel—it was Israel that, in 1948, saved the reputation of the United Nations as a viable organization. The United Nations in that year, as a fledgling organization three years old, was very much in need of being saved by Israel from this terrible damage to its reputation.

4

The Situation in the Middle East

Consolidated version of statements made in the UN General Assembly in the years 1980–1983.

Contrary to the misconceptions fostered by the traditions of this debate, the Middle East is not confined to an area constituting 0.4 percent of the total land area properly referred to as the Middle East. The Middle East is a vast region; it straddles an unbroken land mass considerably larger in size than the United States of America or China. The twenty-one Arab states, and they are by no means all the states of the Middle East, have a combined area of 5,500,000 square miles, that is to say, over ten percent of the world's land mass. The Middle East is also rich in mineral resources, not the least of them oil, on which much of modern civilization finds itself dependent.

This previously unknown wealth is at the root of one of the central and inherent contradictions in the area. New-found riches have not brought harmony or social accord to the peoples of the region. The contradictions of extreme wealth alongside abject poverty are accompanied by the tensions between social progress and political extremism. Repression and the flagrant abuse of whole social groups—the denial of human rights and the exploitation of civilian populations by undemocratically established regimes—all combine to destabilize the area on a scale which has undeniable implications for the situation in the world at large.

In accordance with prescribed ritual, attempts will be made to turn this debate on "The Situation in the Middle East" into another orchestrated attack on Israel, in total disregard of the fact that the situations with which we are concerned include the war in the Persian Gulf, the Soviet occupation of Afghanistan and the armed standoff between Syria and Jordan, to mention only three of the conflicts in the region. These troublespots, with grave implications for international peace, should certainly give rise to concern on the part of the General Assembly and should have a prominent place in any serious discussion of the situation in the Middle East.

I do not wish to question for a moment the importance of such items on the Assembly agenda as the Comorian island of Mayotte, or the islands of the Glorieuses, Juan de Nova, Europa and Bassas da India. However, so long as this Assembly reserves a special place on its agenda for such questions, while turning a blind eye to the numerous conflicts in the Middle East threatening international peace and security, the General Assembly will justly be accused of having an eclectic field of vision and of continuing to practice its notorious double standard on matters affecting the Middle East.

There are islands in the Middle East, too. What has happened, for example, to the Greater Tunb, the Lesser Tunb and Abu Musa, that are claimed by both the United Arab Emirates and Iran? Each of those three islands sticks out like a sore thumb in the middle of an international waterway through which large parts of the world's oil supply are transported. They have been the subject of a long-standing dispute, and in view of recent events surrounding them, certainly deserve mention in the course of any debate on the situation in the Middle East.

The Middle East is an area in which conflicts are chronic and endemic. It is a volatile area, where most of the countries and regimes suffer from instability. Each of the manifold conflicts in the region has a genesis and a dynamic of its own. Moreover, because of the centrality of the Middle East on the international stage, many of these conflicts impinge on countries beyond the region, particularly in Africa, and in certain cases have serious implications for global peace and security as well as for the economies of most states represented here.

The sources of instability in the Middle East fall, broadly speaking, into three categories: internal upheavals *inside* countries of the region; conflicts *between* states of the region; and subversion and aggression from countries *outside* the Middle East. To those three categories one should add another source of instability, of more recent vintage, namely the misuse of staggering oil wealth by certain countries in a manner which threatens the security and well-being of other countries both inside the region and beyond it.

I have cited just three examples of these phenomena. I could, in fact, have reeled off as many as three dozen conflicts of one kind or another which are plaguing the Middle East at this very moment: Algeria and Morocco are at odds with one another; Libya has troubled relations with almost all of its neighbors, from Tunisia on the west to Sudan on the east and south; the two Yemens have been at each other's throat over the past few years; the Gulf states are far from being the best of neighbors and Iraq has long-standing designs on Kuwait. None of these conflicts is mentioned on the Assembly agenda. Each one, however, more than merits a place as a separate item in its own right.

In this context the problem of the Palestinian Arabs is clearly not the central issue of the area or indeed of our times. Bitter and complex as it is, the Arab-Israel conflict is but one focus of Middle East tensions and violence among many and, as such, is far from being the most crucial. In fact, the Arab-Israel conflict is the product of those broader tensions rather than its cause, and virtually all of those tensions would have to be addressed even if Israel had not served as the ever-useful scapegoat for Arab failings and inadequacies.

One of those failings was highlighted in the 1980 yearbook of the Stockholm International Peace Research Institute (SIPRI) in the following words:

> The explosive rise in crude oil prices has brought new and quick wealth to some Middle East countries, which has been used for expensive purchases of modern arms and military equipment as well as for investments in respective infrastructure projects.

The link between Middle East oil and arms is indisputable. The four main oil exporters are also the leading importers of arms in the Middle East and North Africa. That they are also the four most self-righteous debaters in this Assembly is not incidental either. Saudi Arabia, the major power of the Arabian Peninsula, for example, spent 14.5 billion dollars on military equipment in 1979, more than seven NATO countries—Belgium, Canada, Denmark, Italy, the Netherlands, Norway and Portugal—combined.

The military clashes of Iran and Iraq have likewise required recent massive expenditures. In 1979 Iraq received more arms than any other Third World country, and that was before Saddam Hussein al-Takriti marched his legions across the Shatt el Arab. In her book "The Game of Disarmament," Nobel Peace Prize winner Alva Myrdal noted in 1979 that soon:

> Kuwait with only around a million inhabitants will have one of the world's most sophisticated modern air defence systems.

One can only presume that this defense system will be needed against its land-hungry neighbors to the north.

While this Assembly has apparently abundant time to seize every conceivable pretext to assail my country, it obviously has no time to address itself to the trivialities I have referred to, despite the fact that we are ostensibly discussing the situation in the Middle East. I shall therefore try to analyze briefly only some of the current conflicts in the area. Let me, however, note by way of introduction to a short representative cross section, that since 1948 there have been thirty successful coups d'état in the Arab countries and at least forty-four unsuccessful ones. Twenty Arab heads of state and prime ministers have been assassinated, and there have been more than eighty-two recorded political murders. Most of these unhappy events have involved subversion on the part of other "fraternal" Arab states.

In looking more closely at some of the principals involved in the twelve *armed* conflicts currently raging in the Middle East, let us halt first on the eastern flank of the area.

There, on the northern shores of the Persian Gulf, two unstable régimes continue to batter one another and dispatch to mass slaughter the flower of their youth. Iraq's war with Iran has continued unabated since September 1979. As the *Christian Science Monitor* correspondent noted on 19 November 1982:

> Arab and Persian soldiers continue to perish, immense sums of money are being fed into the war machines and the potential for a genuine crisis in the oil-rich Gulf remains unlimited.

Interestingly, though not surprisingly, this Assembly has not seen fit to discuss that war, nor are we aware of any exhibition on United Nations premises devoted to the unfortunate victims of this totalitarian frenzy, as well as to the more than two million dislocated of the Iraqi-Iranian war; a vast refugee problem created by Iraqi aggression, which dwarfs by far even UNRWA's inflated figures for the Palestinian Arab refugees. One wonders whether the time has not come to consider the establishment of a special agency on the lines of UNRWA to deal with this acute refugee problem.

During the past two decades the rulers of Iraq have reached the pinnacle of power in the bloodiest of fashions. As Lawrence Minard wrote in the *Forbes Magazine* on 18 August 1980:

> President Saddam Hussein has emerged as one of the most brutally repressive rulers in recent history.

Distinguished delegates will recall that not long before the publication of the article in *Forbes Magazine*, Saddam Hussein al-Takriti was involved in the firing squad murder of fifteen top Ba'ath Party leaders, some of them his closest advisers. What begins at the top, of course, permeates down through the ranks of the régime, and the vicious repression of human rights and political freedoms in Iraq is now well documented. In its Annual Report for 1981, Amnesty International expressed concern over the large number of executions carried out in Iraq and noted that since 1974 that organization has received information regarding an average of one hundred executions a year.

Since obtaining its independence in the 1930s, Iraq has systematically suppressed its ethnic minorities. Hundreds of Assyrian Christians—men, women, and children—were slaughtered by the Iraqi army in 1933. During World War II, there was a coup d'état in Iraq that brought to power Rashid Ali al-Keilani, who was notable for his collaboration with the Nazis and for the bloody pogroms that were carried out against the Jewish community in Baghdad. For almost a quarter of a century after World War II, the Iraqi authorities methodically engaged in the ruthless oppression of their Kurdish minority, resulting in the massacre of thousands upon thousands of Kurds in the mid-1970s. And that was by no means the end of this tragic story. In its letter of 14 January 1977 to the Secretary-General of the United Nations, the International League for Human rights presented evidence of:

> . . . Iraq's forcible deportation of 300,000 Kurds from their homes in the northern mountains to the southern deserts; the confiscation of Kurdish lands without compensation and the settlement of Arab citizens in those areas; the incarceration of 30,000 former members of the Kurdish fighting force in concentration camps where they have been beaten and tortured, in contravention of the Iraqi Amnesty Law of 1975; the execution of 227 Kurds and imprisonment of over 200 others for political reasons. The Iraqi Government further has prohibited the use of Kurdish in schools, has shut down Kurdish newspapers, has forbidden Kurdish ownership of land in oil-rich areas. . . .

The time has certainly come to consider the establishment by the Assembly of a committee on the exercise of the inalienable rights of the Kurdish people in Iraq, as well as the establishment, within the United Nations Secretariat, of a special unit on Kurdish rights in Iraq. Since Iraq has been a respected member of the United Nations Commission on Human Rights, it would no doubt wish to sponsor the resolutions to this effect and might even meet the financial expenses involved from its oil revenues.

Repression in Iraq is of course not limited to the Kurds. Many prisoners, from all groups within Iraqi society, are subject to vicious torture. Human rights monitors found it necessary to publish a special report in April 1981, detailing medical and other evidence of the frequent use of torture. Despite all this, the *Christian Science Monitor* reported in the previously mentioned article that:

> It seems likely that Hussein will endure—if for no other reason than the ruthlessness with which he has dispatched his foes at home. . . .

That conclusion of the *Christian Science Monitor* found a suitable illustration in the town of Ad Dujayl in July 1982, in an incident that came to light only recently, and which the Iraqi authorities have tried to hide from international view. According to the London *Economist* of 4 December 1982, Ad Dujayl, forty miles north-east of Baghdad, has been erased from the map.

Following an attempt on his life, Saddam Hussein al-Takriti decided to make an example of this centre of disaffection:

> There were about 150 casualties in the two hours of fighting that followed the attempted assassination. After that 150 families simply disappeared. The remaining men were sent off to northern Iraq; the women and children were sent south. Bulldozers then demolished the town.

To the west of Iraq lies Syria—a country whose régime brings together the various causes of conflict in the Middle East and which has itself been a cause of chronic regional instability. It would, of course, be superfluous to dwell upon the well-known mutual non-relations of the two fraternal Ba'ath régimes in Damascus and Baghdad. The severe international problems created by Syria derive, to a great extent, from its internal situation.

From the end of the Second World War until the present régime came into power in 1970, there were a dozen coups d'état in Syria, most of them bloody. The present régime is a minority one, made up mostly of members of the Alawite sect. It rests on the bayonets of the brothers Hafez and Rifa'at Assad.

The state of emergency declared as long ago as 1963 is still used by the régime to justify widespread violations of basic human rights, including those formally guaranteed by the Syrian constitution.

A most recent example of Syrian inhumanity to Syrian occurred, of course, in the city of Hama where, in February 1982, according to the ingenious explanation of the distinguished representative of Syria, some "deviants" were liquidated. In fact, as *The Washington Post* reported on 3 May 1982, the city was subjected to three weeks of relentless artillery and tank fire by forces loyal to the Assad brothers. Entire neighborhoods were reduced to rubble, thousands of persons were killed and an estimated twenty thousand children orphaned. Other reports, among them the B.B.C., note that the number of those murdered exceeded fifteen thousand. In the light of Syrian comments on the matter, we may therefore be forgiven for presuming that Syria probably regarded the liquidation of 15,000 "deviants" and the orphaning of 20,000 children as a not untoward event in that country, and devised to suitably celebrate the conclusion of Syria's term as a member in good standing of the United Nations Commission on Human Rights. In 1980 alone, scores of political figures were assassinated, hundreds killed in riots in Aleppo, Homs, Hama, and Latakia.

Like its neighbor Iraq, Syria is also indicted by international monitoring bodies for the plethora of torture and summary executions, and is the subject of one of the longest individual country reports published in recent years. It is worth noting that these bodies were also concerned about allegations that

Syrian security forces were responsible for the assassination abroad of prominent exiles opposed to the bloody rule of the Assad brothers. In so doing, the leaders of Syria were, of course, only following the example set by the fraternal Libyan régime of Muammar Khaddafi which, starting in January 1983, will grace the United Nations Commission on Human Rights with its membership. It is only fitting that as Syria's term expires, it should be succeeded by a régime equally committed to respect for human rights.

The internal troubles in a Middle Eastern country such as Syria often have direct implications on its external behavior and frequently induce the government concerned to engage in foreign adventures, in the hope of diverting attention from its troubles at home. To illustrate this point, one need only look at Syria's relations with its Arab neighbors—Lebanon, Jordan and Iraq.

There are, however, aspects of Syria's aggression against its Arab neighbors that tend to be forgotten as one act of violence comes hard on the heels of the other. The most criminal and overt of these acts of aggression is Syria's rape of Lebanon. Ever since the end of World War II, Syria has had designs on Lebanon, which it sees as part of "Greater Syria." It has habitually regarded Lebanon as part of Syria, and for that reason has never had diplomatic relations with Lebanon. We will, no doubt, hear very shortly a Syrian representative trying to brush off this strange state of affairs by claiming, as the Syrians usually do, that his country has no need for diplomatic ties with Lebanon because of the "fraternal relations" prevailing between the two countries. Some "fraternal relations!"

In November 1980, another stillborn Arab summit took place. Its conception, gestation, and birth pangs were all illustrative of the situation in the Middle East. At its conclusion, King Hussein of Jordan declared that Lebanon was "dominated and held captive" by foreign forces, clearly alluding to Syria. As reported by The New York Times of 28 November 1980, King Hussein also accused Syria and its cohorts of stabbing an Arab brother state in the back.

The truth is that during the civil war, which began in 1974 in Lebanon, Syria exploited the opportunity to invade Lebanon on the pretext of assisting the Government of Lebanon to restore peace. Having ruthlessly massacred Palestinian Arabs at Tel al-Zaatar and elsewhere, Syria then turned on the Christians in Lebanon, and in the process not only laid the country bare but also tore it apart. Syria's barbarities against the Lebanese did not end with the conclusion of the civil war in 1976. In 1978 the world was appalled and outraged as Syrian forces indiscriminately bombarded populated areas in Beirut. Syrian artillery relentlessly shelled the city for days, killing hundreds of innocent men, women and children, and turning hundreds of thousands more into refugees. Syria continues to occupy 45 percent of Lebanon, with about forty thousand soldiers, and has no intention of leaving. On 15 May 1983, an official close to President Assad was quoted in The New York Times

as saying, "Syria cannot ever pull out of Lebanon at any point in the future.
. . . Our troops stay where they are, regardless of what they think in
Washington and in time certain measures will be taken against Lebanon."

We all know by now what those measures are. Within the Beka'a, Syria has
consolidated its foothold by introducing Syrian currency and by encouraging the cultivation of hashish under direct Syrian control. Syrian forces and
their surrogates have shelled Lebanon's coastal cities, including Beirut, and
have been similarly engaged in Lebanon's north. Significantly, Syrian-backed
atrocities against the civilian population of northern Lebanon coupled with
Arafat's hiding behind Tripoli's civilian population have been met with
callous indifference on the part of Arab governments. In fact, this silence was
sharply criticized on 28 October 1983 by the Jerusalem Arabic newspaper
Al-Fajr:

> The Arab countries have been utterly silent since the beginning of the
> Syrian plot. The continuation of this Arab silence can only be inter-
> preted as participation in this crime, which is being committed in front
> of the Arabs' eyes.

In the same vein, Issam Anani, a lawyer in Jerusalem, was reported in *U.S.
News and World Report* dated 12 December 1983 as saying: "The lesson
from the war in Tripoli is that we must turn our backs on the Arab States
which did not lift a finger to come to our rescue." Besides bombarding
Tripoli, the Syrians have, since May 1983, moved between 5,000 and 10,000
Syrian Alawites into Tripoli, as part of their bid to consolidate Syrian
dominance there (report of the American Friends Service Committee—10
August 1983). All of this is inexcusable under the United Nations Charter,
yet this Organization has refrained from addressing itself to the problem in
any form.

The case of Syria also offers a prime example of subversion from outside
the Middle East region. For many years now Syria has been penetrated by
the Soviet Union, which has used Syria as its proxy to destabilize the region
in furtherance of its imperialistic objectives. On 8 October 1980, Syria
signed in Moscow a Treaty of Friendship and Cooperation with the USSR.
Treaties of this kind are a standard weapon of Soviet diplomacy. In the last
few years they have been used in the Middle East with Iraq in 1972; with
Somalia, in 1974; and with Southern Yemen, in 1979.

They have also been used outside the region, as for example with Viet
Nam, where that Soviet client was quickly emboldened to attack its neigh-
bors. The signing of the Soviet-Syrian Treaty should be worrisome to Syria's
Arab neighbors, especially in view of the five thousand Soviet military
"advisors" in Syria and the vast arsenal of sophisticated weaponry that the
Soviet Union has put at Syria's disposal.

One should recall that it was the Soviet treaty of friendship of 1978 with Afghanistan that was used as the formal pretext for the "fraternal" Soviet invasion of that country. Since the Amman summit, we have also witnessed the massing of Syrian troops on its border with Jordan. Jordan promptly responded in kind, and there have been moments in that crisis when the two countries were within a hair's breadth of open hostilities.

Except for brief interludes of ostensible calm in the eye of the Syrian-Jordanian hurricane, Syria has sought at various opportunities to undermine Jordan's independence and sovereignty. Syrian intervention and subversion in Jordanian affairs have been heightened particularly during Assad's fourteen-year rule. In September 1970, Syria exploited Jordan's confrontation with the PLO terrorists by invading northern Jordan and temporarily occupying a strip of Jordanian territory, which included the town of Irbid. In November–December 1980, Syria massed troops along Jordan's border in a bid to intimidate the Jordanian Government. More recently, Jordanian diplomats have fallen victim to Syrian-sponsored assassination attempts in New Delhi and Athens. On 5 November 1983, King Hussein of Jordan told the Amman newspaper *Al-Rai:*

> Regarding the attempt on our two ambassadors, we have irrefutable evidence that the Abu Nidal organization, which is very active in Syria, is behind these attempts, and we also have information that Syria is seeking to disrupt security inside Jordan by enlisting some elements to create disturbances and carry out terrorism.

Syria's aggressive activities are derivatives not just of its fanatical hostility toward my own country, but also of two other factors which, when mixed together, form a dangerous combination. One of the foundations on which Syrian policy is grounded is that country's radicalism and its relentless effots to turn the Syrian Ba'ath Party and ideology into the dominant force in the region, just as that party and ideology have achieved supreme status within Syria itself. This source of Syrian conduct has evinced itself primarily in the Syrian régime's rivalry with its counterpart in Iraq. But for its present preoccupation with Iran, the Iraqi regime has for a long time sought similar objectives.

On more than one occasion, the Syrian-Iraqi feud has exploded into violence as Iraqi officials and institutions have become the target for Syrian-sponsored terrorism and vice versa. Terrorist groups in the service of these two rival régimes have often switched "loyalties." In fact, this was demonstrated also by the Abu Nidal terror group's transfer of its headquarters from Baghdad to Damascus.

Moreover, Syria's rivalry with Iraq has also been manifested in Syrian support for Iran. Thus, in 1982, Syria sealed Iraq's oil pipeline to the

Mediterranean. As a consequence, Iraq's oil exports—already in decline due to the ravages of the Iran-Iraq war—declined even further. Iraq now exports 650,000 barrels per day instead of the pre-war 3 million barrels per day (*Time*, 24 October 1983). As could be expected, such Syrian support for Iran has been reciprocated by Teheran in such places as Lebanon, where Iranian agents have carried out barbaric terrorist operations.

The mutual endearment of the two fraternal Ba'ath leaders has been expressed not just in deed, but in word as well. Thus, the Syrian media have time and again sharply attacked Iraq's Saddam Hussein al-Takriti, as, for example, in 1980 when the official Syrian newspaper, *al-Baath*, described him as a "pervert" and on 4 May 1982, when Radio Damascus called upon the Arab world to aid "the imprisoned and persecuted Iraqi people to eliminate the regime of terror and treachery in Baghdad, headed by the hangman Saddam Hussein." The Iraqis have not been idle in reciprocating these compliments in their exchanges with their Syrian brothers. Thus, on 22 July 1983, the Iraqi press printed a call by Iraqi Moslem clergy to "execute" Syria's Hafez al-Assad "for his being a tyrant responsible for the slaughter of thousands of innocent Moslems, Palestinians and Syrians."

But Syria is far from being the only source of instability in our region. I have referred to the cruel war between Iraq and Iran, where the toll in human lives mounts month by month, if not day by day.

Ostensibly, Iraq launched that war because of a long-standing border dispute with Iran. But Iraq's aggression against Iran has revealed its true face. When it calculated that Iran had been so exhausted by internal convulsions that it could not strike back effectively, Iraq tore up the treaty which it had concluded with Iran only five years earlier. Moreover, since invading Iran, Iraq's appetite has increased, and now it has extensive territorial designs on Iran.

The president of Iraq announced in the National Assembly in Baghdad on 4 November 1980, that:

> . . . the longer a nation stays in a territory the more rights it gains. . . . Khomeini must realize that war creates additional rights over and above the pre-war rights.

Iraq's contempt for the fundamental rules and principles of international law goes even further than that. On 11 December 1981, the Iraqi Mission to the United Nations circulated the first issue of its new publication, entitled *Qadissiyat Saddam*, which translates loosely as *"The Crusades of Saddam"*—a fitting name for a publication of a UN Mission. Let me congratulate the Iraqi Mission on this auspicious event. For it *is* an auspicious event. It does not happen often that one comes across such an interesting document.

It is certainly worth perusing this bizarre publication, since it contains revealing insights into the mentality and *modus operandi* of the Iraqi tyrant. Its *carte de visite* can be found on the front page, and carries the following message: "President Saddam Hussein: 'We are ready to cooperate with Iranian opposition to topple Khomeini regime'. . . ." This theme is elaborated in greater length on page four, where the Iraqi News Agency reports from Baghdad that in addressing the Iraqi National Assembly the previous month, "President Saddam Hussein has reiterated Iraq's readiness to cooperate unconditionally with the Iranian opposition to topple Khomeini's regime."

One does not have to be enamored of the policies and actions of Iran to grasp the gravity of this most revealing statement that the Iraqi Mission to the United Nations had the audacity to publish under its own auspices. It amounts to an open and unashamed admission by the Iraqi dictator that he is engaged in the subversion of the regime of a neighboring state, in clear defiance and violation of the general rules of international law and of the United Nations Charter, which prohibit intervention in the internal affairs of other states.

This, of course, will not prevent Iraqi representatives in the United Nations and elsewhere from continuing to masquerade as the champions of international law and international legitimacy.

If Syria is the chief menace in the east, Libya is the major threat to our region in the west. That is not to say that Libya has adopted a hands-off policy in our immediate vicinity. On the contrary, Colonel Khaddafi's regime has bloodied its hands in many nefarious activities designed to undermine stability in our part of the region and enable Khaddafi to fulfill his scheme of becoming the Arab world's second Nasser. Thus, Libya has aligned itself with the forces of aggression in Lebanon and has supplied arms for the use of Syria's proxies in that land. Moreover, Khaddafi's unremitting hysterical hatred of my country is also well known.

However, for the time being, Libya's dictator has chosen to focus most of his efforts in North Africa, the Middle East's western half. At one point or another, Libya has sought to subvert every one of its neighbors: Egypt, Sudan, Tunisia, and Morocco. Khaddafi's dream of an Islamic empire has also directed his attention to the other nations of Africa. Currently, his forces are busily entrenching themselves in northern Chad as part of Libya's effort to subdue that state. This Assembly should not forget that a few years back Khaddafi attempted to impose a merger on Chad and even forcibly annexed that country's uranium-rich Aouzou province. Other nations in Africa have also felt the effects of Libyan subversion and intervention although all such activities have predictably been ignored by this Organization.

Arms supplied to Libya by the USSR—presumably arms for peace—have turned up in Ireland, the Philippines, and Ethiopia; and Colonel Khaddafi's irresponsible adventurism has involved his soldiers in other countries, such as Uganda, in abortive attempts to salvage such enlightened régimes as that of Idi Amin. Khaddafi's involvement in the Middle East is at least as great as his involvement in Africa. His neighbors on Radio Tunis described him on 5 February 1980, as:

> a man struck with paranoia who misappropriates the riches of his country and uses them for accumulating arms, financing terrorists from all sides and spreading chaos in the Arab countries.

His fellow African and Arab President, Numeiry of Sudan, stated it more succinctly. Khaddafi, he said, has: "a dual personality—both evil" (Quoted in *The New Republic*, 7 March 1981).

Since the coup d'état in 1970 which brought him to power, Colonel Khaddafi has spared no effort to nip all potential opposition in the bud. In recent years, his campaign has been intensified and expanded to include even alleged opponents who live abroad. Many Libyan emigrés have been terrorized by assassination threats and attempts, while their families in Libya have suffered at the hands of the state secret police. Khaddafi initiated this particular phase of his campaign to tighten control when he announced, on 27 April 1980, that Libyans living abroad would be liquidated if they did not return immediately. The following day, the official Libyan newspaper, *El Zahaf el Akhdar*, reported that the program of physical liquidation had begun. On 23 December 1982, Libya's official news agency, JANA, quoted Khaddafi as saying, "The revolution has destroyed those inside the country, and now it must pursue the rest abroad." In a report entitled *Political Killings by Governments* (1983), Amnesty International listed some fifteen known cases of such Libyan assassination plots in Europe, the United States, and the Middle East. The victims included even two children, aged seven and eight, who fortunately survived the attempt to poison them.

From the safety of Tripoli, Colonel Khaddafi had much to say on the events in Lebanon. On the anniversary of the Libyan revolution on 1 September 1982, he referred once again to his immortal advice to the Palestinians to commit suicide:

> I would have liked the Palestinians to enter into a suicidal battle to the end, since it would have been better for them that way.

Once again Khaddafi said aloud what other Arab rulers, for tactical reasons, really think, but have deemed preferable to conceal. In suggesting suicide to the PLO, Colonel Khaddafi remained faithful to the real precepts of the Arab rulers' perceptions of the PLO. Colonel Khaddafi's pronouncements were, superficially at least, in sharp contradistinction to those of the PLO's patrons at the United Nations who have sought to camouflage their genuine motives behind a flurry of continued activity and the reckless rhetoric of hastily resumed emergency special sessions, sessions which characterize the Arab leaders' predilection for hypocrisy and deceitfulness, even toward their own Arab "brethren."

Therein lies the real reason for the inordinate amount of time devoted to this subject. The rhetorical barrage here is intended to deaden the sounds of reality and truth so clearly perceived by the entire world with regard to the Arab world's true position toward the PLO and its role in Lebanon.*

There is another country which can claim to be a defender—and bank-roller—of the PLO: Saudi Arabia. Its ruling house has rightly been de-scribed as the only family business to have been accorded membership in this Organization. In Saudi Arabia, more than anywhere else in the Middle East, one finds that highly unstable combination of an almost feudal society in possession of staggering wealth, which makes Saudi Arabia a danger not only to the Middle East, but to the world as a whole.

I shall not discuss Saudi Arabia's appalling human rights record, since that is a matter of common knowledge. But I am bound to make a few remarks about the purposes to which Saudi oil wealth is being put.

In the first place, Saudi Arabia is indulging in a buying spree of arms the likes of which the world has never known. According to *World Military and Social Expenditures 1981*, pages 26–27, in 1978 Saudi military expenditure was virtually equivalent to that of all the members of the Organization of African Unity put together. The same publication gives the Saudi population as just under 9 million, as against the combined population of the OAU countries of about 415 million. For the years 1977–1980, Saudi Arabia ranks second in absolute terms among the Third World's major weapon-importing countries, as indicated in the SIPRI yearbook for 1981, entitled *World Armaments and Disarmament* (p. 198). The other countries I have men-tioned in this survey of the Middle East—Iraq, Libya and Syria, all rank, together with Saudi Arabia, in the top six of the Third World's major weapon-importing countries, according to the same source. These disturb-ing facts have not gone unnoticed by the Secretary-General, who draws attention to them in a slightly different form in his report to the General Assembly entitled "Study on the relationship between disarmament and development."

The enormity of Saudi Arabia's arms appetite is growing year by year. It will come as no surprise to distinguished delegates that as of now, Saudi Arabia ranks number one in the world for military expenditure per capita. On 3 May 1981, the Saudi Ministry of Finance announced (according to *The*

---

*On Arab attitudes to the PLO see Chapter 8, Section E, below.

New York Times of the following day), that $25 billion of its total budget for that year of $90 billion has been allocated for military expenditure. This arms allocation is equal to that of the United Kingdom and exceeds the combined allocations of Canada, Belgium, Norway, Denmark, Italy, Luxembourg, the Netherlands and Turkey, which together make up over half the membership of NATO (see *The Military Balance 1981–1982*, published by The International Institute for Strategic Studies in London in 1981). Saudi Arabia has no demonstrable need for the weapons it buys, except for offensive purposes. The experience of the past clearly demonstrates that even if its ability to use its arms is limited, Saudi Arabia is prepared to place its arsenal at the disposal of other Arab countries with which it makes common cause.

Being immensely wealthy, Saudi Arabia prefers to sit back and bankroll the PLO to the tune of over $100 million a year. It prefers—to give another example—to do everything in its considerable political power to try to subvert the Camp David Peace Accords. To that end, it has engaged in economic warfare against Egypt by halting the economic aid it once extended to that country. In parallel, it has called for a holy war, or *Jihad*, against Israel, in total violation and defiance of the principles of international law and of the United Nations Charter, which prohibit not only the use of force but even the threat of force, and it has used its enormous assets to blackmail countries in an overt attempt to force them to desist from providing any support and assistance—both moral and material—to the real peacemakers in the Middle East.

Over and beyond its regional designs, Saudi Arabia, while posing as a moderate, has taken control of OPEC and through OPEC has squeezed the world at large, by regulating the flow of its oil and the price thereof as best suits its own political ends. As a result, Saudi Arabia has probably done more than any single country to jeopardize the world economy, and particularly to inflict insufferable economic burdens on the developing countries of the Third World, which now find they can afford neither oil nor development.

As the president of the Republic of Costa Rica stated before the General Assembly:

> We should not forget that the poor countries bear the brunt of rising petroleum prices and of recession. . . . Recession exacerbates pressures upon the poor countries by reducing the prices of their products and the volume of their sales. . . . Petroleum prices will continue to rise while markets for our impoverished countries, subject to the deflationary and protectionist measures of the rich countries, will continue to shrink.
>
> If poverty is not to prevail among our nations, it is therefore imperative that morality prevail in international economic and trade relations.

The Zambian scholar Siyanga Malumo observed in his article "African Economics and Oil Price Increases" (published in *International Relations*, London, May 1980):

> . . . African economies have suffered more since the beginning of the oil price jump in January, 1974, than at any time since the beginning of colonization of the continent. . . .

Not only are the Middle Eastern petro-hegemonists extorting excessive prices for their oil, thus further impoverishing developing countries; they also use the wealth gained thereby for aggressive purposes against other states inside the region, and even beyond it.

The conflicts just discussed are but a sampling of the more than thirty conflicts that are currently ravaging the Middle East, and that perpetuate regional instability. If this Assembly sincerely seeks to address the situation in the Middle East as it really is, it must take into account the problems just described and it must not allow itself to move blindly along the irrelevant and tendentious course adopted over the years. If, however, instead of addressing the many *real* problems of the Middle East, it will repeat *ad nauseam* what has been said in the endless discussions of the Arab-Israel conflict, this Assembly will only bring itself and the United Nations as a whole into even greater disrepute.

Regrettably, if past performance is any guide, this is what must be anticipated by any realistic observer of the United Nations scene.

5

Jerusalem

Based on statements made in the UN Security Council in March and April 1979 and in June 1980, as well as in the UN General Assembly in November 1979.

Jerusalem has known many foreign rulers during the course of its long history, but none of them ever regarded it as their capital. Only the Jewish people has always regarded it as the center and sole focus of its national and spiritual life.

The Jews of Jerusalem have the longest unbroken historical association with the Holy City, and for the last century and a half they have been the majority of the city's population.

As the representative of Israel, let me state here again that Jerusalem, one, undivided and indivisible, shall remain forever the capital of Israel and of the Jewish people.

While Jerusalem contains holy places and shrines held sacred by three great religions, it is also a vibrant, living, growing city—the home of some four hundred and twenty thousand people whose well-being depends on the city's peace and progress. It is the heart and center of a country, and the capital of a nation.

Jerusalem is a city which should be approached with veneration and respect, with reverence and serenity. It should not be an object for political expediency or a pretext for incitement or agitation.

The problems of the Arab-Israel conflict are complex enough. For their solution they require a spirit of reconciliation and a willingness to reach mutual accommodation. They require honest dialogue and genuine negotiation. This is particularly true with regard to Jerusalem.

Jerusalem, with its holy places venerated by Judaism, Christianity and

Islam, is an especially emotive subject. Consequently, it calls for particular care and sensitivity in keeping with its dignity and singular character.

Let me sound a note of warning. A dangerous dimension has been injected into our discussions. We have heard in our deliberations, right from the beginning, the shrill voice of hatred, incitement and fanaticism. As the representative of a people who, throughout the ages, has been the traditional victim and target of this despicable phenomenon, I feel duty-bound to caution against succumbing here to an evil that has brought so much misery not only in the past but even in our own time.

One of the manifestations of this intolerance and incitement here has been an attempt by the foreign minister of Pakistan to obliterate even the name of Jerusalem, by which it has become known and venerated for the past two millennia. The name of the city is, of course, derived from the Hebrew, "Yerushalayim," meaning the City of Peace.

The attempt made here to obliterate this historic name is not the first of its kind. It was preceded, among others, by Rome, an imperialist power of another age which, having crushed Jewish independence and sovereignty in the Land of Israel, then set out to obliterate the name of the country and of Jerusalem, renaming the latter Aelia Capitolina. But Jerusalem and its historic name cannot be obliterated. Its historic unity cannot be jeopardized by transparent political exercises. Attempts to rewrite and falsify here the history of the Jewish people, of three thousand years of Jerusalem and of the cultural and spiritual history of mankind, are doomed to failure.

Let me appeal that the voices of intolerance and prejudice are not permitted to prevail. Let us all substitute reason for prejudice and reconciliation for incitement.

The Jordanian representative referred to Jerusalem in an intolerant and parsimonious vein with regard to the role of Jerusalem in Jewish history and the role of the Jews in the history of the city. The city of Jerusalem has been the heart and soul of the Jewish people since King David three thousand years ago established it as the capital of Israel. As the center of Jewish life, hope and yearning, Jews for thousands of years have prayed daily for their return to Jerusalem and have reaffirmed the Psalmist's oath:

> If I forget thee, O Jerusalem, let my right hand wither. Let my tongue cleave to the roof of my mouth if I do not remember thee, if I do not set Jerusalem above my highest joys. (Psalm 137:5–6)

At the same time the Government of Israel has always been guided by the deep concern of other faiths for Jerusalem. Its religious and historical sites are precious to Christians and Moslems as well as to Jews. Israel is mindful of the historical treasures and manifold spiritual heritage of Jerusalem.

Israel's policy with regard to Jerusalem's holy places is governed by the

Law of Protection of Holy Places of June 1967. Under this law unrestricted access to holy places is guaranteed to members of all faiths.

In this regard it is relevant to recall that for nineteen years between 1948 and 1967 Israeli Muslims were barred by Jordan from praying in mosques in the Old City of Jerusalem. They gained access to them only in 1967 when the city was reunited.

It is therefore an affront to history that Jordan should complain to the United Nations about Jerusalem. For Jordan stands condemned as the first country in modern history to bombard the Holy City. It was Jordan which, intent on destroying the fledgling State of Israel and on unlawfully grabbing territory for itself, attacked Jerusalem in 1948, in clear defiance of the principles of the United Nations Charter. It placed Jerusalem under siege and opened fire on its inhabitants and on its historical and religious sites. Jordanian forces attacked and destroyed the densely populated Jewish quarter of Jerusalem's Old City with mortar shells and seized the eastern part of the city, including the historic walled section which contains religious shrines holy to Jews, Christians and Muslims.

Between 1948 and 1967 Jerusalem was a city cut in two by barbed wire and minefields. In flagrant violation of the 1949 Israel-Jordan General Armistice Agreement, Jordan barred access by Jews to their holy places and cultural institutions.

Further, the Jordanian Government began to eliminate systematically every trace of Jerusalem's Jewish past. Fifty-eight synagogues, some of great antiquity, like the seven hundred year-old Hurva Synagogue, were wantonly destroyed and desecrated. Those that were not razed to the ground were converted into toilets, stables, and henhouses filled with dung heaps, garbage, and carcasses. In the process, hundreds of Holy Torah Scrolls and books reverently preserved for generations were plundered and burned to ashes. On the Mount of Olives, a hallowed spot for Jews for centuries, 38,000 of the 50,000 tombstones in the ancient Jewish burial ground were torn up, profaned, broken into pieces and used as flagstones, steps, and building materials for public latrines and Jordanian army barracks. Large areas of the cemetery were leveled and converted into parking areas and gas stations. Through the devastated remains of the graves, the Jordanian Government cut an asphalt road to provide a shortcut to a new hotel built, irreverently, on the top of the Mount of Olives.

During the entire period, as these foul acts of desecration were being perpetrated against places holy to the Jewish people, the world remained silent. When, may I ask, was there a Security Council meeting while synagogues were burned, Jewish graves defiled, and Jewish shrines closed off?

Whereas the Jordanian Government destroyed the ancient Jewish quarter in the Old City, drove out all of its inhabitants and subsequently barred Jews from entering, even as tourists, Jerusalem today is an open city, open to all its residents—Jews, Moslems and Christians—and to members of all faiths from all nations.

But the commission established by the Security Council boldly accepted the charge that Israel is attempting to "judaize" Jerusalem (mark the word—I shall refrain from reminding members which lexicon it is taken from). Thus, Israel is accused of establishing a "Jewish quarter" in the Old City. The commission apparently did not know—or did not wish to know what every child knows—that for centuries upon centuries there was a Jewish quarter in the Old City, until the Jordanians obliterated it after 1948. As pointed out by Abbot Leo Rudloff in a letter to *The New York Times* (17 July 1979):

> . . . to call the old city of Jerusalem "Arab Jerusalem" is a misnomer. What about the Greek quarter, the Armenian quarter, the large Jewish quarter of that city? The old city was made *Judenrein* through expulsion, destruction of synagogues, and desecration of the Jewish cemetery.

Abbot Rudloff was in charge of the Benedictine Monastery on Mount Zion in Jerusalem from 1949 to 1969, that included the entire period of the Jordanian occupation and wanton pillage of Jerusalem.

According to the report prepared by the commission, "since 1967 . . . the Arab population has been reduced by 32 percent in Jerusalem and the West Bank." Members will recall that the correct figures were put before the Council in my statement on 13 March 1979:

> When Jerusalem was reunited in 1967, the number of its non-Jewish residents was about 70,000—roughly one quarter of the population. The non-Jewish population has risen since to about 95,000.

> The population of Judea, Samaria and the Gaza District, which was 965,000 in 1967, has risen by about 20 percent, now reaching a figure of approximately 1,150,000 inhabitants.

Throughout the ages and up to the end of the British Mandate over Palestine in 1948, Jerusalem has always been a united city. It was temporarily and artificially divided between 1948 and 1967.

While persecution and insecurity reduced the number of its Jewish residents periodically, Jews throughout the world have always clung to Jerusalem and have longed to return to it. Since modern population statistics first became available in the early nineteenth century, those statistics have consistently shown the existence of an uninterrupted Jewish majority among the city's residents. Until 1948, about two thirds of its population were Jews. The rest included Arabs as well as other non-Arab communities.

All those who are sincerely concerned for the well-being of Jerusalem cannot possibly wish to see a return to the situation which prevailed from 1948 to 1967.

It was during the Jordanian occupation of the eastern part of Jerusalem that stagnation set in in East Jerusalem and there was considerable emigration from it, since Jordan discouraged economic development in Jerusalem with a view to ensuring the primacy of Amman. Particularly hard-hit were the Christian residents under Jordanian occupation, and their numbers decreased significantly during that period, from 19,000 in 1948 to 11,000 in 1967.

When Jordan, in 1952, declared Islam to be the official religion of the realm, that declaration was made applicable also the Jordanian-occupied part of Jerusalem. As a result, Christian holidays were no longer recognized as official holidays of the Christian citizens. Christian civil servants were required to take their weekly holiday on Friday. They were permitted to absent themselves from their jobs on Sunday only until 11 A.M. Christian schools were required to remain closed on Fridays.

In 1953, a Jordanian law imposed severe restrictions on the purchase of land by religious institutions affiliated with "foreign religious organizations." In 1965, Jordan completely prohibited the acquisition of ownership or possession of land within the walled city of Jerusalem without prior special authorization by the government. This resulted in preventing the construction of any Christian church or place of worship within the Old City.

In October 1966, the Jordanian Government took further measures with a view to discriminating against Christian ecclesiastical institutions and clergy, such as the abolition of the exemption from customs duties previously granted to them.

A Jordanian law passed in 1955 was, from then on, strictly enforced also against Christian educational institutions. It required them to abandon foreign languages of instruction and to substitute Arabic for them. The mandatory teaching of the Koran was also introduced then.

After the Six Day War of 1967, our position was presented by the then foreign minister of Israel, Mr. Abba Eban, to the UN General Assembly on 21 and 29 June 1967, respectively. A detailed account of the administrative and municipal measures taken on 27 June 1967 by the Government of Israel with regard to the reunified city of Jerusalem was set out in Mr. Eban's letter to the Secretary-General of 5 July 1967, and was reaffirmed in a letter of 17 September 1978 from the prime minister of Israel to the president of the United States. That letter was annexed to the Camp David Framework Accords of the same date, and it reads as follows:

I have the honor to inform you, Mr. President, that on 27 June 1967—Israel's parliament (the Knesset) promulgated and adopted a law to the effect: "the Government is empowered by a decree to apply the law, the jurisdiction and administration of the State to any part of Eretz Israel (Land of Israel - Palestine), as stated in that decree."

On the basis of this Law, the Government of Israel decreed in July 1967 that Jerusalem is one city, indivisible, the capital of the State of Israel.

There is thus no substance to the allegation that Israel is in the process of altering the existing situation in Jerusalem. It is erroneous to suggest that the Government of Israel proposes to alter the status of Jerusalem, which has been and remains the capital of Israel.

As I have already indicated, we are all aware that religious and historical sites in Jerusalem are precious to Christians and Muslims as well as to Jews. This is expressed in Israel's policy with regard to Jerusalem's holy places. Under the Law on Protection of Holy Places of 27 June 1967, unrestricted access to all the holy places is guaranteed to members of all faiths.

Article 1 of the law provides:

> The Holy Places shall be protected from desecration and any other violation and from anything likely to violate the freedom of access of the members of the different religions to the places sacred to them or their feelings with regard to those places.

Article 2 stipulates:

> (a) Whosoever desecrates or otherwise violates a Holy Place shall be liable to imprisonment for a term of seven years.

> (b) Whosoever does anything likely to violate the freedom of access of the members of the different religions to the places sacred to them or their feelings with regard to those places shall be liable to imprisonment for a term of five years.

During the nineteen years of Jordanian occupation of the eastern part of Jerusalem, there had been no legislation to protect the holy places in Jerusalem. Instead, as already stated, Jordan systematically razed the Jewish quarter within the walled city of Jerusalem.

Since 1967 Jerusalem has once again become a city open and accessible to all. Sacred buildings have been rebuilt; places of worship rededicated. Millions of Moslem and Christian tourists and pilgrims, in addition to Jewish visitors, have visited Jerusalem since 1967 and have prayed and worshipped freely at its mosques and churches. These tourists and pilgrims include hundreds of thousands of citizens of hostile Arab states; they too have been afforded freedom of access to, and worship at, their respective holy places. All these visitors can attest to the complete freedom of access to, and worship at, all the holy places by the adherents of all faiths unprecedented in the history of the city.

The measures taken by the Government of Israel to secure the protection of the holy places are only one part of its effort to ensure respect for universal interests in Jerusalem. Israel has abundantly displayed its will and capacity to secure these universal interests. It has ensured that the holy places of the three great monotheistic faiths are administered by the respective religious authorities which hold them sacred, so that for the first time in the city's history the universal character of the holy places has found effective expression.

Israel, for its part, will continue to work for the peace and well-being of Jerusalem and its people, as well as for the preservation of the special place that Jerusalem holds in the hearts of people of diverse faiths around the globe.

Let me give you a short quotation from a book published in 1811 by Chateaubriand, the famous French statesman and writer, after a visit to the Land of Israel in 1806 and 1807.

> Gaze upon the space between Mount Zion and the Sanctuary. There dwells that small people, different from all others who live in the Land. . . .
>
> In order that your amazement should be complete you should see this people in Jerusalem. There you will see these masters of this Land of Judah, the lawful owners of the Land, living as strangers and servants in their own land, and, in spite of all the pressures upon them, waiting for the Redeemer to come and redeem them. . . .
>
> Persians, Greeks and Romans have vanished from the earth, but one small nation, more ancient still, lives on. And if there is one thing in human history which can be called a miracle—I think this is it.

This surely epitomizes how the world has regarded Jerusalem throughout the centuries, and no amount of wilful distortion and downright lies in this Organization can do away with so fundamental a fact of world history.

6

Jewish Settlements in Judea and Samaria

A

General

Consolidated version of passages from statements made in the United Nations Security Council in March and July 1979, and in February 1980.

The association of the Jewish people with its homeland, Eretz Israel, the Land of Israel, including Judea and Samaria, unique in historic circumstances, has become an integral part of world history, inextricably entwined in the texture of world culture. Here at the United Nations constant attempts have been made over the past thirty years to obscure this inseparable bond that exists between the Jewish people and the Jewish homeland; a bond that antedates the establishment of the United Nations by some three thousand years. No amount of distortion and fabrication in this building can undo so central a fact of the political, spiritual, cultural and religious history of the world.

The historical dimensions of the eternal Jewish ties with the Land of Israel have been described by the prominent British historian and theologian, Dr. James Parkes, who stated on page 10 of his book *Whose Land?* that:

> The Land of Israel is intertwined far more intimately into the religious and historical memories of the Jewish people; for their connection with the country has been of much longer duration—in fact, it has been continuous from the second millennium B.C.E. up to modern times— and their religious literature is more intimately connected with its history, its climate and its soil. The Land, therefore, has provided an

emotional centre which has endured through the whole of their period of 'exile' and has led to constant returns or attempted returns culminating in our own day in the Zionist Movement.

Unlike the two other major religions, Dr. Parkes continues:

[Judaism is] tied to the history of a single people and the geographical actuality of a single land.
(Page 136).

This self-evident truth also found its expression as a matter of course in the League of Nations Mandate for Palestine which stressed "the historical connection of the Jewish people with Palestine and . . . the grounds for reconstituting their national home in that country." The mandatory power was also entrusted with the duty to encourage "close settlement by Jews on the land, including state lands and waste lands not required for public purposes."

A function of this profound historical and spiritual tie of the Jewish people to the Land of Israel has been the existence of an uninterrupted Jewish presence in the Land since ancient times.

But the right of the Jewish people to its land is also sustained by more recent realities. In Jerusalem, for example, Jews have constituted a majority for at least the last century and a half. At the end of the British Mandate in 1948, Jews accounted for more than two-thirds of the population of the Holy City.

In referring to present-day Jerusalem, the representative of Jordan asserted that the distance from Bethlehem to Ramallah was forty kilometers. The truth of course is, as any map will show, that the real distance is twenty-two kilometers, about half of what he asserts. The representative of Jordan apparently needs the gross exaggeration to advance his preposterous claim that the city of Jerusalem now constitutes one-fifth of Judea and Samaria. Again, the facts are that the total area of Judea and Samaria is six-thousand square kilometres. The area of Jerusalem is one hundred and eight square kilometres, i.e. less than two percent of the area of Judea and Samaria.

In Hebron and Shechem (Nablus) Jewish communities existed from the thirteenth century until the present century. In the case of Hebron, the ancient Jewish community ceased to exist in the mid-1930s only after scores of its members—including many theological students—were brutally massacred by their Arab neighbors in 1929. The attackers did not spare women, children, or the elderly. They destroyed Jewish houses, razed synagogues and burned Torah scrolls, bringing a centuries-old Jewish presence to a temporary halt. This brutal pogrom was yet another illustration of that spirit of tolerance and brotherly love of which the Jordanian representative spoke so animatedly in this Council. Villages such as Atarot, Neve Ya'akov, Bet

HaArava, Qallia, Revadim, Massuot Yitzhak, Ein Tzurim and Kfar Etzion existed in Judea and Samaria until 1948. South of Gaza, Jews lived in villages like Kfar Darom and Be'erot Yitzchak.

In a letter published on 17 July 1979 in *The New York Times*, the former head of the Benedictine Monastery on Mount Zion in Jerusalem, Abbot Leo Rudloff wrote:

> There have always been Jewish settlements on the West Bank. Hebron, a city with many ancient historical ties with Israel, had a prospering Jewish community until most of them were slaughtered during the Arab riots of 1929–1936; the rest fled.

> The [Benedictine] monastery owned, and still owns, land on the West Bank. One of these was, before my time, sold to Jewish pioneers. One of my confreres told me that he saw a photo of the stripped and partly mutilated bodies of the young settlers after an attack by Arabs. Now the Jews have resettled Hebron, and the above-mentioned piece of land became the nucleus of what is now the Gush Etzion. Are those re-settlements "illegal"?

The continuous Jewish presence in Judea and Samaria as well as in the Gaza District, was brought to an abrupt but temporary end by the aggression of the Arab armies in 1948. The Jordanian occupying authorities drove out every Jew remaining in the Jewish quarter of the old city of Jerusalem, and for that matter, anywhere in Judea and Samaria. What they achieved by the naked use of force, they formalized in their laws. Article 6, paragraph 3, of the Jordanian Nationality Law of 4 February 1954 expressly prohibits Jews from holding Jordanian citizenship. Another Jordanian enactment stipulates that the sale of land to a Jew is punishable by death, a sentence already pronounced in Amman on several residents of Judea and Samaria. Not only do such laws constitute unadulterated anti-Semitism reminiscent of the infamous Nuremberg laws of Nazi Germany, but they also stand in flagrant violation of the Universal Declaration of Human Rights and of the international law of human rights in general. The present Jordanian allegations are thus nothing other than a public reaffirmation of that same policy of official anti-Semitism. Anyone who asserts that it is illegal for a Jew to live in Judea and Samaria just because he is a Jew, is no better than an advocate of *apartheid*.

However, discrimination on the part of the Hashemite Kingdom of Jordan has not been directed solely against Jews. For all the solicitousness which it today pretends to show toward its Palestinian brethren, Jordan's record in Judea and Samaria from 1948–49 to 1967 was such as should disqualify that country from requesting this debate at all. During the nineteen years in which it illegally occupied those areas, the Jordanian Government deliberately curtailed their economic and educational development so that they could not compete with the primacy of the territory which became the Kingdom of Trans-Jordan in 1946 and which previously had been the eastern part of mandated Palestine. Hence from 1948 to 1967, agriculture in the areas concerned was kept at a subsistence level. Industry was virtually non-existent and no infrastructure was developed. The Jordanian occupation authorities oppressed the local population and brutally suppressed the riots which broke out at frequent intervals. During those nineteen years, scores of Arabs in Judea and Samaria were killed and hundreds wounded by the Jordanian army.

The attitude of local residents toward the Jordanian occupiers can be gauged by an interview with Arab residents of Judea and Samaria which appeared in the Beirut daily *Al-Hawadith* on 23 April 1971:

> Those arriving from the West Bank define the situation thus: We have not forgotten nor will we ever forget the type of rule which degraded our honor and trampled the human feelings within us, a rule which they built by their inquisition and the boots of their desert men. We have lived a long period under the humiliation of Arab nationalism, and it pains us to say that we had to wait for the Israel conquest in order to become aware of human relationships with citizens.

Jordan's real attitude toward the Palestinian Arabs persisted after 1967—and if proof is needed, one has only to recall the ruthless killing of thousands of Palestinian Arabs in Jordan in September 1970. In contrast to this dismal record, the State of Israel has carried out in Judea, Samaria and the Gaza District an immense and constructive program of development marked by human concern and respect for the Arab identity of the inhabitants.

The population of Judea, Samaria and the Gaza District which was 965,000 in 1967 has risen by about 20 percent, now reaching a figure of approximately 1,150,000 inhabitants. Health and medical services have been greatly improved, resulting in a sharp decrease in the death rate and a considerable increase in the birth rate.

Education for this population has been expanded. The number of children in schools rose from 222,000 in 1968 to 375,000 in 1975. The number of institutions of learning increased from 987 to 1299. Two universities and two colleges are functioning where none existed before 1967. The number of teacher-training seminaries has increased tenfold.

I would like to say something about the question of water, because that highly emotive issue has been exploited in this debate.

First, a few plain facts about the water problems of Judea and Samaria. The reality is that the untapped water resources in these areas are meager. The rainy season is relatively short and only a small portion of that water can physically be captured and used for irrigation. The wells and springs of the region are not abundant. They cannot be overexploited lest they reach too high a degree of salinity. Such overuse can create an irreversible deterioration. Political considerations aside, any governing authority in the region must be aware of these facts. Under Jordanian occupation, less than 1.5 percent of the nearly four thousand square kilometers which are potentially arable were irrigated. Indeed, the gross exaggeration by the Jordanian representative of the available quantity of water is completely at variance with his Government's sound hydrological policies before 1967 of avoiding over-use by tightly controlling the drilling of new wells and the exploitation of springs. Israel has maintained this policy, as befits a nation that has made pioneering progress in the field of water conservation and irrigation science and whose experts are invited by many countries to help make the desert bloom.

No political rhetoric here can belie facts which are clearly demonstrable on the ground. The area of irrigated land cultivated by the Arab population of Judea and Samaria has increased by 160 percent since 1967. Improved drilling and pumping installations have assured the Arab inhabitants of a more stable and regulated flow of water, which has been a major contributing factor to the spectacular agricultural progress of the past decade. The supply of drinking water has tripled. In many Arab villages no longer does water need to be hand-carried from wells, for running water has now been brought to households.

It is nonsense to suggest that Israel has "plundered" the water resources in Judea and Samaria. Altogether the available water supply in those areas is about 100 million cubic meters a year. Israel's annual requirements are in the region of one thousand seven hundred million cubic meters a year. Indeed when short-falls occur in Arab towns in the areas in question, they are supplied from Israeli sources.

Income from agriculture has increased 2.6 times in real terms. The significant mechanization of agriculture is shown in the fact that the number of agricultural tractors rose from 130 in 1967 to 1750 in 1976—an increase of 1300 percent. Unemployment has been practically eliminated. In the Gaza District it has fallen to 0.6 percent, including the refugees. The gross national product has increased at an average annual rate of 14 percent.

Income and standard of living have risen most significantly. Private individual expenditure per capita, calculated at constant 1968 prices, has risen in Judea, Samaria and Gaza by nearly 100 percent. Income per capita has risen even more, indicating the creation of considerable savings. The number of automobiles licensed in Judea, Samaria and the Gaza District rose from about 5,000 in 1967 to over 25,000 in 1976. Only two to five percent of the population of the territories in question had television sets or electric refrigerators in 1967. The figure in 1978 was well over thirty percent.

Of the 16,600 officials in charge of administration, 16,000 are Arabs. The civil and religious laws are applied by Arab magistrates. Elections were held in 1972 and 1976. In 1976 women voted for the first time. The relevant electoral law reserves to the government the right to name additional members of the municipal councils and to choose the mayors. That was the practice during the Jordanian occupation. Israel has never tried to influence the election results, no matter what the political opinions of the voters or the candidates. In 1976 participation in the voting was 85 percent despite the methods used to intimidate the population into boycotting the elections.

Freedom of religion and worship is fully guaranteed. The holy places of each of the religions are administered by the representatives of those religions.

Two bridges over the Jordan, becoming more and more crowded every day, ensure a link between the Arab population and the countries of the Arab world. There is movement in both directions. Arab students of the territories in question can go to the Arab countries of their choice to study and can return to their homes at will.

From 1968 to 1976, 5.5 million persons crossed the bridges in both directions. In 1977 alone, more than one million persons and almost 60,000 vehicles crossed the Jordan. Of the persons who crossed, 63 percent were inhabitants of the territories, 30 percent were inhabitants of various Arab countries, and 7 percent were tourists.

That is the general picture of this so-called Zionist hell, which exists only in the perverse imagination of Israel's enemies. I could go into further details and figures at greater length, but I think that the foregoing information suffices to dispose of the ludicrous contention regarding "de-Arabization" of Judea and Samaria.

I have already referred to the inalienable rights of the Jewish people to the Land of Israel. A corollary of this is the right to live in any part of the land. We do not regard ourselves as foreigners in those areas. The Israeli settlements in Judea, Samaria and the Gaza District are there as of right and are there to stay.

It has never been the aim of Israel to exercise control over the lives and activities of the Arab inhabitants there. We seek to live as equals with them, not to replace them.

Incidentally, many of the present-day Jewish villages in Judea, Samaria and the Gaza District have been established on Jewish-owned land, expropriated in 1948 by the Jordanian or the Egyptian Governments. Most of them have been set up on government and public lands which had been barren for centuries. In those very few instances in which private land has been involved, acquisition for public purpose was in accordance with the pertinent Jordanian law and full compensation was offered.

The Israel villages in Judea, Samaria and the Gaza District were inhabited in 1979 by about ten thousand individuals. To assert that that number, in the midst of 1.15 million Arabs, constitutes a "demographic change"—"erosion"—"cannibalization" and what-not is both ludicrous and racist.

The right of Jews to live in Judea and Samaria has also been challenged here by some on legal grounds. As is well known, with the termination of the Mandate over Palestine on 14 May 1948 the armies of seven Arab states, including the Trans-Jordan Arab Legion, illegally crossed the international boundaries, in clear violation of general international law and in breach of the Charter of the United Nations which prohibits the use or even threat of force against the territorial integrity or political independence of any state. The armed aggression of those Arab armies was aimed at crushing the fledgling state of Israel, and the governments which dispatched them had the effrontery to make formal announcements of their illegal action to the Security Council.

The violation of the international boundaries of Palestine by the Arab armies having constituted an act of armed aggression, the consequent illegal occupation by them of any territory previously forming part of the mandated territory of Palestine could not give rise to any legitimate claim of sovereignty—*ex iniuria ius non oritur*. Thus, the purported "annexation" of Judea and Samaria by Jordan in 1950 was in violation both of general international law and of the Israel-Jordan General Armistice Agreement of 1949. It is not without interest to note in this connection that even the Arab League in 1950 threatened Jordan with expulsion from its ranks because of that purported "annexation."

On 5 June 1967 King Hussein spurned an official message from Israel delivered through the United Nations intermediary inviting him to stay out of the six-day war which began that day. Instead, the Jordanian occupants of Judea and Samaria opened fire on Jerusalem and all along the armistice lines with Israel and, as a result of their renewed aggression, lost control of Judea and Samaria. Thus, *when the Israel Defence Forces entered Judea and Samaria in June 1967, in the course of repelling the renewed Jordanian aggression, they ousted from those territories an illegal invader who enjoyed, at the most, the right of an occupant.* However, the rights of such an occupant under the international law of belligerent occupation are self-terminating upon the conclusion of the occupation and no rights survive for him thereafter.

Eminent authorities of international law throughout the world have repeatedly stated in recent years that, in the light of the facts and the applicable law, Israel has better title to any territory of the former Palestine mandate than any other state. The distinguished authorities include Professor Eugene Rostow of Yale Law School, Professor Elihu Lauterpacht of the University of Cambridge, England; Professor Julius Stone of the University of Sydney, Australia; and Professor Stephen Schwebel of Johns Hopkins University, a former member of the United Nations International Law Commission, and a judge of the International Court of Justice since 1981.

The latter, in an article published in 1970 in the *American Journal of International Law* rightly stated:

> *Where the prior holder of territory had seized that territory unlawfully, the State which subsequently takes that territory in the lawful exercise of self-defense, has, against that prior holder, better title.*

He then concluded: *"Israel has better title in the territory of what was Palestine, including the whole of Jerusalem, than do Jordan or Egypt."*

When Israel is thus on record with a well-defined legal position with regard to the inapplicability in the present instance of the Fourth Geneva Convention, it is not enough for members to reject it out of hand, as has been done in most cases here. Differences of opinion are legitimate, and they deserve serious consideration.

Suffice it for me to say here that the terms "occupying power" and "occupied territory," in fact have a well-defined meaning in international law and refer to the seizure by one power of territory under the sovereignty of another power. Since Jordan in no way constituted a legitimate sovereign in Judea and Samaria, the Fourth Geneva Convention cannot be said to apply to Israel's present administration of Judea, Samaria and the Gaza District.

Furthermore, even if the laws of belligerent occupation were for some reason applicable here, it would have to be pointed out that Article 49 of the Fourth Geneva Convention bans forcible transfers, not voluntary acts of individuals taking up residence in the areas under consideration. Moreover, it must also be remembered that Article 49 of the Convention was written in the wake of the mass expulsion from their lands of population groups by the Nazis, in order to make room for the settlement of Germans in those areas, in place of the original inhabitants. As the leading treatise, Oppenheim-Lauterpacht's *International Law* states (vol. II, 7th edition, p. 452), the provision contained in Article 49 of the Geneva Convention is:

> a prohibition intended to cover cases of the occupant bringing in its nationals for the purpose of displacing the population of the occupied territory.

I repeat, *"for the purpose of displacing the population of the occupied territory."* Thus, for this reason, too, Article 49 of the Convention does not apply here.

In addition, in this particular instance, consideration should be given to the fact that Israel not only applies the principles of the Fourth Geneva Convention, but goes significantly beyond them. The Geneva Convention, for example, allows for the application of capital punishment. Israel has never applied the death penalty in the territories in question, despite some atrocious crimes committed there.

The Geneva Convention does not provide for access by local populations to courts of the administering power. Israel allows the people in these territories to have access to Israeli courts, whether the cases are against individuals, against the Government of Israel or against any of its officials, including military officers in these regions.

There is no provision in the Geneva Convention requiring that movement of the local population outside the territories be facilitated. Israel facilitates such movement in both directions, including movement to the Arab countries which regard themselves as being in a state of war with Israel. In particular, it facilitates pilgrimages to Mecca. The Geneva Convention says nothing about trade abroad by the territories in question. Israel facilitates such trade, including trade with Arab countries.

The Geneva Convention accepts the jurisdiction of military tribunals of the administering power. Israel goes further than that and requires that the presidents of those tribunals should have been lawyers for at least six years and that they should be members of the bar and fully qualified. Similarly, the civil and religious tribunals, made up of local judges, continue to function in these regions, applying civil and religious laws that were already in force.

The Geneva Convention makes no provision for elections. Under the Israeli administration, free and democratic elections have been held twice for the municipal and local councils, and in 1976 women were allowed to participate in them for the first time.

The argument has also been raised that the presence of Israel villagers and farmers in Judea and Samaria constitutes an obstacle to peace. Let me point out right away that due to Jordan's "Judenrein" policies there was not one Israeli farmer living in Judea and Samaria between 1948 to 1967 and yet there was no willingness on Jordan's part at that time either to conclude peace with Israel.

Moreover, far from constituting an obstacle to peace, the Israel villages are in fact a vital deterrent to war. Even a cursory glance at a map of the region shows clearly that along Israel's narrow central coastline, where eighty percent of Israel's population lives, the distance between the pre-1967 armistice lines and the Mediterranean Sea averages between 9 and 15 miles, or about the distance from the northern tip of Manhattan Island to the World Trade Center. Until 1967, all of Israel's major towns and cities were within range of medium Arab artillery and Jerusalem was within light mortar range of Arab forces. Villages of the kind we are discussing have proved to be an effective form of early warning system.

If anything, developments on our eastern front have only vindicated Israel's long-standing security concerns and confirmed the importance of the villages in that regard.

Arab rejectionists regard Judea and Samaria, as well as the Gaza District and southern Lebanon, as the most important bridgeheads through which they might realize their dream of a war of annihilation against Israel.

Ever since Judea, Samaria and the Gaza District have been under Israel control, they have tried to reconvert them into forward bases. In this they have allocated the PLO a special role, and set them the task of using the territories as bridgeheads for acts of hostility, terror, sabotage and subversion against Israel and its civilian population.

As part of their "grand design" the rejectionists would obviously like the territories, leading to the outskirts of Jerusalem, Tel-Aviv and every other town and city in Israel, to be cleared of any Israeli presence that may stand in the way of their armies' aims and bellicose designs. Israel sees no reason to oblige them.

Perhaps countries thousands of miles away, unfamiliar with the perils of protracted conflict and hostile neighbors, can turn a blind eye to these harsh facts. Israel cannot. Other states enjoy considerable security and strategic depth. Israel does not. Other states have not been subjected to the impact of four wars of aggression launched by hostile neighbors in the span of three decades. Israel has. Other nations do not know what it is like to be ringed by countries that consider themselves to be in a state of war and which are arming for yet another war of annihilation. Israel does.

In the light of past experience and present realities, Israel has no grounds for underestimating the intentions and belligerent activities of the Arab rejectionists, or what would be even more foolhardy, of ignoring them.

Any discussion of the situation in Judea, Samaria and the Gaza District which does not take into account Israel's fundamental right to self-preservation and its legitimate concern for its security and defense, is meaningless. Similarly, any UN commissions which are established without regard to the background of persistent Arab aggression against Israel for over thirty years are detached from reality and lack coherence. This is all the more so when— as in the case of the commission established by the Security Council to study the question of Jewish settlements in Judea and Samaria—its conclusions were predetermined by the resolution that established it.

No one would, I think, deny that the present situation in those territories raises many problems which can only be solved through direct negotiations. Had most Arab governments, and not least of them Jordan, been prepared to follow the road of peace rather than ongoing hostilities these problems could have been satisfactorily solved long ago.

Had there been any readiness by the instigators of this debate to recognize the Jewish people's inalienable right to self-determination, national sovereignty and independence, had there been any will on their part to live in peace with Israel, the issue of Jewish settlements in Judea and Samaria would not have arisen in the first place. Only because we are faced with a group of states that have rejected peace out of hand and only because these same states remain obsessed with and totally committed to a campaign of relentless hostility (or, as they call it, "rejection"), is every issue being manipulated and blown up out of all proportion to its importance in the conflict. As Professor Fred Gottheil of the University of Illinois told the United States House of Representatives Committee on International Relations on 12 September 1977:

> Jewish settlements on the West Bank is an issue today only because the existence of Israel is an issue. . . . The issue of Jewish settlements in the West Bank today is simply one thin layer that emanates from and partially conceals the core of the conflict, namely, the non-recognition by the Arab states of Israel's right to exist.

Since the heart of the Middle East conflict remains not the Israel presence in Judea and Samaria but the refusal of many of our neighbors to recognize the basic national rights of the Jewish people, I cannot conclude without a reference to that issue. While much is being claimed here and elsewhere in the name of the Palestinian Arabs, we will undoubtedly hear little about the Jewish people's inalienable right to the Land of Israel and its right to self-determination, national independence and sovereignty. It should, therefore, be recalled that even after our independence was crushed by the legions of imperial Rome nineteen centuries ago, the Zionist passion—the longing to return to Zion—remained the focus of Jewish national culture. In prayers, in literature, in daily customs and on the Sabbath, on festivals, and on Holy Days, in the grace over meals, in marriage ceremonies and in mourning, Jews constantly expressed their hope and belief in the return to Zion and the reconstruction of their homeland.

Throughout those long centuries there remained a physical continuity of Jewish life in the Land of Israel often in face of the most adverse of circumstances.

When the Government of Hashemite Jordan and its neighbors come to recognize these realities, the Council will be relieved of debates like this one and the peoples of the area will be able to move rapidly toward a negotiated, just and lasting peace in the Middle East.

B

Specific Questions

The very formulation of the agenda item before us as "the situation in the occupied Arab territories" is intended to imply that the territories in question are nothing but Arab. This in itself already reflects a biased approach. I feel duty-bound to rectify this fallacious concept. While the final status of the territories in question is to be resolved through negotiation and agreement, it is imperative that it be clearly understood that the Jewish people and the State of Israel have the right in principle, as well as in law and in terms of national security, to a permanent presence in Judea, Samaria and the Gaza District.

In 1948 Jordan illegally occupied Judea and Samaria; however, the fact that Jordan and other Arab states failed in their armed aggression aimed at destroying Israel does not legitimize their violation of international law. On the other hand, armed aggression precludes them from invoking in any form the benefits of a General Assembly resolution that they themselves both rejected and destroyed by force of arms.

Most of these Arab states have not changed their fundamental attitude toward Israel, and they are now engaged in a determined effort, of which this debate is part, to frustrate the ongoing peace process. The Arab states concerned reject the peaceful settlement of the Arab-Israel conflict through negotiation, in accordance with the purposes and principles of the United Nations Charter. Instead, they strive to impose their own solution, if not in one fell swoop, then in stages.

This approach, aimed at the destruction of a nation and a member state of this Organization, underlies this debate, in the course of which the Security Council has been treated to discourses in which the massacre of the Jews of Hebron in 1929 was shamelessly justified. It should be remembered that the ancient Jewish community of Hebron was made up of pious Jews—elderly, religious, and defenseless. But in this debate, focused on the restoration of the Jewish presence in Hebron, the bloody pogrom visited upon them half a century ago has been casually brushed off as a necessary and justified act.

The Government of Israel has repeatedly stated its position of principle that Jews have the right to live in any part of the Land of Israel and that Jews are not foreigners in any part of the Land of Israel. This mere reiteration of a position of principle was turned into a flimsy and dubious excuse to call for an urgent meeting of the Security Council, based on an exclusivist—I dare say racist—proposition. That proposition asserts that since the ancient Jewish community of Hebron was liquidated through the brutal massacre of 1929, the city is to be kept forever *judenrein*. For the benefit of those who may not be familiar with the term, let me explain that it means "cleared," or "emptied of Jews," in accordance with the racist tenets of an ignoble era in the first half of this century. All of us know that the struggle against those racist tenets was one of the main objectives of the nations which brought our Organization into being. And now, thirty-five years later, the Security Council is being called upon to sanction and perpetuate a racist crime. This racist approach is carried to preposterous extremes, and to a point that attempts are being made to erase even the name of the city of Hebron, by which it has been known over the millennia, simply because the name Hebron attests to the historical association of the Jewish people with the city. It is not by accident that of the four cities in the Land of Israel held holy by the Jewish people, the first one, chronologically, was Hebron, the city of the Hebrew patriarchs.

Predictably, the commission's second report suffers from all the deficiencies of the first, both on the factual level and in terms of the conclusions drawn therefrom. It is permeated with a wholly uncritical approach, heavily slanted in favor of Israel's enemies. And once again no consideration whatsoever has been given to the highly detailed information published by the Government of Israel, information I presented to the Security Council.

For example, there is the sheer ignorance evidenced in the commission's report when the settlement of Elon Moreh is equated with Qaddum, while anyone who bothers to read a daily newspaper knows that these are not the same. But let us overlook such a minor point. Instead, let us look at the substance of the matter. In that report, note is taken of the decision of the Government of Israel to move the settlement of Elon Moreh to a new site, in the light of a ruling given by Israel's Supreme Court, sitting as a high court of justice. Then in paragraph 49, the report "deplores the efforts of the Israeli Government to side-step that decision." Members of the Council should be aware that the Government of Israel has not side-stepped that decision and that it has been implemented.

The report alleges that in recent months large tracts of private Arab land, totalling forty thousand dunams, have been "confiscated" for the purpose of expanding settlements. This is a falsehood. No such land has been requisitioned at all.

Some land has been "closed" by the military authorities of the area for the purpose of training without the use of live ammunition. A closure order of this kind is temporary. It does not affect ownership. Moreover, even while the order is in effect, the owners are able to use their land and cultivate it. If the military activities cause any damage, the owners are entitled to receive compensation.

The report mentions the decision by the Government of Israel on 16 September 1979 to permit Israeli citizens to purchase land in Judea, Samaria and the Gaza District; it goes on to state that the decision rescinds a previous one which, according to the commission, had hitherto prohibited Israeli citizens and organizations from purchasing land in those areas. This too is false. In accordance with Order No. 25, issued by the military governor in 1967, and in conformity with international law, land purchases were permitted, subject to authorization by the administering authorities. The cabinet's decision of 16 September 1979 was thus purely of an administrative nature, without in any way affecting the provisions of the order of 1967.

The report draws attention to a decision adopted by the Government of Israel, on 14 October 1979, to expand seven existing settlements. The authors of the report were unable to conceal their bias, since, when referring to the land to be used for this purpose, they found it necessary to insert the words "allegedly not privately owned by Arab inhabitants." The fact is, that the land in question was not—I repeat, not—privately owned in any of the cases covered by the Government's decision. All of the land used was either legally owned by Jewish individuals, or was state-owned. The relevant decision taken by the Government began explicitly with the words:

> There will be no confiscation or requisitioning of any private land whatsoever. Any expansion of the settlements or allocation of land to them will be done from state-owned land, after strict and detailed scrutiny by the Attorney-General.

In this connection we were also treated to a turgid and confusing lecture by the Ambassador of Jordan concerning different categories of land. Anyone who is at all familiar with land law is aware of the elementary distinction existing between privately owned lands and state-owned lands. The laws which apply in Judea and Samaria are based on the Ottoman legislation which has been in effect in the region since 1858. Minor changes were made in that law during the time of the British Mandate and under the Jordanian occupation of Judea and Samaria. There have been no changes whatsoever in the law since 1967 when Judea and Samaria came under Israeli control.

The commission's report regurgitates the false allegations that Israel is siphoning off the water supplies of Judea, Samaria and the Gaza District. This is another striking example of the commission's refusal to consider the official information readily available to it, including information which I offered at considerable length on this topic in previous debates.

To compound the demonstratively false nature of their charge, the authors of the report describe the conditions prevailing in the village of Al-Auja as a "case in point." According to the report, the villagers protested that their economy was being ruined because Israeli wells and the water network supplying the nearby settlements had drastically depleted the village's water resources.

As the authors of the report think that this is a "case in point," let me address myself to it in some detail.

There are two villages situated in the Auja basin: Auja Fawka and Auja Takhta. The inhabitants earn their livelihood from agriculture, working their own plots of land or those of several landowners who live elsewhere. Most of the water they consume comes from the Auja Springs and from several shallow wells in the area.

The Auja Springs flow from the ground at an elevation of twenty meters above sea level, at an annual rate of about 10 million cubic meters, which fluctuates radically in direct relation to the amount of rainfall in the region. In a year of plentiful rain, the flow can reach as much as 25 million cubic meters; in a year of drought, it can drop as low as 1 million cubic meters, or less. In the drought year of 1962–63, under the Jordanian occupation, the springs produced only 1.1 million cubic meters of water.

The wells sunk in the area by the Mekorot Water Company of Israel reach a depth of 190 metres below sea level, fully 210 metres below the level of the Auja Springs, and there is no interflow or physical connection whatsoever between the two. Therefore, the claim that the Mekorot wells affect the flow of the spring waters is entirely unfounded.

The drastic reduction of the flow of the Auja Spring waters between July and November of 1979 resulted from (a) a drastically curtailed flow of spring water, resulting from the cumulative effect of sparse rainfall in the three years from 1976 to 1978; and (b) the severe drought of 1978/79, when annual rainfall levels were 70 to 80 percent below average. Given the overall tenor of the commission's report, it comes somewhat as a surprise that those drought years were not blamed on Israel.

The heavy rainfalls of December 1979 brought about a renewed flow from the Auja Springs. If the abundant rainfall continues, the spring water will undoubtedly prove adequate to permit the irrigation of crops as in the past. The flow has already been renewed and that in itself is ample proof that its recent cessation cannot in any way be attributed to the Jewish villages in the vicinity.

I could go on quoting chapter and verse to refute the so-called "findings" of the report, but to what purpose? Not only are the "findings" wrong, but the whole report is permeated with an uncritical approach. That uncritical approach in turn was predetermined by the commission's mandate.

7

The Golan Heights

I

Abbreviated and consolidated version of statements made in the UN General Assembly and Security Council between 16 December 1981 and 29 January 1982.

By way of orientation, let me describe the area which is at the center of this debate, the Golan Heights. We are talking about a miniscule area of only about four hundred fifty square miles in all. But the strategic importance of the Golan Heights is out of all proportion to their size. They are situated about three thousand feet and more above the territory around the Sea of Galilee and the Hula Valley below, and dominate them completely.

As far back as 1947, Jewish villages and kibbutzim in the Hula Valley were attacked by the Syrian army. Following Israel's independence in May 1948, Syria was in the forefront of the Arab countries that invaded our newly-established state, while Syrian guns on the Golan wrought havoc on the agricultural and fishing communities below.

Ever since 1948, Syria has claimed that no international boundary exists between it and Israel. Thus, during the negotiations that preceded the signing of the Israel-Syrian General Armistice Agreement of 1949, Mr. Tarazi, one of the Syrian negotiators, declared: "There is no international border between Israel and Syria. There *was* a political border between Syria and Palestine. We have to sign an armistice agreement not on the basis of a political border but on the basis of an armistice line."

In this way, Syria maintained its rejection of the former mandatory frontier, and insofar as the armistice lines between 1949 and 1967 followed that frontier, Syria insisted that the armistice agreement signed on 20 July 1949

119

include a clause to the effect that the armistice demarcation lines were defined without prejudice to the ultimate settlement. Moreover, in an explanatory letter in conjunction with the armistice agreement, dated 26 June 1949 and addressed to the then Israel minister for foreign affairs by the United Nations negotiator, the late Dr. Ralph Bunche, he wrote as follows:

> Questions of permanent boundaries, territorial sovereignty, customs, trade relations and the like must be dealt with in the ultimate peace settlement and not in the Armistice Agreement.

Until 1967, despite the armistice agreement whose preamble indicated that its purpose was "to facilitate the transition . . . to permanent peace," Syria adamantly refused to conclude peace with Israel and instead constantly harassed Israel from the Golan Heights. The Syrians had in their gunsights not only much of what is called the Galilee Panhandle but also much of northern Israel in general and no small part of Israel territory in the upper Jordan Valley as well.

From its positions on the Golan Heights, Syria frequently bombarded Israeli towns and villages below, and attacked Israel farmers tilling their land. The situation between our two countries reached one of its worst points when, in 1964, the Syrians decided to interfere with the construction of the Israel national water carrier, which draws fresh water from the Sea of Galilee. Those endless incidents initiated by Syria were regularly brought to the attention of this Council.

Writing in the London *Daily Telegraph* of 1 June 1973, its Middle East correspondent, John Bulloch, accurately described some aspects of civilian life in the northern part of Israel under well-entrenched and trigger-happy Syrian gunners:

> Before 1967 the Syrian gunners were up on the plateau; their guns could deal death up to a range of twenty miles. No fishing was then possible in the Sea of Galilee, farmers had armour plating on their tractors and children slept in shelters at night.

Among those who visited the Israel-Syrian frontier in those days was Sir Alec Douglas-Home, a former prime minister of the United Kingdom. He wrote in the London *Daily Mail* of 22 April 1974:

> A few months before the 1967 war, I was visiting Galilee, and at regular intervals the Russian-built forts on the Golan Heights used to lob shells into the villages, often claiming civilian casualties. Any future pattern for a settlement must clearly put a stop to that kind of offensive action.

It is easy to forget the circumstances that brought Israel on the Golan Heights in 1967. Syria had turned the heights into a vast launching pad containing huge reserves of artillery and armor, poised for descent on Israel. In the course of the Six Day War, in 1967, Israel was bombarded ferociously from the Golan Heights. Israel fought back, in self-defense, because had the Syrians been able to come down from the heights, the possible outcome was—and remains—too terrible to contemplate. The Israel Defense Forces stormed the fortified heights in the face of lethal fire in order to liquidate the Syrian positions. We paid a heavy price, but the heights were captured after two days of heavy fighting. Thus, nineteen years of Syrian harassment and aggression were brought to an end. The Syrian army was driven back, out of range, and no longer able to directly threaten Israel's villages in Galilee and the Hula Valley.

For the last fourteen and a half years, since June 1967, Israel has repeatedly appealed to Syria to come to the negotiating table and make peace. Syria has refused adamantly. Peace with us is unthinkable. For that reason, Syria refused also to accept Security Council Resolution 242.

Then, in 1973, Syria launched the Yom Kippur War against Israel, from the Golan Heights. Indeed, in the early stages of Syria's sneak attack on the holiest day of the Jewish calendar, the Syrian advance columns broke through the Israeli defenses, and at one point it even looked as though they might succeed in advancing further. If the Syrian army had still been in control of that strip of territory in October 1973, it would have been able, with relative ease, to penetrate deep into Israeli territory, and Israel would have then been forced to wage a bitter defensive battle within the populated areas of Upper Galilee and the valleys.

Syria accepted Security Council Resolution 338 of 22 October 1973, only because having been defeated in the Yom Kippur War, it was greatly interested in regaining the territories which it lost in that aggression against Israel. At the signing of the disengagement agreement at Geneva in 1974, the Syrians were careful to be represented only by army officers, so as to emphasize the fact that from their point of view there could be no negotiations beyond a military agreement with Israel. The Syrians went even further. They refused to sign that disengagement agreement with us, and requested that the Egyptians sign it on their behalf. It must be pointed out that that disengagement agreement, which is still in effect, did not relate to the subject of the international boundary between our two countries, and thus has no bearing on it.

Syria's bellicose attitude notwithstanding, Israel has persevered in its repeated calls to Syria to make peace with us. And what has been Syria's reponse? It has been to spearhead the rejectionist Arab camp against Israel. It has consistently tried to outrival rejectionist Arab states, such as Iraq, in its subversive activites against the Camp David Framework Accords for Peace in the Middle East.

And there were also other actions by Syria, of which the Government of

Israel was bound to take serious note. On 8 October 1980 Syria signed in Moscow a Treaty of Friendship and Cooperation with the Soviet Union. That treaty, a stock item of Soviet diplomacy, or, rather, one of its standard weapons, guaranteed the uninterrupted and massive flow of sophisticated weaponry, which the Soviet Union had been pumping into Syria for some time.

Israel was also bound to keep a wary eye open to Syrian activities in Lebanon. For, quite apart from what the Syrian army of occupation had done to that country since 1976, it has been perfectly clear to us that Syria has designs to threaten Israel's northern border by outflanking the Golan Heights, if possible, and attacking Israel through southern Lebanon. While Syria keeps the terrorist PLO as a buffer between it and the UNIFIL area of operation in southern Lebanon, it controls the PLO completely, just as it controls almost everything else in Lebanon.

More than that, this year Syria made two further worrisome moves, from Israel's point of view. First, it stepped up its subversive activities to incite the local Druze population of the Golan Heights against Israel. Secondly, it has been tightening its links with Libya, with which it is now in the process of establishing a confederate union. In this it no doubt has the blessing of the Soviet Union, which has a clear interest in promoting the Tripoli-Damascus Axis.

Syria was also the prime mover in bringing about the collapse of the Arab League Summit held at Fez, in November 1981. And we all know precisely what the problem was. On the agenda of the summit was the so-called "Fahd Plan," which was, essentially, an assault on Israel's existence and a prescription for the dismantlement of Israel in stages. However, there was one point in the plan which some could possibly construe—by a wide stretch of the imagination—as implying the most indirect form of acceptance of Israel. Even that very oblique point, negated by the rest of the plan, was nonetheless too much for the Syrians to stomach.

Syria's foreign minister made it perfectly clear where his country stood. Thus, he declared that:

> to speak of co-existence with Israel would be tantamount to granting Israel legitimacy. And talk of withdrawal to the 1967 lines would be tantamount to recognizing Israel's right to four-fifths of Palestine.

He therefore suggested that the Arabs should wait a hundred years or more until Israel is weakened, and then the Arabs could act. In fact, Foreign Minister Haddam was only echoing a similar statement, which had been made some two weeks before by his prime minister. At a ceremony inaugurating a dam in the Euphrates basin on 17 November 1981, Prime Minister Al-Kassem declared, as reported on Damascus radio: "The Syrian masses and the whole nation declare, no recognition, no peace and no negotiations with Israel."

And even more recently, on 13 December 1981, President Assad of Syria was reported by the Kuwaiti news agency to have declared in the Kuwaiti newspaper *al-Ra'i al-'Amm* that "even if the PLO recognizes Israel, Syria will not be able to recognize it."

There is a limit to how long any country can live under such threats, particularly military threats backed up not only by a sizable arsenal but also by the political will to use it. For fourteen years, Israelis and the Druze inhabitants of the Golan Heights have lived well together. I do not think anybody will be taken in by the selective quotations that we heard read from today's *New York Times* by our Syrian colleague. What he did not quote are some rather revealing passages in the same article. Thus, for instance, reference is made there to Mr. Salman Abu Salah, a Druze resident of the Golan Heights who pointed out, according to the article:

> In order to make the people feel free and express their opinion openly, the Israelis should treat the Golan Druze just like any other citizens of Israel. The State of Israel should forgive the Druze who opposed yesterday's decision, because in the situation they are in, they had to oppose it.

He then went on to say that after 1967 the Druze realized "that it is good for me to live here and that we can integrate into the State of Israel. The Syrians treated the Druze in a cruel way. From little issues they made big issues, in which they could hang people, deport them, and maybe hang them before trial." It would have been nice if our Syrian colleague had been kind enough to include these passages, too, from the article which he brought to our attention.

All daily life on the Golan Heights, both of the Israeli residents and of the Druze inhabitants, is with Israel. The authorities on the Golan Heights, military and civilian, are Israelis. They certainly cannot wait a hundred years and more, as the Syrian foreign minister would wish, in order to register births, marriages and deaths. When, for example, matters of law, both civil and criminal, were brought before the courts, it became progressively more incongruous to apply Syrian law. The policemen to whom the local residents turned, the lawyers who represented them and the judges who sat in the courts, were all Israelis.

For all these reasons, the Government of Israel and the Knesset decided last Monday to regularize the situation by applying Israel law, jurisdiction and administration to the Golan Heights.

The Israel law on the Golan Heights does not in the slightest manner diminish the rights of the people living there, including, of course, their property rights and their right to education and religious worship according to their traditions. All these are fully safeguarded.

It has been suggested that the Golan Law adopted by the Knesset does not accord with the provisions of Security Council Resolution 242. We believe this to be incorrect. Resolution 242, which, as I have already pointed out, was rejected by Syria, did not determine any boundaries. In laying down the guidelines for the negotiated settlement of the Arab-Israel conflict, Security Council Resolution 242 stressed the need for "secure and recognized boundaries." The former armistice demarcation lines between Israel and Syria were in no sense boundaries, and they certainly were neither secure nor recognized. This very aspect of the problem was also clearly brought out by the then Permanent Representative of the United States, Ambassador Arthur Goldberg, when, on 15 November 1967, he told the Security Council:

> Historically there have never been secure or recognized boundaries in the area. Neither the armistice lines of 1949 nor the cease-fire lines of 1967 have answered that description. . . . Now such boundaries have yet to be agreed upon.

Indeed, the pre-1967 armistice demarcation lines were an open invitation for Syria to attack Israel, which, as I have pointed out, it did regularly. Since 1967, the range and accuracy of the modern weaponry in Syrian hands have been greatly extended. No responsible government, whose first duty is to preserve the lives and safety of its citizens, would agree to return to the totally insecure armistice lines which obtained before 1967. Countless visitors to the Golan Heights, including former presidents of the United States, have been impressed by the strategic importance of the area and have urged Israel never to give it up. Certainly, every government of Israel since 1967 has declared that it would be impossible to return to the pre-1967 lines.

I should like to take this opportunity to appeal once again to Syria to start negotiations with us directly, with a view to achieving an agreed settlement on all the outstanding issues between our two countries, including the question of the international boundary between them. I do this despite past failures to evoke a positive response from Syria.

Whenever Israel has indicated its willingness to make peace with Syria, the latter has invariably responded with its typical bellicose attitude. That attitude has been reflected over the years in countless declarations made by the leaders of that country.

On 1 November 1954 Faris al-Khoury, then prime minister of Syria, stated on Radio Ramallah that:

> It should be clear that the implementation of . . . UN resolutions will not oblige the Arab states to make peace with Israel.

On 31 May 1956, the representative of Syria to the United Nations, the notorious Ahmed Shukairy, who later became one of the founders of the terrorist PLO, emphasized that:

> Everything enacted by the United Nations since 29 November 1947 should be written off; the establishment of Israel, its membership in the UN and all other resolutions will have to be revoked.

In the same vein, at the fifth emergency special session of the General Assembly on 17 July 1967, George Tomeh, another Syrian representative to the United Nations, indicated that:

> On behalf of all the Arab delegations, . . . we now confirm, as we have stated in the past, our non-recognition of the State of Israel. . . . That denial of recognition to that state should be reaffirmed time and again. . . .

In one of the most revealing commentaries ever broadcast over Damascus radio, that Syrian government-controlled broadcasting station, on 22 December 1976, pointed out that:

> The map that the Arabs are presenting to Israel includes not only Jerusalem, Nablus, Gaza, Sinai and the Golan—but, first and foremost, Tel Aviv, Haifa, Jaffa and Nazareth. In other words, the Arabs are not merely demanding to get back the West Bank and the Gaza Strip, as Palestinian soil; rather, they are demanding their rights throughout their occupied land since 1948. The slogan of "the restoration of the Palestinian people's rights" has found a more favorable reception, at the international level and in world public opinion, than the slogan of "the liberation of Palestine"—meaning the liquidation of Israel. It must be noted, however, that these two slogans mean one and the same thing.

This same idea was reiterated in a slightly different fashion by Syrian Foreign Minister Abdul Halim Haddam on 13 September 1980, to the Qatar daily *al-Raya:*

> We are not concerned merely with the Golan or the West Bank. There is a matter of basic principle connected with the presence of the Zionist entity in the Arab homeland. . . . The problem must be viewed as part of the overall struggle with the Zionist foe. And the Arab nation will retrieve every inch of territory in and outside Palestine.

It is unconscionable that a state like Syria should be permitted to unleash repeated acts of aggression, with the aim of conquering and even destroying a neighboring country and then, having been repulsed, should be permitted to manipulate the means and machinery of the United Nations, to invoke international law in a selective and distorted manner and to find fault with legislation which seeks, in the absence of peace or even of negotiations aimed at reaching peace, to normalize the situation in the area in question.

The representative of Syria in his statement referred to the definition of aggression adopted by the General Assembly in 1974. So, too, did the representative of Jordan. With their characteristic selectiveness, they failed to mention Article 1, which contains the central definition of aggression. That omission is most revealing. I invite the representative of Syria to listen closely to the text of that article:

> Aggression is the use of armed force by a State against the sovereignty, territorial integrity or political independence of another State or in any other manner inconsistent with the Charter of the United Nations as set out in this definition.
> Explanatory note: in this definition the term "State" is used without prejudice to questions of recognition or to whether a State is a Member of the United Nations.

Article 2 then goes on to state:

> The first use of armed force by a State in contravention of the Charter shall constitute *prima facie* evidence of an act of aggression.

It is quite evident why the representative of Syria should have omitted any reference to these articles. He knows, as do we all, that this is precisely the conduct that his country has been guilty of over the past thirty-three years in its attitude toward Israel. Since the definition of aggression so clearly incriminates his country, he simply disregards it. But if he so conveniently forgets those central provisions, it certainly does not mean that the rest of us have also forgotten them.

Here we have before us the root cause of the Arab-Israel conflict: the refusal of the rejectionist Arab countries, including Syria, to come to terms with Israel's very existence and its right to exist, irrespective of territories and boundaries. They regarded the very establishment of my country as illegitimate in 1948 and they've had no change of heart, in this regard, since. They consequently set out to destroy the State of Israel by force of arms in clear violation of the United Nations Charter and of the definition of aggression adopted by the General Assembly. They are still committed to this criminal objective.

Syria, and those in the same rejectionist camp with it, deny the right of a sovereign state, a member of the United Nations, to exist and live in peace as is the right of every sovereign country and every state member of the United

Nations. This attitude violates not only the basic notions of equity, but also the United Nations Charter, which states that

> All Members, in order to ensure to all of them the rights and benefits resulting from membership, shall fulfil *in good faith* the obligations assumed by them in accordance with the present Charter.

I should like to express the hope that any further consideration by the Security Council of this matter will focus constructively on the attainment of peace through negotiations between the states directly concerned and on the prevention of the threat or use of force. In this connection, I should like to repeat here that, for its part, the Government of Israel stands ready, now as always, to negotiate unconditionally with Syria, as with its other neighbors, for a lasting peace, in accordance with Security Council Resolutions 242 (1967) and 338 (1973).

II

Statement in exercise of the right of reply made in the UN Security Council on 14 January 1982.

This is the seventh meeting of the Security Council on the agenda item before us since the sixth of January. We have met virtually every day since Wednesday of last week to deliberate on what presumably is the central issue confronting the international community. Certainly a deliberate attempt is being made here to create that impression, however false, and to that end, apparently, mobilization has been ordered within a certain group of states to lend their support to creating that artificial impression. Thus, we have had here a procession of states participating in this debate, among them Bulgaria, Mongolia, Czechoslovakia, the Sovereign and Independent Republic of the Ukraine, the German Republic—which for some reason calls itself democratic—Hungary, Poland, and the equally democratic Republic of Afghanistan. There is one problem, though, dealing with this category, and that is the intriguing absence of the Sovereign and Independent Republic of Byelorussia, which so far has not made its appearance. But who knows what lies in store for us?—it may still appear.

Some of us have had the feeling over the past few weeks that there may be other international problems confronting the international community. This Council, it would seem, is not aware of their existence. Not for the first time, there seems to be a certain divergence between the real world and the world as experienced and viewed by this Council. Whatever doubts may have persisted in our minds with regard to the priorities of the Council were certainly dispelled this afternoon by the appearance of Poland. We have been looking forward very much indeed to this statement. Some of us were hoping against hope that we might find enlightenment on some of the problems confronting us. It is true that the representative of Poland did speak about solidarity—solidarity with Syria. It is indeed gratifying to know that he supports solidarity, although it is not quite clear whether he writes it with a small or a capital S.

But this is not the only problem that the representative of Poland has failed to address himself to. I believe he could have made a useful contribution to this debate. And since he took time out to participate in it, and as he informed us, his foreign minister [on 21 December 1981, one week after the suppression of "Solidarity"] also took time out to address himself to the question before us, he could have educated us on some interesting and pertinent questions in connection with this item. Certainly, some of us would have been greatly interested in hearing about the evolution of his own country's boundaries. I know all these things happened a long time ago—only thirty-six years ago or so, but still, they may be somewhat relevant. But since he did not see fit to enlighten us, I hope he will forgive me if I take the liberty to do so.

Let me very briefly recapitulate some of the Polish boundary problems. In 1941, the Polish Government-in-exile stated its demand for the reestablishment of Poland after World War II within secure boundaries. On 24 September 1941, the acting Polish minister for foreign affairs, Mr. Raczynski, told a meeting of the Inter-Allied Council held in London, that

> The future frontiers of Poland should safeguard the country's security. They should assure Poland's vital need of a wide access to the sea, adequately protected from foreign interference. (Whiteman's *Digest of International Law*, volume 3, page 284)

These demands were reaffirmed in the General War Aims, formulated by the Polish National Council in 1942:

> Poland should maintain the security of her frontiers by having a large access to the sea and by obtaining a frontier with Germany which should be extended sufficiently towards the west, as well as straightened and shortened.

I anticipate the possible objection that all these demands were made by the *London*-based Government-in-exile. So let me inform the representative of Poland that on 22 July 1944, the Soviet-sponsored Polish Committee of National Liberation, better known as the "Lublin Committee," issued a manifesto to the Polish people, in which it called on them:

Introducing Joseph Mendelevitz to the UN Press Corps, June 1981.

Honorary Doctorate ceremony, Yeshiva University, June 1981. *From left:* Norman Lamm, Yehuda Z. Blum, Stanley Stern, Dr. Israel Miller. *(Photo courtesy of Yeshiva University.)*

Conferring on the floor of the Security Council chamber before the meeting. *From left:* Brian Urquhart, Under-Secretary-General for Special Political Affairs, Yehuda Z. Blum (Israel), and Ole Algard (Norway). *(UN photo by Milton Grant.)*

At 12th Annual "Solidarity Sunday," 22 May 1983, with Senator Moynihan and Ambassador Kirkpatrick. *(Photo by Richard Lobell.)*

With Mr. Jack Spitzer, December 1980.

With Prime Minister Menachem Begin at the UN Special Session on Disarmament, June 1982.

With members of Israel's UN Mission at General Assembly, 1983. *Right to left:* Yehuda Milo, Yehuda Z. Blum, Arye Levin, Aharon Ofry. *Second row:* Aharon Jacob. *(Photo by Isaac Berez.)*

Addressing the Security Council. *(UN photo by Yutaka Nagata.)*

At a press conference with UN correspondents.

With Pope John Paul II, October 1979. *(Photo by Arturo Mari,* L'Osservatore Romano.)

At the Zionist Organization of America–International Leadership Conference, Miami, Florida, 27 October 1979. Secretary of State Alexander Haig and Mr. Ivan Norich, President of ZOA. *(Photo by Alexander Archer.)*

With Jane Fonda, Soviet Jewry Solidarity Sunday, 1981. *(Photo by Michele Singer.)*

With Jaime de Pinies (Spain) conferring before meeting. *(UN photo by Yutaka Nagata.)*

With UN Secretary-General Javier Pérez de Cuéllar. *(Photo by Isaac Berez.)*

With Egyptian Ambassador Ismet Abdul Meguid (Foreign Minister from 1984).
(Photo by Alexander Archer.)

With Japanese Ambassador Nishibori. *(Photo by Alexander Archer.)*

With Mayor Ed Koch. *(Photo by Alexander Archer.)*

Addressing the UN Press Corps.

Conferring with U.S. Ambassador to the UN Jeane Kirkpatrick before meeting.
(*UN photo by Yutaka Nagata.*)

Oleg A. Troyanovsky, President of the Security Council (January 1982) chats with Yehuda Z. Blum prior to a meeting. *(UN photo by Yutaka Nagata.)*

Addressing the UN General Assembly. *(UN photo by Yutaka Nagata.)*

With U.S. President Jimmy Carter. *(Photo by David Rubinger.)*

With Henry Kissinger at dinner at the residence of Ambassador M. Rosenne in honor of President Chaim Herzog, Tuesday, 22 November 1983. *(Photo by Robert A. Cumins.)*

Delegation of Israel headed by Moshe Dayan, Minister of Foreign Affairs. (*UN photo by Saw Lwin.*)

To struggle for restoration to the motherland of Polish Pomerania, Opole, Silesia and East Prussia; for free access to the sea, for Polish frontier posts on the Oder. Poland never again will be threatened by German invasion.

A year later, at the Potsdam Conference, these Polish demands were basically acceded to. Let me quote again from Whiteman's *Digest of International Law:*

> Pending the final determination of Poland's western frontier, the former German territories east of a line running from the Baltic Sea immediately west of Swenemunde and thence along the Oder River to the confluence of the Western Neisse River and along the Western Neisse to the Czechoslovak frontier, including that portion of East Prussia not placed under the administration of the Union of Soviet Socialist Republics, shall be under the administration of the Polish State, and for such purposes should not be considered as part of the Soviet zone of occupation of Germany.

I would like to know whether the representative of Poland can enlighten us about the Polish administration in those areas. Is the population of those areas in 1982 identical with that of 1945, for instance, in cities like Wroclaw and Sczeszin and Poznan? And if the administration is Polish, what law and what jurisdiction apply in those areas pending the conclusion of a peace treaty?

I believe the relevance of my questions is now fully evident to the representative of Poland. Is there no limit to hypocrisy, Mr. Wyzner?

But Ambassador Wyzner is not alone; he is in good company. I have here in front of me a sample of some other participants who came to the support of Syria, very appropriately so. Let me start with this interesting pair, Vietnam and Cuba, two countries of the tropical gulag; two countries that have introduced onto the international scene the tragic phenomenon of boat people; two countries that are engaged in international aggression in Asia and Africa and elsewhere; they come before this Council to sermonize about the need to combat aggression. How apt and how appropriate it is indeed that they should come to the support of Syria!

Another participant is Iraq. There cannot be the slighest doubt as to the sincerity of the Iraqi statement! The Iraqi lamentation in this particular case is as sincere as was the lamentation of the Syrian ambassador last June in this Council on the Iraqi complaint about the destruction of their nuclear reactor. What Iraq *really* thinks about its neighbor, was brought to our attention last week in a press release from the Iraqi mission, issued on 5 January 1982, as an official publication of the Permanent Mission of Iraq to the United Nations. In that press release we read:

The Iraqi Federation of Friendship Societies with Peoples of the World believes that the world public opinion should be informed of the dirty, inhuman and immoral crime which was committed by a gang of criminals of the Assad and Khomeini régimes, by detonating and demolishing the Iraqi Embassy in Beirut and due to which scores of innocent people from the Embassy staff and others fell victim.

I think I can stop here. I need not even refer to Iraq's contribution to international peace and security; it is too well known.

Who else rushed to Syria's support in this Council? Libya, of course—another country well qualified to speak on matters of international aggression. But in this particular case, Libya perhaps may be forgiven, for it has special links with Syria—a confederation or union. Perhaps the Syrian representative could enlighten us on the current state of relations between the two countries. Therefore, it was not unexpected, and certainly not inappropriate, for Libya to make an appearance here. I think it was also helpful, because there are certain things which the Syrian representative wishes to conceal from this Council, but about which his Libyan allies have no such compunction. Let me quote to the Council what Colonel Khaddafi, the level-headed ruler of Libya, told the National Council of Libya last week, on 5 January 1982:

The Saudis said that the enemy must withdraw from the occupied Arab territories. That is not the problem. The problem is the existence of the enemy himself; the existence of the enemy itself conflicts with that of the Arab nation. Either we stay or Israel stays. Anything else is nonsense. The Arabs have the right to tell the whole world that the Zionist entity constitutes a danger to Arab existence and therefore the Arabs should fight it.

This is, in fact, the position of the Syrian representative, just as it is of his ally Muammar Khaddafi, even if here in the Security Council he tries, somewhat unsuccessfully, from time to time to tone down the thrust of his argument.

I have already made reference to the German so-called Democratic Republic, which appeared together with the Democratic Republic of Afghanistan and the Democratic Republic of Yemen. What these three have in common is that they are all equally democratic. They surely must be very proud of their own contributions, and of each other. They fully confirm the saying that birds of a feather flock together.

The representative of Hungary was also good enough to participate in this debate. While he was speaking, I was reminded of a Hungarian proverb; "Kinek vaj van a fején, ne menjen ki a napra." In English it runs: "He who carries butter on his head should not go into the sun." The amount of butter that has been spoiled here in the course of this debate is enormous indeed.

The representative of Jordan made his second statement here today. He spoke, among other things, of the double standard applied by the United Nations with regard to Israel and the Arab-Israel conflict. He is right. Were it not for the double standard, against my country, the situation in the Middle East would have been very different a long time ago. Were it not for the fact that this Organization has been willing to tolerate for thirty-four years the ongoing aggression against my country by practically all its neighbors—until recently all its neighbors—the situation in the Middle East would have been very different. But the United Nations, for reasons well known to all of us, has been willing to tolerate the fact that in violation of its Charter, Arab countries, including Jordan, have totally disregarded not only the prohibition against the use of force, but also against the threat of force; and have been disregarding the Charter provisions that call for the peaceful settlement of international disputes. Yes, indeed, there *is* a double standard. But I could not help feeling, at the same time, that the representative of Jordan also injected a humorous dimension into our debate. He, of all people, introduced the draft resolution supporting the Syrian complaint. I think members of the Council may be interested in an official announcement made by the Government of Jordan only last night, and broadcast on Amman radio. In that announcement, the Jordanian Ministry of the Interior blamed Syrian intelligence for an explosion which occurred in a shop in Amman just three days ago. That blast injured five people, including an employee of the Indian Embassy, as well as one of the persons who planted the bomb. The Jordanian announcement blames a Syrian diplomat, Hisham Mustafa Kanbar, for recruiting two Jordanian civilians for Syrian intelligence. The Syrian diplomat prepared the bomb with his own hands, instructed the two in its use, and personally gave it to them on the morning of the explosion. One of them was injured when the bomb exploded in his hands while he was attempting to plant it in the store. The other escaped across the border into Syria. Following the explosion, the Syrian diplomat left Amman for Syria. All this is in the official announcement of the Jordanian Government.

The Jordanian Ministry of the Interior concludes:

> The Government of Jordan deplores the criminal explosion and emphasizes that such acts conducted by diplomats serving in Jordan stress that without any doubt, the Government of the above-mentioned diplomat [that is Syria] strives by way of such despicable actions to continue to sabotage the effort—the Arab effort—to achieve Arab solidarity, and this at a time when the Government of the said diplomat declares its devotion to this solidarity.

So it is all the more heartening to see that the Ambassador of Jordan is still devoted to this show of solidarity for a country which has been accused by his own Government of being involved in acts of sabotage and terrorism in his country.

This solidarity is manifested in the parallel selectivity with reference to the definition of aggression. The representative of Syria himself reminded us that Syria was a member of the committee that prepared the definition. This only aggravates the attempts by the representative of Syria to mislead the Council.

In his statement he asserted:

> In resolution 100 (1953) of 27 October 1953, the Council asked Israel to suspend drainage in the demilitarized zone, another request which went unheeded.

The representative of Syria was apparently under the illusion that nobody would check on his statement. We did. And what we found was rather interesting. First, the resolution has an operative paragraph, which reads:

> The Security Council notes with satisfaction the statement made by the Israel representative at the 631st meeting regarding the undertaking by his Government to suspend the works in question during (the) . . . examination (of the works in the demilitarized zone).

Nor is that all. We also looked at the verbatim records of that meeting of the Council. In paragraph 4, the then representative of Israel told the Council:

> I am empowered to state that the Government of Israel is willing to arrange such a temporary suspension in the demilitarized zone for the purpose of facilitating the Security Council's consideration of this question.

In paragraph 6 he stated:

> The Government of Israel in hereby accepting this idea, wishes in every way to assist the Security Council in its examination of the problem.

In paragraph 8, the representative of Pakistan, Mr. Zafrulla Khan, stated:

> For my part, I welcome the statement by the representative of Israel.

But perhaps the most interesting quotation that we found is that of Mr. Zeineddine of Syria, in paragraph 15:

The statement just made by the representative of Israel does indicate some change in the Israel Government's view.

We have come a long way since 1953, and the Ambassador of Syria now apparently believes that falsification of the Council's records can proceed with impunity.

8

The War in Lebanon

A

Background of the Lebanese Tragedy

Consolidated excerpts from statements made in the UN Security Council on 31 May 1979, and 6 June 1982.

Israel supports the national sovereignty and territorial integrity of Lebanon within its internationally recognized boundaries. Prime Minister Menachem Begin stated in the Knesset on 7 May 1979:

> I hereby announce in the name of the Government of Israel that our state does not have any territorial demands on Lebanon. We support the territorial integrity and national sovereignty of Lebanon.

The Government of Israel wants peace in and with Lebanon. To this end it has made and will continue to make all endeavors possible. Despite Lebanon's ongoing problems and their complexity, Israel believes that the time has nonetheless come to exert all efforts to move toward a negotiated peace between Israel and Lebanon. In keeping with this primary objective of Israel's foreign policy, the prime minister of Israel extended a direct appeal to the president of Lebanon, inviting him to a meeting with a view to reaching a negotiated peace treaty between Israel and Lebanon. He said in the Knesset:

> I have the honor to invite the president of Lebanon, Mr. Sarkis, to come to Jerusalem to meet with me. For my part, I am prepared to leave by civilian airplane for Beirut. The subject of our conversation—whether it

takes place in Jerusalem or in Beirut, or perhaps in a neutral place—will be one: the signing of a peace treaty between Israel and Lebanon.

As has been acknowledged by the Secretary-General in several of his reports concerning the United Nations Interim Force in Lebanon (UNIFIL), the situation in the south of Lebanon cannot be detached from the situation in the country as a whole. Attempts to do so will not enhance the cause of international peace and security, and are bound to fail.

The tragic reality prevailing in Lebanon must be recognized by all of us. We are all painfully aware that the situation prevailing in the south of the country is merely one symptom of a much larger problem. The internal problems of Lebanon are of long standing. They were greatly aggravated by the arrival of large numbers of armed PLO terrorists. With its far from gentle expulsion from Jordan in September 1970 and its exclusion from other Arab countries, the PLO took advantage of Lebanon's inherent weaknesses to establish operational bases and headquarters there. Indeed, the erosion of Lebanon's sovereignty began in the early 1970s, when the PLO set up what was virtually "a state within a state" in Lebanon, principally in southern Lebanon, where one of the areas was even dubbed "Fatahland."

Over the last few years, with increasing intensity, the PLO turned southern Lebanon into a staging post for its murderous incursions into Israel. Names like Avivim, Ma'alot, Kiryat Shmonah, Nahariya and Misgav Am came to denote the scenes of bloody massacres of women and children.

All of these acts and many others were perpetrated by PLO terrorists operating from Lebanese territory. Nor were the PLO's terroristic activities confined to Israel. A reign of terror swept Lebanese villages in the south, as the PLO gradually tightened its grip over the area. Moreover, southern Lebanon became the training ground, logistic center and refuge for members of the terrorist international from all over the world. Their activities have plagued numerous countries and the international community at large.

From the early 1970s on, Lebanon lost much of its sovereignty over its own territory to the terrorist PLO. But in the brutal and bitter war in Lebanon between 1974 and 1976 the country also lost its independence to Syria, which saw in the steadily deteriorating situation in Lebanon an opportunity to realize its long-standing ambition to swallow up Lebanon within what the Syrians refer to as Greater Syria, "Suriah al-Kubra" in Arabic. Between 1974 and 1976 Syrian allegiances jockeyed and changed for reasons of political expediency to suit Syria's own purposes. At one stage the Syrians presented themselves as the protectors of the Christian Lebanese against the PLO, and did not hesitate at that stage to bombard and demolish PLO strongholds such as Tel el-Zaatar. Later on, roles reversed and the Syrians turned brutally on the Christians with horrifying results, mercilessly bombarding civilian centers, killing uncounted thousands of civilians and turning up to a million Lebanese into refugees. Indeed, the images of Syria's indiscriminate brutality in Lebanon are familiar to anyone who watches television news. Most vivid are the pictures of the merciless Syrian siege of Zahle, the largest Christian city in the Middle East. That siege went on for weeks and by the time it was lifted, it had resulted in more than one thousand casualties. In all these activities, both the Syrian army of occupation and the terrorist PLO have been aided, abetted, trained, equipped and financed by the Soviet Union, whose attempts at destabilizing and subverting the Middle East as a whole are well known and whose sinister role in the Lebanese tragedy is common knowledge.

As a result of all this, Lebanon has been in recent years—and still remains—a country occupied by alien forces. Syria still maintains in Lebanon a sizable portion of its army—that is about 25,000 troops and upwards and the PLO still has over 15,000 armed terrorists operating in the country, of whom more than 2,000 are positioned south of the Litani River. About fifteen hundred of these terrorists are located in the so-called "Tyre Pocket" and around seven hundred are deployed in some forty pockets and nests within the UNIFIL area of operation, with the clear intention of using that area as a springboard in their attempts to terrorize Israel's civilian population, particularly in the northern part of our country. As long as these non-Lebanese elements are allowed to operate within and from Lebanon, no real progress will be achieved toward return of the effective authority of the Government of Lebanon throughout the length and breadth of that country. Peace cannot be restored in Lebanon, and the Lebanese Government cannot re-establish its effective authority, while a massive Syrian army of occupation holds down the bulk of the country and while PLO terrorists, trained and armed by the Soviet Union, are given free rein on Lebanese soil.

Ever since its occupation of Lebanon in 1976, Syria has denied the Government of Lebanon any semblance of free and independent political decision-making and action. No decisions affecting Lebanese national policies, either internal or external, are taken any more by the Government of Lebanon and no longer are those decisions made in Beirut, its capital. They are now made by its "fraternal" neighbor, Syria. To rub it in, Syria, along its border with Lebanon, has eliminated all remaining vestiges of Lebanese sovereignty and authority, especially in the Beka'a Valley. International frontier demarcations between the two countries have been removed, Syrian currency has been introduced, and Lebanese government signs have been taken down and destroyed. The statements of the representative of Lebanon in this Council must also be viewed against this background.

To the outsider it may seem that Lebanon has been divided into spheres of influence, principally between the Syrians, who keep their army in the north of the country, and the terrorist PLO, that operates throughout much of the south. The fact is that the PLO in Lebanon operates under complete Syrian control. It is Syria which oversees the supply of PLO armaments and logistic facilities. It is Syria that decides how that terrorist organization is to be deployed and what tasks it will undertake within the framework of wider Syrian designs.

The terrorist groups operating under the umbrella of the murder organization calling itself the PLO are subverting the situation in the south of Lebanon, just as they have been doing in the rest of the country. There are some two thousand armed PLO terrorists south of the Litani River, mainly in the Tyre area, and they constitute a threat to three tangible targets: the citizens of Israel, particularly in the north; the villagers in southern Lebanon; and the men of UNIFIL in the fulfillment of their mandate.

Beyond that, there are another ten to twelve thousand armed PLO terrorists in areas of Lebanon north of the Litani. Taken together, these terrorists constitute a menace to the restoration of the authority of the Government of Lebanon in all parts of that troubled country.

Recently, there has been a marked escalation in the criminal acts against Israel perpetrated by the terrorist PLO from Lebanese territory. There has also been an increase—if such were possible—in the barbarity of these outrages, as demonstrated in the brutal and abominable killing of a little girl of four and her father on the beach at Nahariya on 22 April 1979, on which I reported in my letter of 22 April 1979 to the Secretary-General. The ostensible aim of these atrocities, beyond mass murder for its own sake, is, to judge by statements made by the terrorist PLO itself, to try to subvert the ongoing peace process in the Middle East.

Israel is in possession of information from reliable sources that a decision has been taken to step up violence by the terrorist PLO in southern Lebanon. This is undoubtedly the cause of the heightened tension in the area in the last few days.

The Secretary-General has also confirmed that the majority of the recent acts of violence in southern Lebanon were initiated by the terrorist PLO, euphemistically referred to in United Nations jargon as "armed elements."

In my letter of 9 May 1979, I spelled out the catalogue of violence against Israel in recent months by PLO terrorists operating out of Lebanon. I also indicated that in almost every case, it was through its news agency in Beirut and on its radio station broadcasting from Lebanon that the terrorist PLO has openly boasted of its responsibility for these criminal activities.

Let me reiterate that Israel's actions are specifically directed against concentrations of terrorists in Lebanon. The unfortunate fact is that for years now, the terrorist PLO has chosen to take cover behind refugees in camps and Lebanese civilians in towns and villages throughout the country.

This fact is well known and beyond dispute. Moreover, the terrorist PLO marauds with complete freedom throughout Lebanon in total disregard for Lebanese sovereignty. Who of us has forgotten the extraordinarily candid speech made on 14 October 1976 by Ambassador Ghorra, the former Permanent Representative of Lebanon? Addressing the General Assembly, he described in detail "the constant Palestinian intervention in the internal affairs of Lebanon and the intolerable encroachment on its sovereignty."

Ambassador Ghorra reminded us that in 1973 President Suleiman Franjieh "denounced the illegal occupation of parts of Lebanese territory by Palestinian elements." He recalled that the terrorist PLO did not respect the many accords which were concluded with them over the years to limit their presence and activities in Lebanon. He then went on to say:

> The Palestinians increased the influx of arms into Lebanon. . . . They transformed most of the refugee camps, if not all, into military bastions. . . . Common-law criminals fleeing from Lebanese justice found shelter and protection in the camps. . . . Those camps in fact became centers for the training of mercenaries sent and financed by some other Arab states. . . .
>
> Palestinian elements belonging to various . . . organizations resorted to kidnapping of Lebanese—and sometimes foreigners—holding them prisoners, questioning them, torturing them and sometimes killing them. . . . They committed all sorts of crimes in Lebanon and also escaped Lebanese justice in the protection of the camps. They smuggled goods. . . . They went so far as to demand "protection" money. . . .
>
> It is difficult to enumerate all the illegal activities committed by those Palestinian elements. . . .

In striking at the terrorist bases from which the PLO's murder gangs launch their criminal raids against the civilian population in Israel, my Government is exercising its inherent right of self-defense. Like any other government, the Government of Israel has the right and the duty to take all the measures necessary to protect the lives and safety of its citizens.

A state's right to take the measures necessary to hold and to foil hostile activities emanating from across its boundaries is a principle well recognized by international law and by international practice alike. What is more, the very toleration by a state on its territory of armed bands engaged in hostile activities against another state is considered a breach of international law on the part of the state tolerating the presence of such bands on its territory, irrespective of whether such state is unwilling or unable to curb such activities.

This principle is clearly expressed by Fawcett in "Intervention in International Law, A Study of Some Recent Cases" (103 *Recueil des Cours*, 1961, vol. II, pp. 347, 361–63, 365–67):

> Where incursion of armed bands is a precursor to an armed attack or itself constitutes an attack, and the authorities in the territory from

which the armed bands came, are either unable or unwilling to control and restrain them, then armed intervention, having as its sole object the removal or destruction of their bases, would . . . be justifiable under Article 51 [of the UN Charter].

Israel's response to the PLO's criminal acts is thus what any self-respecting, sovereign state would do in the circumstances.

Indeed, how many states represented here would sit back passively and watch their own women and children being killed and wounded by terrorists? As the representative of a country that is one of the prime targets of international terrorism, I can only repeat that the Government of Israel is duty-bound to take all measures necessary to protect the lives and safety of its citizens. Israel expects that the territory of Lebanon will not be permitted to serve, as it has in the past, as a launching pad for harassment of, and indiscriminate terror against, its citizens.

Let me conclude by repeating what I said at the outset: Israel sincerely desires peace with and in Lebanon. Israel also desires that the national sovereignty of Lebanon and the effective authority of its government be restored within that country's internationally recognized boundaries.

B

Operation "Peace for Galilee"

Abbreviated version of statement made in the UN Security Council on 6 June 1982.

In the Council's meeting of 5 June 1982, the distinguished representative of Lebanon made what was apparently a slip of the tongue. Since slips of the tongue are not likely to be recorded in the minutes of the Security Council, and because of the revealing nature of the case in point, I should like to commit it to posterity. Ambassador Tueni called upon the Council to consider "the aggression against Israel."

Ambassador Tueni was, of course, right. Israel indeed has been the target of ongoing aggression for many years. Yet this Council has not evinced the slightest interest in all those acts of warfare, violence and terrorism which, in their totality, manifest the ongoing Arab aggression against my country. Let me assure Ambassador Tueni that this Council will remain equally indifferent now to the display of Arab aggression against my country and against my people. This Council cannot even plead ignorance in this regard. Israel has regularly informed the Council over the years of the atrocities attempted and perpetrated by the PLO against Israel, Israelis and Jews around the world. I would even venture to say that we have long been among the most diligent correspondents of the Council in recent years. Permit me therefore to refresh this Council's memory and to remind its members of some of the "highlights" of PLO barbarism in recent years.

On 22 April 1979, four PLO terrorists landed at night on the coast of Nahariya in a rubber dinghy, after setting out from the Lebanese port of Tyre. On reaching Nahariya, the terrorists attacked an apartment building, killing one Israeli civilian, his two small children and an Israeli policeman. This was reported by me to the Security Council on 23 April 1979.

On 6 April 1980, five PLO terrorists of the so-called "Arab Liberation Front" infiltrated Israel from Lebanon and attacked a children's nursery at Kibbutz Misgav Am on Israel's northern border. A two-year-old child and a kibbutz secretary were murdered by the terrorists, and one soldier was killed. One adult civilian, four children and eleven soldiers were injured. I reported this to the Security Council on 7 April 1980.

On 27 July 1980, a PLO terrorist hurled two grenades into a group numbering forty Jewish schoolchildren waiting to board a bus outside a community center in Antwerp, Belgium. One child was killed outright and seven others were wounded, in addition to ten adults and a pregnant woman, all of whom sustained injuries. I reported this to the Security Council on 30 July 1980.

On 29 August 1981, terrorists of the PLO faction "Black June" attacked a synagogue in Vienna, using hand grenades and machine guns. Two worshippers were killed and nineteen people were wounded, including two children and two Austrian policemen. I reported this to the Security Council on 31 August 1981.

On 7 October 1981, an explosive charge went off at a building in Rome housing the offices of Israel's national airline, El Al. Eight people were wounded, and the premises were badly damaged.

On 20 October 1981, a booby-trapped car exploded opposite the Jewish Portuguese Community Synagogue in Antwerp, Belgium, only minutes before special holiday services were due to begin. Three people were killed, and about one hundred wounded.

On 15 January 1982, the PLO bombed a Jewish-owned restaurant frequented by Jewish patrons in West Berlin. The explosion killed a fourteen-month-old girl and wounded twenty-four other people. I reported this to the Security Council on 20 January 1982.

On 3 April 1982, a PLO terrorist shot and killed a diplomat at the Israel Embassy in Paris outside his home in the French capital. The murder of Mr. Yacov Bar-Simantov by a young female terrorist, who shot him at point blank range, was witnessed by his family. Responsibility for the murder was assumed by the "Lebanese Armed Revolutionary Faction," one of the many aliases of the terrorist PLO. Being the seasoned criminals that they are, the

PLO terrorists have developed the technique of adopting such aliases for the purpose of covering up their crimes. This was reported to the Security Council by the Chargé d'Affaires of the Permanent Mission of Israel to the United Nations on 3 April 1982.

And last week, on 3 June 1982, a group of PLO terrorists attempted to assassinate Israel's ambassador to the Court of St. James, Mr. Shlomo Argov, as he was leaving a hotel in central London. They fired at point blank range, seriously wounding the ambassador, who underwent brain surgery and remains in critical condition in a London hospital. I reported this to the Council on 4 June 1982.

This is by no means the sum total of PLO atrocities over the years. Even in the relatively short period of time that has elapsed since the July 1981 agreement on cessation of hostilities, the total of dead and wounded at the hands of the PLO has steadily mounted: it now stands at 17 dead and 241 wounded, in a total of 141 terrorist acts, all of them originating from terrorist bases inside Lebanon. To give some indication of the escalation of terrorist activity in the last few weeks, I would point out that since 9 May— that is, less than one month ago—twenty-eight acts of PLO terrorism have been reported in Israel and abroad and against the area under the control of Major Sa'ad Haddad in South Lebanon.

These and many hundreds of additional terrorist attacks against Israel, Israelis and Jews were regularly reported by us to the Council. All our reports have gone unheeded. This Council has remained unmoved, and did not see fit to act with a view to curbing the criminal activities of the PLO; nor did this Council ever pronounce itself against the harassment by the PLO of Israel's civilian population in the northern part of our country. They have been repeatedly subjected to massive bombardments, shelling, and rocket attacks by the PLO using long-range artillery pieces and Katyusha rocket launchers supplied to them by the Soviet Union.

When is this Council galvanized into action? When Israel, after years of unparalleled restraint, finally resorts to the exercise of its right of self-defense, the fundamental and inalienable right of any state, which is also recognized by the United Nations Charter as the inherent right of members of this Organization. In order to save a terrorist organization from well-deserved and long overdue retribution, this Council is convened in emergency meetings, urgent meetings and every conceivable form of extraordinary session. It is the same Council that, all these years, has not found the time to devote even one such meeting to a debate on the situation in Lebanon as a whole and to the causes underlying that unfortunate country's predicament. It is the same Council that has not found the time to discuss the mass murder and bloodbath perpetrated by the régime of the Assad brothers of Syria last February against the people of Hama—the fifth largest city of that country.

It is the same Council that has not found time over the past nineteen months to discuss the Iraqi aggression against Iran and the resulting misery for millions of people, including more than two million refugees.

It is the same Council that has not seen fit to discuss, since January 1980, the ongoing rape of Afghanistan by the Soviet army of occupation.

It is the same Council that has not found time to discuss in over three years, since January 1979 to be precise, the continuing genocide of the people of Kampuchea, a country which has been subjected to external aggression from Vietnam.

And it is the same Council that has never found time to consider the suppression of the Polish people by a military régime imposed on it from without.

Perhaps I have been a trifle naive. But I have been under the impression that the primary duty of this Council was—and remains—the promotion of international peace and security, not the encouragement of international terrorism or the protection of its practitioners.

Let me ask a simple question: How many Israelis have to be killed by the PLO terrorists for this Council to be persuaded that the limits of our endurance have been reached? How many passengers on civilian buses, how many Israeli schoolchildren, how many Israeli toddlers, how many Israeli women simply doing their shopping, how many ordinary Israeli civilians asleep in their beds, how many of Israel's diplomats, must be murdered by the PLO for this Council to realize that Israel and its people are one of the prime targets of international terrorism and of its foremost exponent and linchpin, the murderous PLO?

The answer is simple. It is grounded in the bitter experience of many years. Given the parliamentary situation in this Organization and the constellation within this Council, Israel cannot expect this body even to deplore PLO barbarism against Israel's civilian population, let alone take any steps with a view to curbing that barbarism.

It thus becomes imperative for the Government of Israel to exercise its legitimate right of self-defense to protect the lives of its citizens and to ensure their safety.

Indeed I would aks how many states represented here would agree to sit back passively and watch their own women and children murdered and maimed by terrorists? How many states represented here on this Council are willing to accept an unconditional cessation of hostilities without guaranteeing what they perceive as their vital interests?

Yet we are still confronted with the strange phenomenon that countries that one day vote against such a call for an unconditional cessation of hostilities when the matter affects them in one part of the world, have no compunction about supporting the following day a similar call in another part of the world.

Reference was made in this Council to the fact that the hit list of the PLO terrorists involved in the assassination attempt in London against Ambassador Shlomo Argov apparently included the resident PLO terrorist in the British capital. If indeed this information is correct, it should not occasion any surprise. After all, the settling of scores in the criminal underworld is a well-known fact of life. And there is no reason to expect this to be any less applicable to the PLO's criminal community. Their constant internecine feuding and reciprocal assassinations have proved over the decades a characteristic and salient feature of Arab terrorism in general and of Palestinian Arab terrorism in particular. The warring factions within the PLO have excelled themselves in this field. Let me give the Council a few examples:

The murder in London in April 1979, of PLO henchman Said Hamami, the man who, in fact, served as the predecessor of the present PLO operative in London who is said to have figured on the latest hit list.

The murder of Ali Yassoun, the PLO operative in Kuwait, in June of the same year.

The murder in Cannes, France, of Zuhair Muhsin, the chief of the Al-Saiqa terrorist faction within the PLO.

The murder of PLO terrorist Na'im Khader in Brussels, in June 1981.

To borrow an expression from English company law, it is not incumbent upon Israel to "lift the veil," with regard to the internal bloodfeuding of the PLO, with a view to researching the mutual relationships of its factions and members. To make such a demand on Israel would be about as reasonable as to demand that the law-enforcement authorities of a particular state should absolve a known criminal of responsibility for his crime simply because he also had the intention of murdering another member of his camp.

The simple and incontrovertible fact remains: all the groups which together constitute that multi-tentacled octopus known as the PLO have their headquarters, training grounds, and bases of operations in Lebanon. This fact is unaltered by the feuding that remains a permanent feature of the PLO's existence and that occasionally erupts into full-fledged violence among the various PLO groups.

Not many weeks past, on 25 February 1982 to be precise, in a remark that did not go unnoticed, Ambassador Tueni told a meeting of the Security Council that "We shall never become accessories to anybody's strategy in the destabilization process that is today tearing the Middle East apart."

Now, Ambassador Tueni has requested a meeting of the Security Council to complain, in substance, that Israel has attacked PLO bases in his country.

Israel has stated on numerous occasions that it has no territorial ambitions in Lebanon; that it respects and honors Lebanese independence and territorial integrity. My Government reiterates this clear policy today. But the least that we are entitled to expect is a full measure of reciprocity.

We are perfectly willing to believe in the earnestness of Ambassador Tueni's declaration, and another equally serious undertaking: "My country,"

Ambassador Tueni said at the same meeting of the Security Council, "is not for hire, nor for sale. It is not negotiable and it is not dispensable."

If all this were true, what, may one ask, are fifteen thousand armed PLO terrorists doing on Lebanese soil with their artillery and tanks? What of the well-documented comings and goings of international terrorist organizations finding succor and enlightenment in the academies of international terror run by the PLO to the glory of murder and rampage? Under what authority are they receiving international delegations, including United Nations committees, on Lebanese soil? Why is the Syrian army of occupation laying down the law in Lebanon? What are twenty-five thousand well-armed Syrian soldiers, one third of the Syrian army, doing in Lebanon, in Beirut, its capital; in Tripoli and in other cities; in the Beka'a Valley which has been annexed to Syria in all but name?

In short, where does Lebanese sovereignty begin, and where do Ambassador Tueni's hollow protestations end?

Over all these years of turmoil in Lebanon this Council has not seen fit to devote any time to discuss the subversion of Lebanese sovereignty, first by the PLO and subsequently by Syria, except for the five desultory minutes which it accorded the topic on 6 October 1978—that is to say, more than three and a half years ago—at the end of which it nervously adopted, without any formal debate, a milk-and-water resolution that avoided even indirect reference to Syria, that was then involved in the massive bombardment and destruction of civilian quarters of Beirut and the large-scale massacre of its population. This pattern of behavior by the Council, totally at variance with the facts and realities prevailing in Lebanon, will also be duly reflected in future deliberations of this Council. The Council apparently is still not aware of the fact that Lebanon is an occupied country, dominated by the Syrian army of occupation and by the PLO's armed terrorists. This bizarre pattern of behavior by the Council may perhaps be understood by its members, but is certainly far from being comprehensible to world opinion. It can only further lower and compromise this Council's already badly shattered credibility on any matter affecting the Arab-Israel conflict.

All these facts are well known by all of us and certainly by the representative of Lebanon. Israel has profound sympathy for the agony of Lebanon and its people, but that sympathy does not absolve the Lebanese representative of the obligation to adhere to at least a minimum of honesty in these debates.

His statement in the Council in the present debate—like so many of his earlier statements—has a ring of duplicity that, regrettably, has come to characterize his country's position. It is essential to realize that from the viewpoint of the Lebanese representative, the true object of the debates is to find a scapegoat for Lebanon's fundamental problems and a way to avoid facing up to them directly and honestly.

This, sadly, has been Lebanon's approach for the last decade and more.

For example, as early as December 1968, Fuad Boutros, the foreign minister of Lebanon, claimed in this Council that: "Lebanon gives refuge to no commando organizations." This was a barefaced lie, and when the president of Lebanon, Mr. Hélou, was pressed about it, he later admitted to Lebanese parliamentarians that the claim was made in this Council "in order to secure Israel's condemnation" (as reported in the Beirut newspaper *Al-Hayat* of 1 July 1969). This mendacious and duplicitous approach continues to find expression in the positions taken by our Lebanese colleague in this Council.

Let me therefore tell him very plainly: had Lebanon been prepared to face its problems honestly over the years and fulfilled its national and international commitments, it might not have come to this sorry pass.

In the normal course of international affairs, a sovereign state assumes the responsibility for the actions not only of its government but also of its subjects and "guests." Lebanon's duty to prevent its territory from being used for terrorist attacks against other states is based on general international law:

> States are under a duty to prevent and suppress such subversive activity against foreign Governments as assumes the form of armed hostile expeditions, or attempts to commit common crimes, against life or property. (Oppenheim-Lauterpacht, *International Law*, 8th ed., vol. I, pp. 292–93)

This principle has been embraced by the General Assembly on numerous occasions, including, for example, in the Declaration on the Inadmissibility of Intervention in the Domestic Affairs of States and the Protection of their Independence and Sovereignty, adopted in 1965, and in the Declaration on Principles of International Law concerning Friendly Relations and Co-operation among States in accordance with the Charter of the United Nations, adopted in 1970.

For Israel, compliance with this principle is a matter of the utmost concern, especially regarding Lebanon. The PLO, the so-called guest of Lebanon, whose variety is legion and whose sense of responsibility is nil, is acting with its customary brazenness in trespassing against the citizens of a neighboring state, Israel. Israel must hold Lebanon fully responsible for any atrocity committed against it when it is conceived and planned in Lebanon, irrespective of whether it is carried out from Lebanon or from any other territory.

Our attitude should hardly appear strange to the Lebanese authorities. They know full well what the scoreboard indicates: it bears witness to assassinations and attempted assassinations; murders and attempted murders, all of which reflect the objectives of PLO strategy—namely, the maximum loss of life and limb among Israelis and Jews, wherever they may be.

When the cessation of hostilities on the Lebanese border went into effect on 24 July 1981, after laborious and protracted efforts by the United States envoy, Ambassador Philip Habib, it soon became clear that the Lebanese Government, for all the protestations of Ambassador Tueni, was unable to enforce it, control it or ensure its continuation. Violations began almost immediately and have continued unabated, culminating most recently in the attempted assassination of Ambassador Argov in London. In the face of great provocation, Israel has been acting with the utmost restraint, but the most recent terrorist outrages make too heavy demands on Israel's patience.

It is customary for the PLO terrorists, as well as for their protectors, financers and supporters, to voice surprise at Israeli acts of self-defense when the limits of forbearance are reached, but the Security Council should consider Israel's situation when confronted with the unending harassment and the indiscriminate and senseless killing of innocent people by the PLO. It also would do well to bear in mind the sinister association of the PLO with one of the super-powers, with the bandits who parade in military uniforms and make use of the PLO in promoting their inter-Arab ambitions, with the potentates who buy insurance by paying ransom to the PLO chieftains. Propaganda has elevated these men to the ranks of courageous freedom fighters. In reality they are cowards, whose custom it is to use men, women and children as human shields in an attempt to ward off the retribution which they deserve.

Israel sincerely regrets any loss of life that may have occurred among persons not directly responsible for PLO activities. The responsibility must be borne fully by the PLO and attributed to its total disregard for human life, be it Israeli or Arab, Jewish, Christian or Moslem. But Israel can not remain unmoved by the repetition of endless murders, sabotage and incitement. Those who overstep the boundaries and see themselves under no obligation regarding the life and property of Israel's citizens must be put on notice. Israel has always sought negotiations with its neighbors with a view to arriving at a peaceful settlement of all the outstanding issues. Israel's neighbors, with one well-known recent exception, have declined to negotiate with us.

Faced with intolerable provocation, repeated aggression and harassment, Israel has now been forced to exercise its right of self-defense to arrest the never-ending cycle of attacks against its northern border, to deter continued terrorism against Israel's citizens in Israel and abroad, and to instill the basic concept in the minds of the PLO assassins that Jewish life will never again be taken with impunity.

The Government of Israel, after all these months of cautioning and warning, has now decided to act, justifiably and within clearly delineated parameters, to free the inhabitants of the Galilee from PLO harassment. The Israel cabinet, in its meeting today, has thus resolved as follows:

> 1. To instruct the Israel Defense Forces to place all the civilian population of the Galilee beyond the range of the terrorists' fire from Lebanon, where they, their bases and their headquarters are concentrated.
> 2. The name of the operation is "Peace for Galilee."
> 3. During the operation the Syrian army will not be attacked unless it attacks our forces.
> 4. Israel continues to aspire to the signing of a peace treaty with independent Lebanon, its territorial integrity preserved.

No one in the Middle East is as eager as Israel to see Lebanese sovereignty restored, its internal strife resolved, the Syrian occupiers removed, the PLO subdued and freedom and tranquillity returned to that war-torn land. Israel will do everything in its power to maintain good-neighborly relations with Lebanon, and the Lebanese leaders know this. If Lebanon is now helplessly given over to its captors, having forfeited its independence, it must not expect Israel to relinquish its responsibilities as a sovereign state. Israel has no quarrel with Lebanon, only with those who have subjugated it.

C

Israel's Assistance to the Rehabilitation of Lebanon

Abbreviated version of statement made in the UN General Assembly on 26 June 1982.

Israel did not participate in the orgy of hatred, misinformation and distortion that went under the name of a General Assembly debate in what by now has apparently become the Seventh Permanent Emergency Special Session of this Assembly. We refrained from participating in that debate out of our firm conviction—shared by so many knowledgeable observers in this building and around the world—that this exercise was not motivated by any genuine concern for the agony of Lebanon and for the suffering of the sorely tried people of that war-torn land. Quite to the contrary, many if not most of the participants in this debate were motivated by considerations not only irrelevant to the restoration of Lebanese sovereignty to the Lebanese people but even inimical to the attainment of that goal. There can be little doubt that the draft resolution about to be adopted by the Assembly also duly reflects this motivation.

Let me therefore at this stage briefly state Israel's position on the situation in Lebanon. I do so in full awareness of the fact that truth has become a rare and increasingly irrelevant commodity in this building. For a decade and more the tragedy of Lebanon has been unfolding in full view of a cynical and indifferent world and has cost the lives of about one hundred thousand persons; about a quarter of a million have been wounded and more than one million Lebanese have been displaced. Since the causes of the tragedy are common knowledge and well-known to all of us, I need not elaborate on them here today.

As far as Israel is concerned, for the past decade and more, Lebanese territory has become the launching-pad and the staging-ground for indiscriminate terrorist attacks on the civilian population of Israel. There have been hundreds of such outrages, the targets of which, deliberately, have been the children of Israel, the women of Israel, the civilians of Israel, as well as the diplomats of Israel.

International terrorism has converted Lebanon into one of its major centers, indeed, into its world headquarters. The terrorist PLO, which has systematically undermined and subverted Lebanese sovereignty ever since the early 1970s, has welcomed to Lebanon its terrorist guests from other parts of the world.

Operation "Peace for Galilee" was prompted solely by dictates of self-preservation and self-defense which is an inherent right of every state, and recognized by the UN Charter. The operation was ordered because of the intolerable situation created by the presence in Lebanon of a large number of terrorists operating from that country and equipped with modern, long-range weaponry threatening the lives of the civilian population of my country.

Israel was stunned in recent weeks by the immense quantity of arms and ammunition found in Lebanon, that had been put at the disposal of the terrorists there, and by the elaborate infrastructure established by the terrorists on the territory of a sovereign state, a member of our Organization.

As unfortunately always happens in times of war, many innocent civilians have been caught up in the hostilities in Lebanon. Israel regrets as much as anybody else, and I daresay more than most, any civilian casualty, irrespective of nationality or creed. As far as Israel is concerned, every civilian casualty is one too many. But we categorically reject and unequivocally condemn the attempt at falsification and the horror propaganda that we have witnessed in recent weeks, here and elsewhere. Wild, unsubstantiated and grossly exaggerated figures of civilian casualties and displaced persons have been deliberately bandied about by some professional and other, not-so-professional, liars. Thus, for instance, in the cities of Tyre, Sidon and Nabatiyeh 460 civilians have lost their lives. Indeed, as I said before, 460 too many. But it is fortunately a far cry from the wild figures that have been mentioned by our enemies and their supporters, some of whom even interspersed their wild accusations with foul and obscene language. According to the best estimates available to us, some twenty thousand persons have become homeless which, again, is a far cry from the equally wild figures mentioned in this connection. The responsibility for all this misery and suffering must be borne fully and squarely by the terrorist PLO and must be attributed to its total disregard for human life—so vividly manifested in its cowardly practice of shielding behind civilians and establishing its encampments as well as arms and ammunition depots deliberately in civilian population centers as well as within hospitals, mosques and schools.

Israel is already contributing its share, bringing relief for the civilian population of Lebanon under its control to the point where, according to the competent international relief organizations, there do not exist any longer problems of food shortages or shortages of medical aid in those areas.

From the start of the "Peace for Galilee" operation the Israel Defense Forces have been at pains to ensure adequate food supplies for the civilian population. To this end, the IDF distributed bread and milk powder, as well as a large number of tents, within forty-eight hours of entry into Lebanese towns and villages. The Israel Ministry of Energy has assumed responsibility for the allocation of fuel supplies. The Israel Defense Forces are repairing the water, electricity and communications systems where damaged, as well as carrying out road repairs.

The Government of Israel has appointed a member of the cabinet to coordinate aid to the civilian population in southern Lebanon and has also set up a committee on humanitarian aid to Lebanese civilians, headed by the director-general of Israel's Foreign Ministry. Last, but not least, volunteer groups formed by Israel civilians are collecting food, clothing and blankets for immediate dispatch to suffering Lebanese civilians. Volunteer fund-raising is being organized and sponsored by various civic organizations, women's groups, the Israel broadcasting service, newspapers and individuals.

Israel has no territorial ambitions whatsoever in Lebanon. We do not covet even one single square inch of Lebanese territory. We do not want to stay in Lebanon, or in any part thereof. But we are entitled to demand that proper arrangements be made so that Lebanon should no longer serve as a staging ground for terrorist attacks against Israel's civilian population. We are entitled to demand that concrete arrangements be made that would permanently and reliably preclude hostile action against Israel and its citizens from Lebanese soil.

Israel fully supports the restoration of the sovereignty, independence and territorial integrity of Lebanon. Israel stands for the restoration of the territorial unity of Lebanon within its internationally recognized boundaries under the authority of its lawful government and free from any foreign intervention. Let Lebanon be Lebanon! Let Lebanon be returned to its own people!

D

Beirut and Sakiet-Sidi-Youssef

Statement made in the UN Security Council on 6 August 1982, following the vote on a draft resolution, supported by France, that called for sanctions against Israel. The draft resolution was vetoed by the United States.

It is not my intention to respond to the statements that we heard from the distinguished representative of the Union of Soviet Socialist Republics. I did so extensively in an earlier meeting today. Let me, therefore, only briefly state that I see no need on my part to respond to the expressions of vilification on the part of the leading imperialist power of our time, the leading expansionist power of our time, the power that has installed the gulags to suppress and oppress its own people. We are in no need of being taught decency and proper behavior by any representative of the Soviet Union.

But I do wish to say a few words and address myself to another member of the Council, and I do so more in sorrow than in anger because we have tremendous respect and admiration for his country. It is not only a great country but its people is a great people—a people that has stood for many generations for those ideals that make life worth living. It is therefore with sorrow that we note that as far as that country is concerned today, 6 August 1982, will live on as a day of shame and infamy. Let me read to the distinguished representative of France a passage from a previous meeting of this Council. Let me do so in his own language:

> Une armée qui installe ses mitrailleuses au milieu de la population civile prend une responsabilité grave à l'égard de cette population. Une ville d'où des pièces tirent sur d'autres troupes ne peut prétendre être une ville ouverte, à l'abri des bombardements.

This was uttered in this Council by the representative of France, Mr. Georges-Picot, on 2 June 1958. In English:

> An army which sets up machine-guns in the center of an area occupied by civilians assumes a heavy responsibility with regard to this civilian population. A town from which guns are fired on troops elsewhere cannot claim to be an open town, immune to bombing.

What prompted that statement by the representative of France was the episode of Sakiet-Sidi-Youssef. For the sake of those members of the Council who may not remember, Sakiet-Sidi-Youssef, on Tunisian territory, was used as a terrorist base from which French troops and French civilians across the

Tunisian border were harassed. And the French representative, rightly, made a point of emphasizing these facts:

> I consider it my duty in order to enable the Council to form an objective appraisal of the situation, to fill in the gaps in the Tunisian statement and to correct certain points which will make it clear to the President and the members of the Council that Sakiet-Sidi-Youssef was not an open town, but a military center of the Algerian rebels, supported by the Tunisian army and administration; a center from which attacks were continually launched against the French forces.

> Long before the incident of 8 February 1958 [which was the reason for the Council discussing the issue] Sakiet-Sidi-Youssef and its mine were used as a training center for the rebels and as a transit point for the supply of arms to the Algerian rebellion. What amounted to a rebel garrison—averaging five hundred to seven hundred men—was permanently established at the mine, while the families lived in the village. Units of recruits were stationed there, drew arms, and for six weeks carried out intensive military training consisting of technical instruction on the spot, combat exercises in the hills to the north of the mine buildings, firing practice in the hills, and so on.

The French Government therefore concluded that in order to stop those terrorist activities it had to act. And how was that action characterized? Here I quote from the meeting of the Security Council on the same day, again from the statement by Mr. Georges-Picot:

> The French retaliation was no more than an act of legitimate self-defense. The local command in particular took constant care to avoid civilian losses, opening fire only as a last resort. A commando unit of armed Tunisian civilians, on the other hand, did not hesitate to set fire to two dwelling houses nor deliberately to use the village school as a base for directing fire on the French garrison, thus making itself responsible for the death of the head of the school and of his family. . . . While the fighting was going on, the Remada school was used by Tunisian armed units as a point from which to fire against the *bordj* occupied by the French troops.

And the conclusion? It is to be found in the address by Mr. George-Picot at the previous meeting:

> France is justified in contending that the Tunisian Government has taken advantage of all the facilities accorded to it by France in order to give open and constantly increasing encouragement to supporters of a rebellion on French territory and that, in doing so, Tunisia has committed a definite breach of faith. The Tunisian Government has also

failed to fulfil its obligations under the United Nations Charter, which requires it to live in peace and as a good neighbor with the other members of the United Nations. Its attitude is directly contrary to the spirit of decisions taken by the General Assembly, which, in its resolution concerning the situation in Greece, called upon "Albania, Bulgaria and the other states concerned to cease forthwith rendering any assistance or support to the guerrillas in fighting against Greece, including the use of their territories as a base for the preparation or launching of armed actions." Are we not facing a similar situation?

We have been exposed here over the years to a great deal of hypocrisy and bigotry and cynicism, and we know well that when it comes to my country a double standard is traditionally applied here. This has become the rule. We do not agree with it. We do not acquiesce in it, but we are not naive. When the representative of France engages in such exercises, I confess we find it very painful indeed, not for our sake, but for the sake of France, which we respect and admire, and which we will continue to respect and admire despite its day of shame.

E

The Arab World's Real Attitude toward the PLO

Statement made in the UN General Assembly on 17 August 1982, on the occasion of the PLO's expulsion from Beirut.

Here we go again. This time we have been summoned for the fourth installment of what may now rightly be termed the Seventh Permanent Emergency Special Session of the General Assembly. Needless to say, the Seventh Emergency Special Session has been tainted in its entirety with illegality *ab initio*, from its very inception in July 1980. It was a contrived exercise from the beginning and contrived it remains. How else does one account for the bizarre fact that this alleged emergency and its precise timing were all decided and predetermined many weeks ago? This blatant and unbridled abuse of the emergency machinery of the United Nations can only further discredit that machinery itself and can only make a mockery of the Organization as a whole.

However, beyond the procedural irregularities surrounding this exercise that flaw in advance any resolutions that may emanate from it, there arise also some other very serious and pertinent questions relating to these deliberations.

One may well ask just why it is that the tragedy of Lebanon is being discussed in a Special Emergency Session on Palestine? Is it not indicative of the true motivations of the sponsors of this marathon exercise? The Lebanese tragedy, after all, has been with us for the last eight years. Why, one may legitimately ask, was there no Emergency Special Session on Lebanon during the eight years of the ongoing slaughter of Lebanese of all faiths and creeds by the PLO and the Syrian army of occupation?

The Syrian army remains till this very day on more than half of the Lebanese territory, despite the fact that it can no longer rely on the fig leaf that covered its nakedness all these years, the so-called mandate of the Arab League. Even that pretext is gone now since the expiry of that mandate last month and the unwillingness of the Lebanese Government to seek its renewal. Nor does one recall an emergency special session to discuss the trampling underfoot of the sovereignty and independence of Lebanon by the PLO that established a "state within a state" in almost two-thirds of that country's territory. There has never been an emergency special session to discuss the terror régime of the PLO toward the civilian population in the areas which fell victim to its tyranny—a tyranny that lasted for a decade and more. It is only now, with the indisputable evidence of the facts on the ground, that the full dimensions of the PLO raging unchecked in the midst of a captive civilian population are being revealed. And with it comes also the revelation as to the true attitude of the various Arab countries *vis-à-vis* the terrorist PLO.

Was it not the truest reflection of the Arab leaders' policy toward that terrorist organization when one of them, in one of his rare lapses into lucidity, loudly advocated collective suicide as the best possible course of action for the PLO? Colonel Khaddafy is a trifle naive in assuming that the idea of suicide might find favor with the PLO—an organization whose business after all is the killing of others. To do him justice, Colonel Khaddafy has never sought to disguise the attitude toward Israel of those Arab régimes which still seek my country's destruction. He has said aloud what other Arab rulers, for tactical reasons, have deemed preferable to conceal. Once again Colonel Khaddafy spoke what his fellow Arab leaders really think. In offering the PLO to commit suicide, Colonel Khaddafy remained faithful to the real precepts of collective Arab thinking on the subject of the PLO. Colonel Khaddafy's pronouncements were, superficially at least, in sharp contradistinction to those of the PLO's patrons in this Organization who have sought to camouflage their genuine motives behind a flurry of continued activity and the reckless rhetoric, of hastily-resumed emergency special sessions, sessions which characterize the Arab leaders' predilection for hypocrisy and deceitfulness, even toward their own Arab "brethren."

Therein lies the real reason for the reconvening of this session. The rhetorical barrage here is intended to deafen the sounds of reality and truth so clearly perceived by the entire world with regard to the Arab world's true position toward the PLO.

The other day in the Security Council the observer of the Arab League treated us to a vivid display of fireworks. He was pleading for a cessation of hostilities in Beirut and one could not but be moved by his apparent sincerity on that occasion. Yet there was the nagging thought that, had all that fervor been directed at the PLO, *before* the Israel Defense Forces were forced to dislodge it from its hideaways in south Lebanon and in Beirut, the calls of the observer of the Arab League would not have been burdened by the hollow ring of insincerity. The terrorists had, after all, hijacked the Lebanese capital and taken its civilian population hostage, true to their well-known, dastardly tactic, as recorded in the ignoble annals of the PLO.

The rude awakening of the observer of the Arab League is unfortunately very much in character for Arab leaders. First they set up and organized the terrorists for the purpose of harassing and eventually destroying my country. Then they dumped them on Jordan. When that backfired, they unloaded the PLO onto the back of Lebanon, which was the weakest link in the Arab chain. The Arab leaders saw in Lebanon an appropriate host for the PLO. Since the PLO larva had metamorphosed into a voracious monster, keeping it in Lebanon was the sensible thing to do. Not only was it kept out of the Arab leaders' hair but it also afforded excellent opportunities: Syria used the PLO presence as a pretext for its military intrusion into the Lebanon, an exercise that was willingly bankrolled by the Saudis and other assorted Arab oil millionaires. The Iraqis, the Libyans, the Iranians, indulged their appetite for subversion, counter-subversion, mutual bombings and assassinations, as well as their hyperactive political schemes—all with the help and operational assistance of the various factions of the PLO. Lebanon, the country that was long touted as the only democracy in the Arab world, became a living symbol of what the Arab leaders' intrigues could really do to a democratic country with no muscle to resist them. And the world slowly but surely grew accustomed to it, and highhandedly ignored it. Lebanon was expendable, and not only in the eyes of the Arab leaders. In the higher echelons of world governments it was not considered good form to talk of the goings on in that hapless country. Certainly it was impolite to mention the tired resignation of the European powers to the ongoing rape of Lebanon; the eleven years of the PLO presence, the nibbling away of Lebanese sovereignty, the civil war, the Syrian invasion and the subsequent bombardments, the killings and the rampage—were all relegated to the inner pages of the frostily sanctimonious newspapers in the West; the frightful casualty figures, in the hundreds of thousands, were hardly ever mentioned by the media. After all, as the Jordanian ambassador said in the Security Council a few days ago, it was all an "internal Arab affair."

Yet who would deny that the sordid details of this "family affair" were an open secret—well known in a passive sort of a way abroad. The world knew, in fact, that the Arab leaders, for their own often diametrically opposed reasons, guided and orchestrated the pernicious activity of the PLO in Lebanon—inside and outside the vast enclaves given over to the domination of the multifarious PLO factions and splinter groups.

The Syrian army that entered Lebanon uninvited in 1976 did but little to control the excesses of the PLO. By establishing a seemingly "hands off policy," Syria was conniving and acquiescing in an activity whose eventual outcome would be Syria's *de facto* annexation of the Lebanon. President Hafez al-Assad never made any secret of his doctrine: Lebanon was part of greater Syria.

Did the other Arab leaders protest the cannibalization of Lebanon? Quite the contrary. The PLO presence in Lebanon was ostensibly sanctioned by a whole series of agreements—the Cairo agreement of November 1969, the Melcart agreement of 1973 and so on. The Syrian invasion of Lebanon was equally sanctioned by the Arab states, *post factum*, and the bills for the exercise of this "brotherly love" were paid out of the till of the Organization of Arab Petroleum Exporting Countries (OAPEC).

I referred earlier to the fervor of the Arab League observer, accompanied by most impressive gesticulations, before the Security Council. Where was that voice all these years, where was this righteous indignation, these eloquent hands? Did the Arab League plead with the terrorists to abandon the shameful tactic of hiding behind the skirts of women in Beirut? Did the Arab representatives beseech the terrorists not to place mortars and rocket launchers on top of hospitals; to abandon the ammunition dumps dug under the sports stadiums; not to detonate the high explosives stocked in the basements of houses and in the vaults of the national museum, in short, to leave Beirut and spare its population the ravages of a war they had engendered? Did the Arab leaders think of the population of Beirut, of Sidon, of Tyre, of Nabatiyeh, when they were so eminently supportive of the terrorists, "heroic" in the sense only of callously engulfing the civilian population with them? Did the Arab League—new or old—attempt to persuade the PLO or Syria not to trespass on Lebanese sovereignty? Did the Arab League attempt to prevail upon the PLO leaders to desist from their harassment of Israel—through a series of operations emanating from Lebanese territory? Was any effort made to modify the PLO dogma of murder of innocent women and children in Israel and Jews worldwide? Did the Arab League attempt to check the sterile and relentless war against Israel, the economic boycott, the blackmailing and blacklisting of those who traded with or visited Israel?

The hands that so expressively portrayed Arab confusion in the Security

Council applauded the child-murderers of Ma'alot, of Misgav Am, of Nahariya, of the Tel-Aviv-Haifa coastal road; yes, they applauded the killers of the Israeli athletes at the Olympic Games in Munich, of the Jewish worshippers in Antwerp, in Paris, in Vienna; of the innocent travelers of El Al and God knows how many more. Those hands were counting the money that bought the weapons all these long years. And where was all that hand-wringing when the PLO massacred the Lebanese villagers, raped their women and extorted their money? Where was that plaintive voice when on the night of 19 October 1976 a thousand armed terrorists attacked the little mountain village of Ayshiyeh in the subdistrict of Jezzin, locked sixty-five men, women and children in the village church and massacred them all in cold blood? And when they perpetrated thousands of other similar atrocities? The hands were applauding the Arafats, the Hawatmehs and the Habashes—all those shady characters in the terrorist hall of shame.

Yes, Lebanon was expendable in the eyes of Arab and some non-Arab leaders, because it was weak. Jordan, too, would have been expendable. The Arab leaders laughed up their sleeves at the discomfiture of the Hashemite King in 1970. If King Hussein had not acted, not bombed the refugee camps and laid siege to the PLO strongholds, shelled the areas where the PLO was resisting, then Jordan too would have been victimized, much like Lebanon. But in the final count it is the PLO itself which is being used by the rapacious, self-seeking and feuding leaders of the Arab world. That truth, so self-evident today, can hardly be denied any longer.

The Arab leaders did everything in their power to perpetuate the Lebanese role of the prostrate host to the PLO—for the simple reason that no one in the Arab world wants any part of the PLO, and for good reason. After all, it is they who created this Frankenstein monster and they know its true character. Who would surrender his sovereignty to the grand masters of international terror? Maintaining them in Lebanon was cheaper, safer; it kept them and their shady connections at arm's length. That is why the Arab governments refused for many weeks to accept the PLO stragglers out of Beirut. The terrorists were finally assigned asylum only after it was proved beyond any shadow of doubt that they were beaten and grossly deflated—and then they were separated into relatively harmless groups. Syria long refused to accept them in spite of the interesting fact that the so-called Palestine National Council is headquartered in Damascus. The Syrians wanted the PLO with its fangs pulled. President Assad knows how to handle this type of PLO. The same is true of the others—all the irrelevant, shamed demurrals notwithstanding. But in a fashion characteristic of the Syrian régime, President Assad will now bill himself in the Arab arena as the savior of the PLO, and generous financial honoraria will be very much in order. There was the compelling final argument, of course; that delaying any longer the decision to accept the terrorists would simply add to other internal embarrassments of the Alawite ruler of Syria.

All these years, then, the Arab chieftains rained encouragement and succor on the terrorists acting from Lebanese territory. They knew Israel could not and would not tolerate forever this dangerous course and would have to excise this malignant growth.

The Arab leaders also knew perfectly well that the terrorists had been using the eleven months of cease-fire, after July 1981, to build up an unprecedented and extraordinary arsenal. They could hardly doubt the purpose. However, knowing also of the Soviet involvement in that feverish arms procurement effort and imagining the Soviets to be the guarantors of PLO ambitions backed or tolerated by the Syrian *gauleiters* in Lebanon, Arab leaders were confident that no great harm would result from the eventual serious bloodletting of the Israelis. They were wrong. The Arab leaders were certainly not ignorant of Israel's concern for its citizens, for its diplomats abroad and for the Jewish victims of terror worldwide. They knew perfectly well they were sowing the wind. They should not now be surprised at the whirlwind. Israel kept back, remonstrated, warned, but was eventually compelled to act in exercise of its right of self-defense with vigor and with decisiveness, reaching for the permanent effect of a more solid peace on its northern border. The threat to Israel's security, the operations from Lebanese soil of international terrorism had to be eliminated at their source.

F

Sabra and Shatila

I

Statement made in the UN Security Council on 18 September 1982.

A crime occurred in West Beirut last night. Civilians were murdered, and we join all those who genuinely express their revulsion and indignation at such crimes. We do so because, in contradistinction to most speakers seated around this table, we are not selective in our respect for human life. But what are the facts? The Israel Defense Forces were deployed west of the refugee camps in West Beirut. The eastern side of these camps were left open, to permit free access to those who were supposed to take control of the refugee camps, in accordance with the provisions of the Habib plan—to be more explicit, the Lebanese Armed Forces. Last Thursday and Friday it was clearly indicated to the Lebanese Government that the time had come for the Lebanese Armed Forces to take over control of those camps.

For reasons best known to the Lebanese Government, the Lebanese Armed Forces did not do so. This morning the Israel Defense Forces discovered what had happened in the refugee camps during the night. In order to protect the inhabitants of those camps from further horrors, they have been surrounded on all sides—for the protection of their inhabitants, it being understood—clearly understood—that we expect the Lebanese Armed Forces to take control not only of the refugee camps, but also of West Beirut in its entirety, of Beirut in its entirety, of Lebanon in its entirety. I can inform the Council that an arrangement has been reached with the Lebanese Armed Forces according to which they will take control of the refugee camps in West Beirut tomorrow, Sunday morning, ten o'clock local time. These are the facts.

But how many of you around this table are interested in the facts? Is it not much more pleasurable to engage in an orgy of hatred? My country has been subjected in this body and in other bodies of the United Nations to many diatribes and orgies of hatred, and having been here for some years, I believe I have become immune to this kind of treatment. But let me tell you in all frankness: this Council has stooped here tonight to new depths of moral degeneration and intellectual depravity. I know that once I am finished, such defenders of the United Nations as the diplomatic mercenary, Mr. Maksoud, will jump up in defense of the Organization. I am not endowed with the gift of prophecy like Mr. Maksoud, this latter-day prophet, who prophesied what I was going to say—but judging from past performance and past experience I believe I shall not be deceived.

A blood libel against my country is being spread here, and some speakers have apparently forgotten that the customary time for spreading blood libels against Jews is Passover, not Rosh HaShana. I can forgive Mr. Ovinnikov such an oversight. He comes from an atheist state,· and such hallowed customs apparently are no longer remembered in those circles in the Soviet Union in which he moves. But, Ambassador Ovinnikov, you are absolutely faithful to the long tradition of *pogromshchiki* in your country. For the benefit of those who do not know the expression, I would invite the Russian interpreters to translate it, for it ominously comes from the Russian language. You are a worthy disciple of the Black Hundreds, Ambassador Ovinnikov. This is the kind of language that they employed in reference to my people. The representative of the state that established the gulags, the representative of the country that has done away with the rule of law, sermonizes here about compassion for innocent human beings. Of course you know exactly what happened last night in West Beirut. You know that people were stood against the wall, *galavoi k'stenke*, with their heads against the wall. Ironically, and not surprisingly, as you know, this is the kind of execution practiced in your country. The notion comes from the Lubianka, that notorious prison in Moscow. That is where they execute people *galavoi k'stenke*. Do not try to apply your notions of humanity and inhumanity to other places around the world, Mr. Ovinnikov!

The representative of the Soviet Union seems to believe that he can use foul language against my country with impunity, and that we shall not reply. We shall reply. There is no right of reply in the Supreme Soviet, I believe. But we are here at the United Nations, and there is still free speech here at the United Nations.

But Mr. Ovinnikov is only one example.

I will not run down the entire list, the sorry procession of liars. I shall give only two or three more examples. One of them is the distinguished representative of Jordan who speaks for a country that exactly twleve years ago massacred thousands of Palestinians. Yes, thousands of Palestinians, in what became known as Black September. I know that was a little "family affair," thousands of Palestinians were massacred. Hundreds of them, including PLO operatives, came fleeing across the Jordan River to find refuge in the "Zionist hell." Yet he comes before the Council, and sermonizes here.

Then we have the representative of Syria, the spokesman for the régime that perpetrated the horrible crimes in Hama, who with his characteristic lucidity took Israel to task. We still do not know the exact number of people massacred there. It ranges from six to twenty-five thousand; Ambassador Fattal has not had the courtesy to inform us of the precise figures. Instead, Mr. Maksoud asks for the floor, for an impassioned speech; Mr. Maksoud, who has set himself up as the new moral monitor of our Organization. Curiously enough he has also spoken on behalf of the Government of Lebanon. I must confess that we, at least, have been under the impression that there is an ambassador from that country in our midst. But if Mr. Maksoud seeks new employment as an examiner of morals and international behavior, he has chosen well. As the observer for the Arab League, he will have plenty to do. He will be able to examine what happened in Hama in Syria; what happened to the Kurds in Iraq and in quite a few other countries for whom he claims to speak here. He can also look forward to a career as a historian. He can look into the massacre of the Palestinians in Jordan, of Lebanese and Palestinians murdered by the Syrians and by the PLO in Lebanon over the years, and so on. I am sure he can look forward to many years of gainful employment.

Let us for a change be honest with ourselves. What we are seeing in Lebanon these days is nothing but the tragic residue of international indifference over many years.

One of our colleagues expressed sorrow over the fact that he was robbed of his afternoon nap. The trouble is that too many people have been napping for eight years in regard to Lebanon. How many meetings did this Council have over the past eight years on Lebanon, Lebanon proper? Anybody who would care to look at the records of the Council will find we continuously and repeatedly asked for such a debate. We were ignored. There are countries that, historically, have posed as the protectors of the Christian community in Lebanon, and everybody knows that the Christian community in Lebanon has been pleading with them over the years, seeking their protection and their aid. They were ignored. The Lebanese Government itself sought the protection of various countries, and was ignored. Syria and the terrorist PLO were given a free hand in Lebanon. When a hundred thousand Lebanese were massacred over the years, this Council was not convened in any meeting, emergency or otherwise. Ambassador Ovinnikov was not interested. Now he has his reasons. It is much more convenient to talk about Beirut than about the Panshir Valley in Afghanistan. We are paying for the callous indifference of this Organization and of its individual members to the agony and tragedy of Lebanon over all these years. But is it not somewhat hypocritical now to pose as people with humanitarian concerns?

A tragedy occurred last night in Beirut. We condemn it. We express our revulsion. We are horrified by it. But search yourselves: are not all of you who have been napping all these years also somewhat responsible for it? I know it is much more difficult to admit such guilt than to bewail the fact that an afternoon siesta did not materialize.

II

Statement made in the UN General Assembly on 24 September 1982, under the presidency of Mr. Imre Hollai (Hungary).

The capital of Hungary, the beautiful city of Budapest, holds a very special place in the modern history of my people. For it was the birthplace of one of the greatest Jewish personalities of modern times, Binyamin Zeev Theodore Herzl, the founder of the modern Zionist movement—the national liberation movement of the Jewish people.

In your address to the General Assembly following your election, you quoted from two great fellow countrymen, the writer Mór Jókai and the Nobel Prize winning scientist Albert Szentgyörgyi. Permit me to invoke here today the memory of another great Hungarian who deserves to be remembered from the rostrum of the General Assembly. It is only fitting that we do so in this year of 1982, for it was exactly one hundred years ago, in the year 1882, that Károly Eötvös, a great Hungarian humanist and fighter for the cause of the oppressed and the downtrodden, rose in indignation to combat the terrible blood libel hurled against the Jewish community of Hungary and against the Jewish people at large in the trial of Tiszaeszlár—

one of the countless blood libels to which my people has been subjected throughout history.

Unfortunately, false accusations against my people are not simply a matter of history. The past months—and in particular the last days and the discussion here today—bear testimony to the lengths to which the enemies of the Jewish people are willing to go in their relentless campaign of vilification of my people and of my country.

A terrible crime was perpetrated in Beirut last week. Innocent men, women, and children were murdered by evil men who lost the image of God and respect for fellow man. The spiritual and temporal leaders of my country, including the president of the state, the chief rabbis and the cabinet, as well as the people of Israel, have all expressed their horror and revulsion at this despicable crime, thus joining the sentiments of outrage of civilized mankind all over the world. We did so not only because of the universal sense of horror that had gripped the people of Israel and the Jewish people but also because, in contradistinction to our detractors, we are not selective in our respect for human rights and we condemn their violation irrespective of the identity of the violators and of the victims. The Government of Israel, in its desire to have various aspects of the Beirut tragedy cleared up, today requested the president of the Israel Supreme Court to head a commission to investigate those aspects.

It has been obvious from the very beginning, and confirmed by the course and tenor of this debate, that this entire ugly exercise is intended to constitute an integral part of the ongoing onslaught against my country for which the United Nations has become notorious, and this despite the well-known and unchallenged fact that the massacre in Beirut last week was perpetrated not by Israelis but by others. As has been rightly stated today by Mr. Norman Podhoretz in *The Washington Post:* "in a morally sane climate, responsibility [for the massacre in Beirut] would have been assigned to the thugs who initiated this particular cycle of murderous horrors and their opposite numbers who responded in barbarous kind." But the atmosphere prevailing here is not that of a morally sane climate and facts have long ago ceased to matter for our enemies and their supporters. In fact, truth has become an increasingly precious and rare commodity in this building, certainly in connection with any aspect of the Arab-Israel conflict. To quote again from today's *Washington Post,* this time from its editorial: "There is a double standard by which Israel is judged, and it is turning out to be Israel's pride."

This Organization has not seen fit to institute any inquiries into the genocide of the people of Kampuchea over the years. It has studiously refrained from looking into the torrent of disturbing reports about the large-scale and ruthless massacres perpetrated against the people of Afghanistan by

the Soviet invaders. It has never evinced even the slighest interest in the
horrible crimes perpetrated by successive Iraqi régimes against the Kurds. It
has remained indifferent to the bloodbath carried out last February by the
tyrant brothers Assad of Syria against their own people in the city of Hama.
It has never expressed the slighest indignation at the terrible crimes of Idi
Amin against his own people; instead, Idi Amin's régime became a respected
member of the United Nations Commission on Human Rights. And last but
not least, this Assembly has treated with callous indifference the plight and
agony of the people of Lebanon through eight long years of PLO and Syrian
terror, involving the deaths of 100,000 Lebanese, the wounding of 300,000
more and the displacement of more than one million.

What we are witnessing in Lebanon these days is the tragic residue and
legacy of international indifference of many years. Anybody who would care
to look at the records in recent years of this Assembly, would find that we
repeatedly drew this Assembly's attention to the root causes of the agony of
Lebanon and asked that they be addressed fairly and squarely. We were
ignored by this Organization which, through its conduct, gave the terrorist
PLO and the Syrian army of occupation a free hand in Lebanon and the
opportunity to brutalize the country and its inhabitants. We are all paying
now for the callous indifference of this Organization over all these years to
the agony and tragedy of Lebanon. Any honest soul-searching would therefore have to raise the question as to the responsibility of this Organization,
of its individual members and of the international community at large for the
agony of Lebanon.

Let me therefore state that given this Assembly's dubious record, Israel
and decent people everywhere will treat this disgusting orgy of hatred and
this hypocritical and cynical exercise to shift the blame for the massacre of
Beirut from those who perpetrated it to those who did not, in the only
manner appropriate to them, namely with the contempt which they deserve.

9

Disarmament Issues

A

General

In its Iraqi-sponsored resolution 33/71A of 14 December 1978, the UN General Assembly, "recognizing that the continued escalation of Israeli armament constitutes a threat to international peace and security," requested the Security Council "to call upon all States . . .to refrain from any supply of arms, ammunition, military equipment or vehicles, or spare parts therefor, to Israel," as well as "to ensure that such supplies do not reach Israel through other parties."
The following is an abbreviated version of the statement made on 27 November 1978, in the course of the debate held in the First Committee of the General Assembly.

The First Committee has hitherto refused to be drawn into the contesting claims about armament by any of the parties to the many international disputes that exist among member states. Despite serious differences in their approach to disarmament, no draft resolution has ever been submitted here to censure any power, even though all sides have sympathizers and allies represented in this Committee.

It is not my wish to enumerate the member states who are currently—or who have been for decades—involved in bitter disputes with each other or member states who are actually in a state of armed conflict with one another. If each of these states were to submit draft resolutions demanding a United Nations initiative to disarm the other, the proceedings of this Committee would degenerate into a sad political farce.

The Iraqi draft resolution, by asking the General Assembly to side with one party to the Israel-Arab dispute, undermines, therefore, the very foundations upon which the United Nations rests its claim to speak for all mankind in the matter of disarmament.

The Iraqi draft resolution, without its political cosmetics, is simply Iraq's appeal to member states of the United Nations to ensure the disarmament of Israel. Yes—there is no doubt that Iraq would like to see Israel disarmed—preferably totally disarmed. This Committee should bear in mind that the Iraqi draft resolution, calling for an arms embargo on Israel, has been submitted by a member state which not only considers itself to be in a state of war with Israel, but has also formally declared Israel's destruction to be its official goal. Iraq declared war on Israel immediately on the establishment of the state and invaded Israel, together with other Arab armies, the very next day. It has refused to sign an armistice agreement with Israel, and still regards itself as being at war with Israel. It has, in addition, rejected all United Nations efforts toward a peaceful settlement of the Arab-Israel dispute, based on UN Security Council resolutions 242 and 338.

This draft resolution must, therefore, be judged in the light of Iraq's official policy. In other words, by demanding an arms embargo on Israel, it is intended to pave the way for Iraq to accomplish its declared aim of destroying Israel. It also, in effect, asks all member states to aid and abet Iraq in this gravest contravention of everything the Charter stands for.

If adopted, this draft resolution would fly in the face of Article 51 of the Charter, which recognizes the inherent right of self-defense of members of the United Nations. Similarly, by attempting to deprive Israel of this inherent right, it would violate the principle of the sovereign equality of all members of the Organization that is inscribed in the Charter.

For this Committee to be able to appraise better the utmost gravity of this draft resolution, permit me to resort very briefly to an analogy taken from the lives of private individuals. A person harboring a grudge against his neighbor decides to gang up with some of his friends with a view to murdering him. They manage to acquire a wide assortment of weapons—submachine guns, hand grenades, explosives, daggers, etc. As they proceed with their preparations to carry out their criminal design, they discover, much to their indignation, that their would-be victim keeps at his home a pistol for the defense of himself and his family. Outraged by this display of intolerable arrogance by their intended victim, the entire group of bullyboys and thugs decides to petition the local police chief with a view to getting their intended target disarmed, so that they can carry out their criminal design without any risk and without any obstruction on the part of their victim.

Does such a scenario seem absurd to you? Yes, indeed, it is. Do we recoil from condoning such a course of action in our private lives? Undoubtedly, yes.

Yet this is precisely what the Iraqi draft resolution would have the General Assembly condone on the international plane. Here we have Iraq, the author and sponsor of the draft resolution before us, openly and unashamedly committed to the destruction of Israel. Together with a number of states equally inspired by this lofty and noble aim, they discover, much to their disgust, that their intended target is unwilling to oblige them and is determined to resist their criminal design. Feigning a sense of outrage, they therefore approach the world organization, the Charter of which imposes on its members the duty to refrain from the threat or use of force against another state and commits the Organization to promote the maintenance of international peace and security. Blatantly and unashamedly they request that the world organization recommend the disarming of their intended victim, so as to facilitate the implementation of their illegal and openly avowed goal—the liquidation of a member state of the United Nations.

It is a measure of the decline of the moral standards prevailing in this Organization that member states dare even to contemplate formally submitting a draft resolution of such a preposterous and sinister nature. If such a resolution were in fact adopted, it would clearly have to be regarded as yet another step in the all-too-well-known process in recent years of drawing the United Nations further and further away from the noble aims and principles enunciated in its Charter.

For many centuries the Jewish people suffered the fate of being the defenseless and disarmed victim of the bullyboys and thugs of succeeding generations of international society. It was this state of defenselessness that lay at the root of Jewish martyrdom that in our generation culminated in the bloodbath carried out by the Nazi-Fascist beast and which cost the lives of one-third of my people—six million innocent human beings, including one-and-a-half million children. Let me remind the Iraqi representative, and the Committee, that one of the staunch collaborators with Nazi Germany during that dark period of world history was the régime of Rashid Ali al-Keilani, prime minister of Iraq, under whose rule there also occurred in 1941 the notorious anti-Jewish excesses and pogroms in Baghdad and elsewhere in Iraq.

When the Jewish people, after many generations of statelessness, reestablished the State of Israel in 1948, we vowed that this would mark the end of the state of defenselessness that had been the fundamental cause of the tragedy of my people, and the present-day bullyboys of international society would have to realize that they could no longer engage with impunity in their assaults on Jewish lives and Jewish dignity. Apparently, some of them do not like this change in the status of the Jewish people. Supported by all those who have consistently fomented trouble in the Middle East and are now opposed to the peace-making process there, they would like to reduce the Jewish people again to that state of defenselessness which it shook off with the restoration of Jewish statehood in the Land of Israel. Let the word therefore go forth clear and loud from this place: the days of Jewish defenselessness are forever over and the State of Israel is determined to resist every assault on its existence and its integrity.

In its preamble, the Iraqi draft resolution asked the General Assembly to be "gravely concerned over the continued and rapid Israeli build-up." I propose that we leave the world of propagandistic claims and concentrate on cold figures, presented by neutral sources of international repute. There is, indeed, good cause for the General Assembly's concern about an arms build-up and the acquisition, within a very brief period of time, of the most sophisticated weaponry on a scale unprecedented in the history of mankind. I am referring to the arms build-up on the part of most Arab states.

The overall picture is staggering: According to the Stockholm International Peace Research Institute (SIPRI) and the International Institute of Strategic Studies in London, orders placed by the Arab states since 1977, for arms to be supplied by 1980, amount to $35 billion, so far. To give these figures some tangible scale, suffice it to say that this sum would, at the present price level, provide the United Nations with a regular budget for the next seventy years.

In this connection, it may not be out of place to mention that all those Arab states that have placed orders for the delivery of $35 billion worth of arms contribute less than 1 percent of the United Nations budget.

If one were to pursue this method of comparison, and as this draft resolution refers to the Middle East, one may also be reminded that the annual budget of the United Nations Relief and Welfare Agency (UNRWA) for Arab refugees is $139.8 million. In other words, one percent of the amount now earmarked for arms by some Arab states would suffice to provide UNRWA with its budget for two and one half years, whereas less than one-fifth of this enormous sum would secure total resettlement for all Arab refugees.

In terms of arms, these $35 billion mean hundreds of the most sophisticated combat aircraft, each so expensive that even some states, permanent members of the Security Council, who are the producers and exporters of some of these new types of planes, can only afford to supply their own armies with relatively few of them.

There exist today three systems of gigantic military alliances in the world: NATO, the Warsaw Pact states and the Arab states. In certain types of military hardware, the Arab states are fast reaching a point of parity (though not always of functional equivalence) with either NATO or the Warsaw Pact states. In certain types of weapons, the total Arab strength has already exceeded either NATO or the Warsaw Pact states.

Who is this enormous arsenal of arms directed against? Hardly against NATO or the Warsaw Pact countries. If one is to confine oneself solely to official statements of Arab governments, there can be no shadow of doubt that some Arab states are investing their inflated oil revenues to acquire such an overwhelming superiority of arms against Israel as to be able to overrun her without undue risk.

Israel believes in her ability, if attacked, to resist this Goliath, as she did in days of old and more recently. However, since the Iraqi draft resolution before us wishes the General Assembly to express its concern about the arms build-up of David—not that of Goliath—some figures of comparison between the two will have to be cited.

The military confrontation of the Arab countries with Israel is truly monstrous in its disproportion. Their population numbers over one hundred million—Israel's population is three million,. They occupy a territory of 5,378,000 square miles—in other words, a territory the size of the whole of Europe and Russia, up to the Ural mountains, or to put it differently, a territory roughly 50 percent larger than the territory of the United States or China. By contrast, Israel's territory is approximately the size of the state of Maryland or New Hampshire. Among the Arab states are some of the richest countries in the world, with per capita incomes equal to or higher than that of the United States, outstripping in wealth and financial power some of the most industrialized countries in the world. A large amount of this income is, as I already pointed out, being spent on armament.

It is of interest to recall the exact extent of Arab superiority, of only the so-called confrontation states, over Israel, in the possession of modern armament and manpower by 1980:

Armed Forces	6 to 1
Combat aircraft	3.8 to 1
Tanks	3.6 to 1
Artillery	10 to 1
Surface-to-air missile batteries	20 to 1

What should Israel's reaction be to these ratios of manifest imbalance between Israel and the Arab states?

If the United Nations had been that impartial tribunal of international equity its founders had hoped it would become, there would indeed have been a case for the UN to adopt a draft resolution asking the General Assembly to express its concern over the world's most gigantic acquisition of arms—on the part of Arab states. The General Assembly would have been justified in expressing its alarm over the Arab arms build-up because, quite apart from the Israel-Arab dispute, the presence of so much powder so close to so much oil is indeed a cause for world concern.

Yet the draft resolution before us does not call on the General Assembly to express grave concern over this colossal Arab arms build-up; it does not recognize "that the continued escalation" of Arab armament "constitutes a threat to international peace and security." No, it merely substitutes the word *Israel* for the word *Arab* and thus asks the General Assembly to become party to an outrageous political hoax; a political hoax because the extent of Arab military superiority over Israel, in terms of arms, is not a secret—it is common knowledge, especially to a committee of the General Assembly in which the representatives of member states are no strangers to military statistics.

Much has been made by the representative of Iraq of the size of the Israel military budget. True, it was the biggest per capita, and I repeat, per capita, military budget in the world. It is not any more. We have been overtaken by Saudi Arabia. Even so, it is much bigger than any Israeli would wish it to be. I doubt whether there is another country in the world that is obliged to spend nearly 30 percent of its gross national product on defense. Yes, my countrymen carry a very heavy burden. We would be very happy if we could devote much more of our resources to development, education and social welfare. However, if the tone adopted by some Arab representatives in this Committee is any indication of their countries' intentions toward Israel, it is little wonder that the Israeli taxpayer has to carry so heavy a burden in order to survive.

In the course of the last year, institutions whose business it is to record figures relating to military budgets have taken note of an important development in this sphere in the Middle East.

The London International Institute for Strategic Studies in a publication entitled "Military Balance 1978–1979" shows Israel spending $3.13 billion on defense as compared to $4.2 billion in the previous years. This represents a reduction of the military budget of Israel by 23 percent, even if we disregard the depreciation in the value of U.S. currency.

This Committee has for years been studying ways and means to reduce military budgets, and we all know the differences of opinion existing in this Committee on the modalities of how to effect these reductions. However, even if one were to use the more simplistic yardstick advocated by the Soviet Union, namely, the reduction of all military budgets by 10 percent, Israel can be said to have exceeded this requirement by more than 100 percent. In fact, Israel is, to the best of my knowledge, the only, or one of the very few countries in the world, that can be said to have done so.

This little publicized fact is even more remarkable if one takes into account that this reduction has been decided on in spite of the feverish arms build-up on the part of some Arab countries.

In an obvious ploy to assure African support for its draft resolution, Iraq has accused Israel of collaboration with South Africa in the nuclear field. This has been done before, and this allegation is included in a resolution adopted by the General Assembly. Given the automatic voting majority at the disposal of Arab states, the presence of an accusation against Israel in a resolution of the General Assembly also ensures its almost automatic adoption, although, of course, it is in itself no proof of its veracity.

The circle, thus created, is truly vicious. First, an accusation, however unfounded, is railroaded through the General Assembly; then the authors of the slander need only quote a United Nations resolution to substantiate, as it were, their originally false allegations.

The special rapporteur of the report submitted to the Third Committee is forced to admit, on the matter of alleged cooperation between Israel and South Africa in military matters and in the nuclear field, that "hard evidence that is not officially denied by one or both sides is difficult to come by." It is difficult to come by because it does not exist, except in the minds of those who stand to gain politically if their allegations are accepted.

The Government of Israel has stated on several occasions that it would not be the first to introduce nuclear weapons into the Middle East. That is an official government statement. It is an official undertaking, of which responsible quarters the world over have duly taken note.

Foreign Minister Moshe Dayan addressing the thirty-second General Assembly (1977) called on Israel's Arab neighbors to join it in direct negotiations with a view to establishing a nuclear-weapon-free zone in the Middle East. Mr. Dayan went on to say:

> Israel firmly believes that such negotiations should lead to the conclusion of a formal, contractual, multilateral convention between all the states of the region, on the lines of such notable precedents as the establishment of a nuclear-weapon-free zone in Latin America and the proposals for similar agreements in the areas of South Asia and the South Pacific. Unfortunately, the Arab states have totally rejected this call by Israel, which, after all, is in the interests of all the people of the Middle East. On this occasion I repeat our proposal.

On the general issues of disarmament, my Foreign Minister had the following to say in the course of the general debate in October, 1978:

> Israel is prepared to play its part in the reduction of the arms race and remains ready to enter into agreements on arms limitation with all states in the Middle East. There is no doubt, however, that the appropriate way to bring about an arms reduction in the Middle East is through peace treaties which would include limitations on armaments within their framework. Indeed, the mere transformation from a state of war to one of peace will move the states involved to dedicate their resources to economic development rather than military arms. (9 October 1978)

I should like to add to my Government's official announcements a quotation from the preamble of an agreement reached between Egypt and Israel at Camp David on 17 September 1978, for the framework of peace in the Middle East. It reads as follows:

> Security is enhanced by a relationship of peace and by cooperation between nations which enjoy normal relations. In addition, under the terms of peace treaties, the parties can, on the basis of reciprocity, agree to special security arrangements such as demilitarized zones, limited armaments areas, early warning stations, the presence of international forces, liaison, agreed measures for monitoring, and other arrangements that they agree are useful.

The statements of the Government of Israel and this extract from the Camp David agreement can be summed up as follows: It has been said that before disarmament can relax world tensions—world tensions will have to be relaxed to provide a propitious setting for disarmament.

Israel's contribution to the reduction of tensions and for providing a propitious setting for disarmament in the Middle East has been threefold. First, on a unilateral level, Israel has considerably reduced its military budget. The reduction of military budgets has been urged in this Committee, not only because it would signify a halt in the world's arms race, but also because of its beneficial psychological impact in areas of international tension. The Middle East is, *prima facie*, an area of international tension, and Israel invites Iraq, the prime mover of the draft resolution before us, and all other Arab states, to follow suit and similarly cut their budgets, by over twenty percent. If they do so, it will be a considerably greater contribution to world peace than all the grandiose speeches in support of disarmament that we so often hear from the Arab side in this Committee.

Second, on a multilateral level, Israel has come out with a proposal toward the creation of a nuclear-weapon-free zone in the Middle East. To our regret, this proposal has been rejected out of hand by Arab governments. Israel is still waiting for a favorable response on the part of Arab governments to the offer extended to all Arab states by the Israel Minister of Foreign Affairs on the matter of arms reduction.

Third, on a bilateral level, Israel's negotiations with Egypt, that led to the signing of the Camp David agreement, as well as negotiations that are presently being conducted, are intended to show the way to peace for all the countries of the Middle East. Even in the field of arms control it means that less money will have to be spent by Cairo or Jerusalem on the acquisition of arms and that more money will go for development, education and health in both countries. Is this not what all our debates and resolutions in this Committee are about?

The task of peace will not be simple for either country. However, in the nature of things, there exist dynamics of peace, as there are dynamics of war.

If Israel and Egypt can gradually undertake the very confidence-building measures described in the agreement just quoted; if both countries reach a point where neither fears the other, then they will have succeeded in the field of disarmament where three hundred-odd General Assembly resolutions have failed.

The Iraqi draft resolution was tabled with the express purpose of harming the process of peace. Instead of establishing a framework for peace, as the Camp David agreement did, Iraq, by its own admission, seeks to establish a framework for war, and its draft resolution is part of it.

If Iraq or any Arab states think that they have reason, in the words of the draft resolution, to be "alarmed" or "concerned" about Israel's intentions, why do they not emulate the example of Egypt and see whether or not, through negotiations, these fears may be dispelled?

If there is a grain of truth in Iraq's posture of alarm, why do not Iraq and the other Arab co-sponsors of this draft resolution respond favorably to the offer made by the Foreign Minister of Israel and negotiate with Israel—and other countries of the region—a Middle Eastern "Tlatelolco," as the countries of Latin America have so wisely done?

Israel is acutely aware of the tragic futility of an armament race that is turning the Middle East into a laboratory in which the world can experiment with novel methods of destruction. Israel does not feel that the Middle East is under an obligation to provide the world's armament industry with constant profits, nor to guarantee them a market for weapons for years to come. We would prefer to boost the import into the Middle East of the modern equivalent of "plowshares" and "pruning hooks," and we call on our Arab neighbors to join us in a common regional effort to make Isaiah's vision a living reality.

I am aware that most members of this Committee tacitly agree with what has just been said. If voting on draft resolutions in the United Nations were secret, the Iraqi draft would have few supporters, indeed. I call on member states to reject this act of war-mongering, calculated to undermine the peace-making process and to vote, instead, for peace.

B

Nuclear-Weapon-Free Zone for the Middle East

Abbreviated version of statement made in the UN General Assembly on 11 December 1979, concerning the Israel proposal for the establishment of a nuclear-weapon-free zone in the Middle East.

The resolution before us is a continuation of the same Iraqi initiative of a year ago that was criticized by the Stockholm International Peace Research Institute and adopted with evident reluctance by the General Assembly.

At this point it may be useful to look at the Iraqi resolution of last year, and especially at subjects that were omitted from this year's follow-up draft resolution. They are principally paragraphs that dealt with conventional armaments.

By abandoning the mention of conventional weapons and by accusing Israel of trying either to acquire, or of possessing, nuclear capability, Iraq has shifted into a far safer area of slander, where hearsay, rumor and speculation can be served up as irrefutable evidence. The draft resolution is doing just this. No "increasing information and evidence" whatsoever has been made public to substantiate the Iraqi allegation that Israel is "aiming at the acquisition and development of nuclear weapons." Therefore, the condemnation of Israel is based on an allegation that has not been proved to anyone's satisfaction, except that of Iraq and its allies.

Israel has enumerated before the First Committee the long list of eighty-seven member states that, in one way or another, find themselves in the same position as Israel. This resolution is, therefore, clearly discriminatory in singling out Israel and not addressing the same request to the majority of member states of this Organization.

This hypocrisy reached its height in the list of the co-sponsors of this resolution, in which the majority are not complying with what Israel is asked to do.

Finally, the submission of the Iraqi draft resolution is nothing but a transparent attempt to divert the world's attention from the frantic efforts on the part of three countries—Iraq, Libya and Pakistan—to establish a new nuclear axis. If one were to express oneself in the language of the draft resolution, there is indeed "cause for alarm" at the increasing information and evidence regarding activities aimed at the acquisition and development of nuclear weapons by these three states.

The Israel delegation wishes to reaffirm our awareness of the danger posed to the survival of the whole of mankind by the existence and spread of nuclear weapons. Israel will continue its commitment to their prohibition and to prevention of their spread.

Ever since the problem of nuclear armaments was raised at the United Nations, Israel has consistently supported resolutions aimed at preventing the proliferation of nuclear weapons. Israel voted in 1968 in favor of the United Nations resolution on the text of the Non-Proliferation Treaty. We did this in the belief that practical and satisfactory solutions will be found for the prevention of the proliferation of nuclear weapons.

The signing of the peace treaty between Israel and Egypt has proven that direct negotiations can solve seemingly intractable problems, and that this path offers the best hope for progress.

Such a development could contribute significantly to the implementation of a process leading to the establishment of a nuclear-weapon-free zone in the Middle East, in the manner in which the Tlatelolco Treaty for Latin America was achieved. As far as Israel is concerned, such direct negotiations, with the participation of all the states in the region, could start without preconditions at any time and in any place.

In this connection, it should be noted that in a vote in the First Committee on another nuclear-weapon-free zone, a significant group of states abstained on the grounds that "insufficient consultations have taken place among the countries" of the region concerned. As one of the delegates explained, his country's abstention was in line with the "basic approach that initiatives and decisions on nuclear-weapon-free zones cannot be taken against the will of the states directly concerned but must be freely and voluntarily pursued by all of them."

There are today two parallel processes in the Middle East—peace-making and war-mongering. These processes have clear ramifications in the field of disarmament. On the one hand, there is an ominous threat to peace in the region in the frantic arms build-up by the so-called "rejectionist front" of Arab states. The "Eastern front" alone (Syria, Iraq, Jordan, Saudi Arabia and other Arab Gulf states) is currently equivalent to NATO in manpower and tanks, and already has twice as much artillery. As we have pointed out in the First Committee, the vast amount of petro-dollars accumulated by several Middle Eastern countries became a significant and independent factor, acquiring a momentum of its own in the accelerated international arms race.

On the other hand, over the past year, we have witnessed the historic breakthrough of the Israel-Egyptian Peace Treaty. As the SIPRI Yearbook of 1979 points out, the link between the Israel-Egypt Peace Treaty and the reduction in the military budgets of these countries is self-evident. Israel, for its part, has reduced its military budget in 1978 by 23 percent. We regret, therefore, that this highly significant measure of confidence-building in the Middle East was not reciprocated by other Arab states. We also regret that the First Committee, devoted as it is to the cause of disarmament, did not take the opportunity to commend the example, set by Israel and Egypt, to other states in the region.

The resolution before us is intended to exploit, for partisan and political ends, the genuine concern felt by some member states for the non-proliferation of atomic weapons. It is, however, nothing but a pretext for the conduct of anti-Israel warfare by some Arab states in the General Assembly of the United Nations.

10

Destruction of the Iraqi Nuclear Reactor

Abbreviated and consolidated version of statements made in the UN Security Council on 12 and 19 June 1981, and in the UN General Assembly on 11 November 1981.

On Sunday, 7 June 1981, the Israel Air Force carried out an operation against the Iraqi atomic reactor called "Osiraq." That reactor was in its final stages of construction near Baghdad. The pilots' mission was to destroy it. They executed their mission successfully.

In destroying Osiraq, Israel performed an elementary act of self-preservation, both moral and legal. In so doing, Israel was exercising its inherent right of self-defense as understood in general international law and as preserved in the United Nations Charter.

A threat of nuclear obliteration was being developed against Israel by Iraq, one of Israel's most implacable enemies. Israel tried to have the threat halted by diplomatic means. Our efforts bore no fruit. Ultimately we were left with no choice. We were obliged to remove that mortal danger. We did it cleanly and effectively. The Middle East has become a safer place. We trust that the international community has also been given pause to make the world a safer place.

These facts and the potentials for a safer world are widely recognized. Several states in the Middle East and beyond are sleeping more easily today in the knowledge that Iraq's nuclear arms potential has been smashed.

But this will not preclude a hypocritical parade here in the Security Council. Nothing will prevent numerous members of the United Nations from the usual ganging-up on Israel. Nothing will stop them from hurling abuse at us, even though they know in their heart of hearts that it is Israel that has relieved them of an awesome menace. Their cant will do this

174

Organization no credit. The sham and charade will not add to the stature of this Council. Pontification will not further the cause of peace.

Israel has long believed in a different, more constructive approach. We advocate the establishment of a nuclear-weapon-free zone in the Middle East, grounded in a multilateral treaty, reached through direct negotiations by all the states concerned. This is the moment for the Security Council to lend its support to Israel's proposal. I shall return to it at greater length toward the end of my statement.

Ever since the establishment of the State of Israel over thirty-three years ago, Iraq has been conspiring to destroy it. Iraq joined several other Arab states that attacked Israel the day after it became independent in 1948. But while other Arab states—Egypt, Jordan, Lebanon and Syria—signed armistice agreements with Israel in 1949, Iraq adamantly refused to do so. Instead, it fomented and supported the unrelenting Arab belligerency and terrorism against Israel. It also took part in the Arab wars against Israel in 1967 and 1973. And it has doggedly rejected any international measure or instrument which might imply even the most indirect recognition of Israel and its right to exist.

On 22 October 1973, when the Security Council called for a cease-fire in the Yom Kippur War, the Baghdad Government announced that Iraq does not consider itself

> a party to any resolution, procedure or measure in armistice or cease-fire agreements or negotiations on peace with Israel, now or in the near future. *(The New York Times,* 23 October 1976)

More recently, the Iraqi ambassador in New Delhi had the following to say at a press conference reported by the Middle East News Agency on 24 October 1978:

> Iraq does not accept the existence of a Zionist State in Palestine. . . . The only solution is war.

And only last year, during the Seventh Emergency Special Session of the General Assembly, the representative of Iraq found it necessary to re-state his government's opposition to the very existence of Israel.

In sum, Iraq declares itself to have been in a state of war with Israel since 1948. Hence, it has rejected all United Nations efforts to seek a peaceful settlement of the Arab-Israel dispute. It has publicly rejected Security Council resolutions 242 (1967) and 338 (1973).

Iraq has missed no opportunity to make it clear that it would not abide by international law in respect to Israel and that it reserves its freedom of action with regard to Israel. This perverse doctrine found expression in the "National Charter" of Iraq, proclaimed by its president, Saddam Hussein, in

February 1980 and circulated at the request of the Permanent Representative of Iraq.

The principles allegedly underlying that Charter were said to include, *inter alia,* the non-use of force and the peaceful settlement of disputes. Yet those principles were specifically excluded with regard to my country on the grounds that it is a "deformed entity [which is] . . . not considered a State." This same Charter committed Iraq in no uncertain terms to all-out warfare against Israel, and enjoined other Arab states to participate in that war, using "all means and techniques."

In a letter to the Secretary-General of 11 March 1980, I drew attention to the fact that this undisguised denial by one member state of the right of another member state to exist is in flagrant violation of the purposes and principles of the United Nations Charter. I observed that it was a matter for surprise that a document so violently opposed to everything that the United Nations stands for should be circulated at all as a document of this Council, whose primary responsibility is the maintenance of international peace and security. The United Nations, and this Council in particular, were unmoved. Such a flagrant violation of the United Nations Charter is apparently perfectly in order. As far as we have been able to ascertain, the Security Council, or for that matter the United Nations as a whole, has never called Iraq to account for this, over the last thirty or so years. It is apparently perfectly in order to use the threat of force against Israel, to train and send in terrorists to commit mindless acts of murder, and to join in Arab wars of aggression against Israel in 1948, in 1967 and in 1973, and then to retreat to safety, using other Arab countries as a buffer between its heroic army and Israel.

Not by accident has Iraq taken a lead among those Arab states that reject out of hand any solution of the Arab-Israel dispute by peaceful means. To translate its words into deeds, Iraq has used its petro-dollars to develop a sophisticated technological and military infrastructure. It sees itself as the leader and linchpin of the so-called Eastern Front, which the Arab rejectionist states established in Baghdad in 1978 against Israel. Despite its deep involvement in a war of aggression against Iran, Iraq has continued to indicate its willingness to send men and matériel to take part in any military hostilities which the rejectionist Arab states may initiate against Israel.

Over and beyond the development of its conventional forces, Iraq has in recent years entered the nuclear armaments field methodically and purposefully, while at the same time piously appending its signature to international instruments specifically prohibiting it from doing so.

As far back as 8 September 1975, Saddam Hussein was quoted by the Lebanese weekly *al-Usbu al-Arabi* as saying that the acquisition of nuclear technology by his country was the first Arab attempt toward nuclear armament. By way of comment on reports that Iraq would be the first Arab country to acquire an atomic bomb, the Iraqi oil minister at the time was reported, on 30 November 1976, in the Kuwaiti paper *al-Qabas,* to have declared a week earlier that all Arab states should participate in a project to produce an atomic bomb. And according to the *International Herald Tribune* of 27 June 1980, Na'im Haddad, a senior member of Iraq's Revolutionary Command Council, stated at a meeting of the Arab League in 1977 that "the Arabs must get an atom bomb."

In brief, this Council is now confronted with an absurd situation. Iraq claims to be at war with Israel. Indeed, it prepares for atomic war. And yet it complains to the Security Council when Israel, in self-defense, acts to avert nuclear disaster.

I would like to remind the representative of Iraq that a state cannot invoke in its favor benefits deriving from certain provisions of international law without being prepared at the same time also to abide by the duties flowing from international law. Arab states, including Iraq, seek to impose on Israel duties stemming from the international law of peace while simultaneously claiming for themselves the privileges of the international law of war.

In recent years Iraq has been the most active Arab state in the nuclear field. Its activities indicate beyond any shadow of doubt that its goal has been the acquisition of a military nuclear option.

In 1974 Iraq attempted to acquire from France a five hundred-megawatt nuclear power reactor of the graphite-gas type, which had been developed in the 1950s primarily for the production of large quantities of plutonium for military use. Although that request was turned down, it was nevertheless agreed to supply Iraq with a seventy-megawatt nuclear reactor of the Osiris type, which is considered one of the most advanced reactors of its kind in the world, and one of the most suitable for the production of weapons-grade plutonium in significant quantities.

Iraq demanded that its supplier provide it with eighty kilograms of weapons-grade nuclear fuel, i.e. uranium enriched to a level of 93 percent. When it comes to research, this type of fuel is generally confined to use in nuclear facilities with an extremely low capacity—from one to ten megawatts.

France undertook to provide it with this weapons-grade uranium. In 1979, France tried to persuade Iraq to accept a far lower grade of uranium, but the Iraqis insisted on the previous deal. To fulfill it, France had to draw from stockpiles in its own military nuclear arsenal.

During 1980, France dispatched to Iraq the first shipment of the enriched weapons-grade uranium concerned, containing twelve kilograms. This shipment enabled Iraq to put into operation a smaller nuclear reactor provided by the same supplier. Israel learned from unimpeachable sources that following the delivery, expected soon, of two additional shipments of weapons-grade uranium weighing about twenty-four kilograms, Osiraq would be completed, and would become operational within the next few weeks and not later than the beginning of September 1981.

This of course is by no means the end of the story. Iraq has also purchased complementary fuel-cycle technology, namely, four research laboratories for the study of the chemical processes of fuel preparation and its recycling, as well as the reprocessing of irradiated fuel. From the nuclear weapons point of view, the most significant is a radio-chemistry laboratory, known as the "hot cell," used for the separation of irradiated fuel and the extraction of plutonium. This project is scheduled for completion in 1981.

Together with the construction of these facilities, Iraq has been energetically investigating the possibility of acquiring nuclear power reactors which operate on natural uranium and heavy water, and produce large quantities of plutonium.

In order to build up the reserve of uranium needed to attain self-sufficiency, Iraq has operated in four parallel directions:

a. It has bought weapons-grade enriched uranium on the international black market;
b. It has acquired uranium through bilateral deals;
c. It has obtained enrichment facilities; and
d. It has begun an intensive search for uranium on its own territory.

Iraq already possesses aircraft capable of delivering nuclear warheads. In addition, it is involved in the development of a new surface-to-surface missile with an effective range of up to three thousand kilometers, also capable of delivering a nuclear warhead. The distance between Baghdad and Jerusalem is eight hundred kilometers.

Despite its protestations to the contrary, Iraq for well-known reasons has not embarked on its large-scale nuclear program for reasons of pure research. And Iraq has certainly not embarked upon its nuclear program because it faces an energy crisis. It is blessed with abundant supplies of natural oil. When not engaged in foreign adventures against one of its neighbors, it is normally one of the largest oil suppliers in OPEC.

No amount of bluster can hide a simple, basic fact: Iraq's nuclear program has had just one aim—to acquire nuclear weapons and delivery systems for them.

Academic and public figures who follow these matters have had no illusions about Iraq's nuclear objectives in the military field. For example, on 5 August 1980, the Paris newspaper *France-Soir* published an article on Iraq's nuclear program containing a warning by the eminent French scientist, François Perrin, who had served as head of the French Nuclear Energy Commission from 1951 to 1971. Referring to Osiraq, Perrin explained that it is fueled by highly enriched uranium which can be used to produce an atomic weapon.

Similarly, on 27 March 1981, Senator Alan Cranston told the United States Senate:

This massive Iraqi nuclear development program is under way despite the fact that Iraq has no parallel program for developing commercial nuclear power.

Senator Cranston went on to say that he had been informed authoritatively that Iraq was pursuing a nuclear weapons capability option.

He explained that Iraq had vigorously embarked on an approach of the Manhattan Project type, that could provide it with nuclear explosives of the Hiroshima size. Senator Cranston's concerns were heightened by the fact that Iraq is governed by what he termed "a radical, militarily aggressive regime which routinely employs terrorism to advance its aims."

The combination of an Osiris reactor and about eighty kilograms of weapons-grade nuclear fuel, together with laboratories for the production of plutonium, would have enabled Iraq to acquire a nuclear weapons capability by the mid-1980s. To produce nuclear weapons, Iraq could have opted for one of two paths:

a. The production of three to four nuclear explosive devices, on the enriched uranium path, by using the fuel supplied for operating Osiraq; or

b. The use of plutonium produced by Osiraq and the reprocessing laboratory for the production of one plutonium bomb a year.

Further cause for anxiety was given by the delivery of weapons-grade nuclear material without proper provision for the return of the fuel rods after use.

Any lingering doubts about Iraq's intentions to acquire nuclear weapons to be used against Israel were removed just two days ago by the Iraqi minister of information. According to *The New York Times* of 11 June 1981, Latif Jassem wrote in the state-run newspaper *al-Jumhuriya* on 10 June 1981, that the Israeli attack on Osiraq last Sunday showed that Israel knew that its "real and decisive danger" came from Iraq.

In plain terms, Iraq was creating a mortal danger to the people and the State of Israel. It had embarked on ramified programs to acquire nuclear weapons. It had acquired the necessary facilities and fuel. Osiraq was about to go critical in a matter of weeks.

Iraq's nuclear activities have troubled many governments and experts around the world. They have asked themselves the following questions:

1) Why did Iraq first try in 1974 to acquire a 500-megawatt nuclear reactor, of a kind designed primarily to produce large quantities of plutonium for military use? Moreover, why is it now trying to buy an upscaled, Cirene-type plutogenic reactor, whose military use is clear, but whose commercial use is not proven?

2) Why did Iraq insist on receiving a 70-megawatt reactor that has no usable application as an energy source, that does not correspond to any peaceful energy plan and that is far too large for Iraq's most ambitious scientific needs?

3) Why did Iraq insist on receiving weapons-grade nuclear fuel, rather than the less proliferant alternative of "Caramel" fuel which it was offered?

4) What is Iraq's demonstrable need for nuclear energy, given its abundant oil reserves?

5) If Iraq has a need of this kind either for the short or long term, why has it not developed a commercial nuclear energy program? Why has it not made any transactions which would be relevant to such a program?

6) Why, if it is genuinely interested in nuclear research, did it rush to buy plutonium separation technology and equipment that cannot be justified on scientific or economic grounds?

7) Why has Iraq been making frantic efforts to acquire natural uranium wherever and however it can on at least four continents, some of which uranium is not under the safeguards of the International Atomic Energy Agency (IAEA)? Why has Iraq taken the highly unusual step of stockpiling uranium before it has built power reactors?

All these questions are fairly intelligible to the layman and must make everyone think. They are certainly intelligible to the expert, who will confirm that they point in one direction only—namely, a weapons-oriented nuclear program.

For the sake of illustration, let me elaborate on one of these questions— Iraq's insistence on receiving weapons-grade nuclear fuel and its adamant refusal to accept a less proliferant variety when offered. The International Fuel Cycle Evaluation (INFCE)—an international body, convened under the auspices of the IAEA, to deal, *inter alia*, with the non-proliferation aspects of the nuclear fuel cycle—was greatly concerned with the already wide production of fissile material in nuclear reactors of the one to five megawatt size, not to speak of a 70-megawatt facility like Osiraq. Consequently, the INFCE set up study groups under the auspices of the IAEA to make recommendations on the subject. The January 1980 report of Working Group Eight, entitled *Advanced Fuel Cycle and Reactor Concepts* is most illuminating.

In the section headed "Measures to Increase Proliferation Resistance," the report recommended that proliferation resistance can be increased by

> enrichment reduction preferably to 20 percent or less which is internationally required to be a fully adequate isotopic barrier to weapons usability of U^{235}.

In another section of the same report, dealing with French reactors of the Osiris type—which would include Osiraq—the authors state:

> The Osiris core was converted from the highly enriched uranium to the low enriched UO_2 Caramel fuel, with startup of the reactor in June

1979. The general success of the work developed on Caramel fuel . . . permits Osiris to be completely loaded with Caramel assemblies.

In layman's terms, had Iraq so wished, it could have successfully operated Osiraq on Caramel-type fuel, thereby at least eliminating the option of diverting weapons-grade nuclear fuel. But it refused to do so, and insisted on receiving weapons-grade enriched uranium.

Three eminent French nuclear scientists have made a serious examination of these and other disturbing questions related to Iraq's nuclear development program:

Georges Amsel, Director of Research at the *Centre National de la Recherche Scientifique*, Unit for Solid Physics at the *Ecole Normale Supérieure;*

Jean-Pierre Pharabaud, Engineer at the *Centre National de la Recherche Scientifique*, Laboratory of High Energy Physics at *Ecole Polytechnique;*

Raymond Sene, Chief of Research at the *Centre National de la Recherche Scientifique*, Laboratory of Particle Physics at the *Collège de France.*

The analysis and conclusions of these three prominent scientists are to be found in a comprehensive memorandum entitled "Osirak et la Prolifération des Armes Atomiques," which they presented to the French Government and public in May of this year.

It is of great interest and relevance to compare their scientific findings and conclusions with the version presented to this Council. It was alleged here that the two "hypotheses"—namely the diversion of enriched uranium and the production of plutonium, for the manufacture of a nuclear weapon—are both groundless.

Let us look at what the French scientists say about each of these hypotheses or, to be more accurate, about these possibilities. Chapter II of their memorandum is entitled "Possibilités de la Prolifération." Paragraph 5 thereof is headed "Les Possibilités d'Obtention d'Explosifs Nucléaires Liées à Osirak."

Concerning the uranium path, they indicate that two options exist:

a. The use of fresh enriched uranium; and

b. The use of slightly irradiated enriched uranium.

Even assuming that the diversion of the enriched uranium were to be detected and that the supplier would immediately halt further deliveries of enriched uranium, the authors of the memorandum conclude that Iraq *already* possesses sufficient weapons-grade material to produce two nuclear bombs.

As regards the production of plutonium, the French scientists observe in their memorandum that by introducing a blanket of natural uranium around the reactor core of Osiraq, plutonium can be produced. After the chemical separation of the plutonium, the yield per annum would be sufficient for one nuclear bomb. This separation can be carried out in the facility based on the "hot cell" installation supplied to Iraq by Italy. This method does not involve any diversion of the enriched uranium fuel. In addition, plutonium production can be accomplished even if the supplier imposes the use of the less enriched "Caramel" type of fuel in the nuclear reactor.

Given the nuclear facilities and materials and the complementary technology Iraq had at its disposal, to try to dismiss in this Council either of these paths leading to the manufacture of a nuclear weapon as "groundless hypotheses," or even to make light of them, is irresponsible. Such an attitude flies in the face of incontrovertible scientific data, readily available to informed observers.

Indeed, it also flies in the face of statements by French officials. As reported in *The New York Times* of 18 June 1981, Dr. Michel Pecqueur, head of the French Nuclear Energy Commission, while trying to defend the agreements between his country and Iraq, conceded that

> in theory the reactor could be used to produce a "significant amount" of plutonium, which means enough for a bomb, by irradiating a large amount of natural or depleted uranium. The plutonium could be extracted in a "hot cell" laboratory supplied by Italy, although the reprocessing is technically difficult.

Then there are the admissions made by the chief nuclear attaché at the French Embassy in Washington who, according to *The New York Times* of 17 June 1981, agreed that Osiraq had what he termed "high neutron flux" which "meant that it could have produced a considerable amount of plutonium." The French official concerned took issue with the estimate of the annual production of ten kilograms of plutonium, and suggested that "five kilograms was a better figure." In other words, the only point at issue is whether Osiraq could have produced enough plutonium for one bomb in a period of 12 months, or in something between 12 and 24 months. And does anyone here seriously believe that there is an essential difference if it were to take Iraq one year or a few months longer to produce a nuclear bomb?

In another article in *The New York Times* of 18 June 1981, two professors of nuclear science and engineering at Columbia University explain how Osiraq provides the neutron bombardment for converting natural uranium into plutonium. In the same article, the chief nuclear attaché at the French Embassy in Washington is quoted as saying that

> the basic design of the French export model, known as Osiris, shows a cavity in the reactor that can hold material for neutron bombardment.

In the course of this debate, great play has been made of the fact that Iraq is a signatory to the Nuclear Non-Proliferation Treaty (NPT), and that its nuclear reactors have been inspected periodically by the IAEA.

Let me again draw the attention of members of the Council to the French scientists' memorandum. Chapter III is entitled "Les Sauvegardes." It is an extensive analysis of the NPT safeguard system and takes up about one-third of the whole paper. Among the more significant points are:

1) The country being inspected has to approve in advance the name of the individual inspector whom the IAEA wishes to designate. The country being inspected can reject the inspector whom the agency has nominated.

Parenthetically, let me mention in this regard that, according to information submitted yesterday, since 1976 only Soviet and Hungarian inspectors have inspected Osiraq.

2) The frequency of routine inspections is a function of the size of the reactor. For Osiraq, this means no more than three or four inspections a year.

3) For routine inspections advance notice is given.

4) In principle, the possibility exists of unscheduled inspections, that is to say, surprise visits. But in practice, advance notice of three or four days is given, even for such unscheduled inspections.

5) The inspectors must have access to everything relating to fissible material. However, they are not policemen; they can only inspect what has been declared. Thus, any "hot cells" and chemical separation facilities constructed in secret elsewhere will escape all inspection.

6) The inspectors within the facility are always accompanied by representatives of the state concerned.

7) The effectiveness of the safeguard measures depends on the cooperation of the country concerned. In this connection the authors of the memorandum observe that for the IAEA and for France, Iraq's good faith has been taken for granted and its assurances at face value, without any guarantees.

8) Experience shows that inspections can be blocked for a certain period without causing any reaction. On this point the authors of the memorandum recall:

> This is what happened on 7 November 1980 at the beginning of the Iran-Iraq war, when Iraq informed the IAEA that the inspectors from the Agency could not at that time come to Baghdad to inspect the two

reactors. A well-informed French source at that time stated: "We are in a completely new situation which was not foreseen in any international treaty."

In brief, there are several serious loopholes in the NPT safeguards system that can easily be exploited by a country, such as Iraq, if it is determined to obtain a nuclear weapon.

The flaws in the safeguards system are now coming out into the open. No less an authority than the former director of safeguards operations at the IAEA in Vienna, Mr. Slobodan Nakicenovic, attested to the inadequacies of the NPT safeguards on Austrian radio on 17 June 1981.

These serious weaknesses were incisively analyzed in a leading article in *The Washington Post* of 16 June 1981, entitled "Nuclear Safeguards or Sham," in which the NPT safeguards system was shown to be hollow. Having asked why the IAEA had done nothing about several suspicious features of the Iraqi nuclear program, the article observed that the NPT

> is written in such a way that a violation does not technically occur until nuclear material—uranium or plutonium—is diverted form its approved use. But this may occur within a few days of its insertion into a nuclear bomb. Since IAEA inspectors come around only a few times a year, the international safeguards system amounts to only an elaborate accounting procedure that relies on the good intentions of the parties being safeguarded.

Iraq's preference for Osiraq and the complementary fuel-cycle facilities pointed toward a premeditated attempt to exploit the limitations on IAEA safeguards regarding this type of reactor for the purpose of embarking on a nuclear weapons program without risking detection. This was so because such safeguards do not apply to research within the reactor.

Moreover, no television or photographic surveillance measures for monitoring between inspection visits were foreseen under the existing safeguards approach for such research reactors. As a result, no means would be available to provide indication of diversion between inspections.

As already mentioned, during 1980 Iraq received a shipment of weapons-grade uranium. Thereafter, Iraq promptly denied IAEA inspection. Such unilateral actions could have been repeated by Iraq on future occasions, when additional shipments of weapons-grade enriched uranium would have been received by Iraq.

As I have already pointed out, parallel to ordering weapons-grade uranium, Iraq purchased large quantities of uranium concentrates to ensure an adequate supply of raw material for its program. These purchases, too, were not subject to safeguards.

As far as the complementary fuel-cycle facilities were concerned, they also had a great advantage for Iraq. They too would remain outside the scope of safeguards as long as Iraq maintained that it was not producing plutonium or nuclear fuel.

In other words, Iraq could proceed with its nuclear weapons program and, once ready, it could exercise its right of withdrawal from the NPT on three months' notice, as provided for in Article X of NPT, without fear of sanctions. Even if an unlikely attempt were made to impose sanctions on Iraq, the process would be ineffectual. To quote "A Short History of Non-Proliferation," a document published by the IAEA: "History has shown that the extent to which international bodies can pose fully effective sanctions on national governments is limited."

In these circumstances, it is surely not unreasonable to raise serious doubts about the efficacy of the NPT safeguards system. There is certainly room for grave reservations when the country supposedly bound by these safeguards makes no secret of its ambitions to obliterate another country.

In this connection, let me refer to a report in *The New York Times* of 19 June 1981, based on information from officials and diplomats at the IAEA in Vienna. One of them has lifted the veil from Iraq's nuclear program. He is quoted as saying:

> If you ask whether Iraq had it in mind to make nuclear weapons one day, then I would say that a lot of people at the Agency thought it probably did. A lot of things Iraq was doing made sense only on that assumption.

Could it be that this was the reason why Israel was muzzled last week in Vienna and denied the possibility of presenting its case to the board of governors of the IAEA before they proceeded to condemn my country?

Over the last few years, Israel has followed Iraq's nuclear development program with growing concern. We have repeatedly expressed our demand both publicly and through diplomatic channels that nuclear assistance to Iraq be terminated. On various occasions, Israeli representatives drew the attention of the United Nations General Assembly and of its First Committee to the frantic efforts being made by Iraq and its supporters to establish a nuclear axis aimed against Israel. The Government of Israel has repeatedly urged the European countries involved to stop assisting Iraq's systematic drive to attain a military nuclear capability, stressing the grave implications of such aid to Iraq for all concerned. We also urged other friendly governments to use their influence in that direction. All these public and diplomatic efforts by Israel went unheeded while, at the same time, the pace of Iraq's nuclear development increased.

I should add that Israel was not alone in its apprehensions. Several neighbors of Iraq and other states in the Middle East also expressed their deep concern to Iraq's suppliers over Iraq's nuclear ambitions—but to no avail.

Precious time was lost, and Israel was left facing the stark prospect that, within a very short period of time, Osiraq would become critical, or in the jargon of nuclear scientists, was about to go "hot."

Israel was left with an agonizing dilemma. Once Osiraq had become hot, any attack on it would have blanketed the city of Baghdad with massive radioactive fallout. The effect of that would have been lethal. Tens of thousands, and possibly hundreds of thousands, would have been grievously harmed.

On the other hand, Israel could not possibly stand idly by, while an irresponsible, bellicose régime, such as that of Iraq, acquired nuclear weapons, thus creating a constant nightmare for Israel. Saddam Hussein's régime has amply demonstrated its total disregard for innocent human life both at home and in its war with Iran. Given the nature and record of that ruthless régime, the vast dangers for Israel inherent in the creation of an Iraqi military nuclear potential are self-evident.

The Government of Israel, like any other government, has the elementary duty to protect the lives of its citizens. In destroying Osiraq last Sunday, Israel was exercising its inherent and natural right of self-defense, as understood in general international law and well within the meaning of Article 51 of the United Nations Charter.

The concept of a state's right of self-defense has not changed throughout recorded history. Its scope has, however, broadened with the advance of man's ability to wreak havoc on his enemies. Consequently, the concept took on new and far wider application with the advent of the nuclear era. Anyone who thinks otherwise has simply not faced up to the horrific realities of the world we live in today. This is particularly true for small states, whose vulnerability is vast and whose capacity to survive a nuclear strike is very limited.

Commenting on the meaning of Article 51 of the Charter, Professors Morton Kaplan and Nicholas de B. Katzenbach wrote in *The Political Foundations of International Law*:

> Must a state wait until it is too late before it may defend itself? Must it permit another state the advantages of military build-up, surprise attack, and total offense, against which there may be no defense? It would be unreasonable to expect any state to permit this—particularly when given the possibility that a surprise nuclear blow might bring about total destruction, or at least total subjugation, unless the attack were forestalled.

Professor Derek Bowett of Cambridge University, in his authoritative *Self-Defence in International Law*, observed:

No state can be expected to await an initial attack which, in the present state of armaments, may well destroy the state's capacity for further resistance and so jeopardize its very existence.

Professor Myres McDougal of Yale Law School, writing in the *American Journal of International Law* in 1963, stated:

Under the hard conditions of the contemporary technology of destruction, which makes possible the complete obliteration of states with still incredible speed from still incredible distances, the principle of effectiveness requiring that agreements be interpreted in accordance with the major purposes and demands projected by the parties, could scarcely be served by requiring states confronted with necessity for defense to assume the posture of 'sitting ducks'. Any such interpretation could only make a mockery both in its acceptability to states and in its potential application of the Charter's major purpose of minimizing unauthorized coercion and violence across state lines.

So much for the legalities of the case. But still we have been accused of acting unlawfully. Presumably it is lawful for a sovereign state to create an instrument capable of destroying several hundred thousand Israelis, but it is illegal to halt that fatal process before it reaches completion.

The decision taken by my Government in the exercise of its right of self-defense, after the usual international procedures and avenues had proved futile, was one of the most agonizing we have ever had to take. We sought to act in a manner which would minimize the danger to all concerned, including a large segment of Iraq's population. We waited until the eleventh hour after the diplomatic clock had run out, hoping against hope that Iraq's nuclear arms project would be brought to a halt. Our air force was only called in when, as I have said, we learned, on the basis of completely reliable information, that there was less than a month to go before Osiraq might have become critical. Our air force's operation was consciously launched on a Sunday, and timed for late in the day, on the assumption that workers on the site, including foreign experts employed at the reactor, would have left. That assumption proved correct, and the loss in human life, which we sincerely regret, was minimal.

We have been told in the course of this debate that one cannot isolate the subject before the Council from the root cause of the Arab-Israel conflict. Israel agrees—and this debate, if nothing else, has been an object lesson of what the root cause of the Arab-Israel conflict really is, i.e., the absolute refusal of most Arab states to recognize Israel and its right to exist.

Take, for example, the new Syrian ambassador, whose maiden speech we had the pleasure of hearing on Tuesday, 16 June 1981. It goes without saying that Syria deeply laments the smashing of Saddam Hussein's nuclear capability. With his bosom friend and ally the representative of Iraq sitting at his side, the representative of Syria made his country's attitude toward Israel patently clear by describing my country as a "cancer in the region," suffering from "congenital deformities." He is obviously a soul-mate of the representative of another Arab state with which his country has fraternal relations, namely the distinguished representative of the Palestinian Arab state of Jordan, who has in the past delicately alluded to bubonic plague and venereal disease in referring to my country. These epithets are more than mere pejoratives. They demonstrate the inability of most Arab states to reconcile themselves to Israel's existence and to its right to exist like any other sovereign state.

This, and only this, is the root cause of the Arab-Israel conflict. There will be no solution to the conflict until the rejectionist Arab states come to terms with Israel, and negotiate peace with us.

But this does not mean that the Middle East is doomed to live under the threat of nuclear war until a comprehensive peace is achieved. Israel has always supported the principle of non-proliferation. In 1968, Israel voted in favor of General Assembly resolution 2373 on the NPT.

Since then, Israel has carefully studied various aspects of the NPT as they relate to conditions prevailing in the Middle East—conditions which, regrettably, preclude its implementation in the region.

The NPT envisages conditions of peace. However, as I have just pointed out, most Arab states not only deny Israel's right to exist, but are also bent on destroying my country and hence reject any peace negotiations with us.

Almost half the states in the new Arab League, with its headquarters in Tunis, are not bound by the NPT régime. And some Arab states, which are parties to the NPT, have entered reservations specifically dissociating themselves from any obligation toward Israel in the context of the treaty.

Moreover, other Arab states, also parties to the NPT, are not only suspected of searching for a nuclear weapons option but are known to have been involved in unsafeguarded transfer of nuclear material. Libya, for instance, was reported in 1979 to be involved in an unsafeguarded international uranium deal between Niger and Pakistan, two states not party to the NPT. Libya has also purchased several hundred tons of uranium from Niger, apparently without involving the IAEA.

Beyond the Middle East, Pakistan is considered to have all its known nuclear facilities under safeguards. But as is also well known, it has embarked in parallel on the reprocessing and uranium enrichment courses through the acquisition of unsafeguarded equipment by exploiting loopholes in the export guidelines of the London Club member states.

In the light of the above, it is clear that the NPT is no effective guarantee against the proliferation of nuclear weapons in the Middle East.

In such circumstances, Israel is of the view that the most effective and constructive step which could be taken would be to establish a nuclear-weapon-free zone in the Middle East—based on the Tlatelolco model, freely arrived at by negotiations among all the states concerned and anchored in a binding multilateral treaty to which they all will be signatories.

Israel has repeatedly given expression to this idea. Since 1974, Israel has proposed it annually in the General Assembly and in other international forums. At the thirty-fifth session of the General Assembly in 1980 Israel submitted a draft resolution on this subject, which spelled out in precise terms our proposal for the establishment of a nuclear-weapon-free zone in the Middle East. To our great regret, this proposal was rejected out of hand by a number of Arab states, first and foremost by Iraq, whose representative even challenged Israel's right to sit on the First Committee. The Iraqi position could only mean than Iraq rejects any possibility of creating a nuclear-weapon-free zone in the Middle East.

Israel's proposal stands. With full awareness of the many political differences between the states of the Middle East, and without prejudice to any political or legal claim, it behooves all the states of the region, for the sake of their common future, to take concrete steps toward the establishment of a nuclear-weapon-free zone in the Middle East.

It is for that reason that in a letter to the Secretary-General of 9 June 1981 Israel further elaborated its proposal and formally and urgently requested all states of the Middle East and states adjacent to the region to consent to the holding in the course of the current year of a preparatory conference to discuss the modalities of such a conference of states of the Middle East with a view to negotiating a multilateral treaty establishing a nuclear-weapon-free zone in the Middle East. The details of our proposal were set out again in my letter of 15 June 1981 which was circulated as an official document of the Security Council.

While obviously not solving the Arab-Israel conflict as a whole, we believe that our proposal, if advanced, would constitute a significant contribution to the future well-being and security of all the states of the Middle East. It is for this reason, too, that Israel has submitted its proposal independent of other efforts being made to reach a comprehensive solution of the conflict. Hence Israel's proposal is an unlinked deal, standing on its own, separate and independent from anything that might delay its fulfillment. Hence, too, we have submitted our proposal without prejudice to any political or legal claim which any of the states concerned may have on any other state.

The Security Council now has a clear-cut choice before it. It can either resign itself to the perpetuation of the well-established pattern of one-sided denunciations of my country, that can only serve as a cover and encouragement for those who entertain destructive designs against it. Alternatively, it can address itself seriously to the perils and challenges that confront us all. If these perils and challenges are successfully met, a historic contribution can be made toward further advancing the cause of peace in the Middle East.

11

Mediterranean–Dead Sea Canal

Consolidated version of letter dated 2 October 1981, addressed to the Secretary-General of the United Nations, and of excerpts from statement made on 16 December 1981, in the United Nations General Assembly. Following feasibility studies, the project in question was suspended for budgetary reasons.

With regard to the water conduit to be constructed by Israel between the Mediterranean and Dead Seas, I wish to convey the following information.

The intention is not to construct a "canal," with all the images conjured up by that term. We are not talking of another Suez Canal or Panama Canal, with ships of all sizes plying in both directions. We are talking about a water conduit, largely an underground pipeline, and hydro-electricity.

The worldwide energy crisis facing mankind has prompted the experts of many nations to concentrate on the search for alternative solutions and new technologies. Israel's efforts to harness the water of the Mediterranean for generating energy must be seen against this background.

The projected conduit, that will link the Mediterranean and Dead Seas, was originally envisaged as early as the nineteenth century. It is designed to utilize the four hundred-meter difference in the levels between the Mediterranean and Dead Seas in order to generate hydro-electric power.

Energy generated in this way has the potential of benefiting the entire region, including the Kingdom of Jordan, as well as Judea, Samaria and the Gaza District. It is worth noting in this connection that hydro-electric power as a cheap and efficient energy source is still not available in Jordan (see the *Jordan Times* of August 1980).

Once the project is concluded, the maximum water-level of the Dead Sea, to be reached probably in the year 2012, will only be equal to that which existed before the water-level of the Dead Sea dropped to its present *niveau* as a result of Jordanian and Israel irrigation projects involving, respectively, the waters of the Yarmuk River and the Sea of Galilee.

It should be noted that the water-level of the Dead Sea has fallen 7 meters since 1955, to 400 meters below sea-level, and continues to fall owing to evaporation. Thus the water that will flow into the Dead Sea from the Mediterranean will raise the level of the Dead Sea, within 20 years of the completion of the Israel project, to its level of 1955.

It must be stressed that the Israel project is not designed to raise the level of the Dead Sea beyond the crest level of the dikes of both the Israel Dead Sea Works and the Jordanian Potash Company. Existing and projected dikes and dams will provide full protection to those facilities.

It should further be noted that Israel's largest chemical industrial complex, as well as hotels and tourist development projects, are located on the shores of the Dead Sea at an altitude identical with that of the Jordanian potash plant. Thus, if only for clear reasons of self-interest, Israel has no intention whatsoever of raising the water-level beyond the level at which these facilities are located.

The results of the research carried out thus far indicate only negligible effects—if any—on the composition and chemical balance of the Dead Sea resulting from the projected mixing of waters from the two seas.

In his letter dated 9 April 1981, the representative of Jordan erroneously contended that the project in question would bring about flooding in the Jordan valley and that sites along the Jordan River would be inundated. In fact, the projected conduit will have no effect whatsoever either on the Jordan River or on the Jordan valley. That assertion by the representative of Jordan also flies in the face of the elementary laws of physics, for the Dead Sea, being, as is well-known, the lowest point on earth, can hardly inundate higher locations, including the Jordan valley.

In the same Jordanian letter it is also alleged that the conduit will traverse "the breadth of the occupied West Bank." This assertion, too, is absolutely at variance with the facts. It is not necessary for present purposes to go into the question of the juridical status of Judea and Samaria (see my letter of 22 November 1978*). Suffice it to state here that nowhere will the conduit even touch the area of Judea and Samaria.

Israel is ready to co-operate fully with the Kingdom of Jordan in the projected enterprise for the mutual benefit of all the inhabitants of the region. Israel has repeatedly suggested to Jordan such co-operation aimed at the joint exploitation of the great potential this project holds in store for both countries.

---

*See Chapter 3, Part I, above.

Since this project can also be highly beneficial to Jordan, it is both astonishing and disappointing that, instead of welcoming such an endeavor, the representative of Jordan has found it necessary to call it a "fiendish plan."

In view of the use by the said representative of derogatory and pejorative terms concerning the Israeli project, it is somewhat surprising that the Government of Jordan should be planning the construction of a canal of its own linking the Red Sea and the Dead Sea. Jordan cannot have it both ways: either its complaints about the potential damage to the Dead Sea are valid and therefore it must not build a similar project of its own, or alternatively—and this is probably more to the point—Jordan simply does not want any competition.

The Arab League states, particularly the oil producers among them, are alarmed because the Israel project will produce an alternative and renewable source of energy, which is wholly independent of oil. It may conceivably serve as a model to other countries, particularly developing countries seeking to break out of the vise, political and economic, into which they have been locked by the Arab petro-hegemonists. In brief, the Israel project is not one which Arab oil blackmailers would wish to go ahead, for very selfish and mercurial reasons.

Nature has endowed the Dead Sea with a unique geographical feature—it is the lowest spot on the face of the earth, lying some four hundred meters below sea-level. That differential between it and the Mediterranean can easily be utilized to generate clean and efficient hydro-electric power, so much needed by Israel and Jordan alike, since neither of our two countries has, as yet at least, indigenous sources of oil. Israel has repeatedly proposed to Jordan co-operation in the joint exploitation of the great potential which this project holds for both our countries. Israel still hopes that Jordan will grasp the opportunity of jointly utilizing the remarkable geographical features of the Dead Sea which are at our common disposal.

With regard to the Gaza District, in his letter dated 13 April 1981, the representative of Egypt has contended that the conduit would lead to "acquisition of territories, confiscation of properties [and] depopulation of whole areas" inside the Gaza District. This contention is unfounded. All that is involved is the laying of a pipeline, approximately five meters in diameter, deep underground. This pipeline will neither adversely affect the population of the Gaza District nor the quality of its water supply. On the contrary, the livelihood of the area's population can only be enhanced by this project.

In any event, the political status of the Gaza District will evolve from the negotiations envisaged in the Camp David framework for peace in the Middle East. The construction of the pipeline in question clearly has no bearing on these negotiations.

The United Nations was conceived as "a center for harmonizing the actions of nations" (Article 1 (4) of the Charter). The hydro-electric project that Israel proposes to build by means of a conduit from the Mediterranean to the Dead Sea is a perfect instance of where the United Nations could encourage the harmonization of the positions of Israel and its Arab neighbor concerned, the Kingdom of Jordan.

12

Universal Declaration of Human Rights— Thirtieth Anniversary

Statement made in the UN General Assembly on 14 December 1978.

It is with a profound sense of satisfaction that I bring, as the representative of Israel, my Government's message on the occasion of the thirtieth anniversary of the Universal Declaration of Human Rights.

The noble principles enshrined in that declaration were first proclaimed to the world some three thousand years ago by the Jewish people and by the prophets of Israel in Jerusalem; to wit, the equality and brotherhood of man, the intrinsic dignity and value of the human being and the ideals of social justice based on eternal peace among nations.

In the very first chapter of Genesis we read:

> And God created man in His own image, in the image of God created He him; male and female created He them.(Genesis, 1:27)

In this short verse the essence of universally applicable human rights is enunciated: the equality of man and woman, irrespective of race, color or creed.

Everything else follows from this basic premise. It is summed up succinctly in the words of the prophet Malachi:

> Have we not one father? Has not one God created us? Why then do we deal treacherously every man against his brother? (Malachi, 2:10)

The prophets of Israel also understood that the equality and brotherhood of man could not be fully realized without universal peace and disarmament.

Nowhere has the vision of eternal peace and universal disarmament been given a more forceful expression than in the words of two prophets of Israel, Yeshayahu ben Amotz and Micha Hamorashti, who—having foreseen the spiritual unity of man under God with his word coming forth from Jerusalem—gave expression to this vision in identical terms:

> And they shall beat their swords into plowshares and their spears into pruning hooks. Nation shall not lift up sword against nation, neither shall they learn war any more. (Isaiah, 2:4; Mica, 4:3)

The Jewish people carried this vision of universal justice and universal peace with it throughout centuries of persecution and discrimination and throughout the darkest periods of world history. It believed in it even in the years of the terrible Holocaust during which it became the main victim of the genocidal practices of the enemies of mankind, the enemies of the United Nations. The Jewish people therefore rallied to the cause of the United Nations and more than one and a half million of its sons fought in the ranks of the Allied forces that eventually crushed the enemies of mankind and brought this Organization into being.

Illustrious sons of the Jewish people were in the forefront of the struggle for promotion of the international protection of human rights. A Jewish lawyer, Raphael Lemkin, whose family had been wiped out in Poland during World War II, was instrumental in writing the Convention on the Prevention and Punishment of the Crime of Genocide adopted by the United Nations on 9 December 1948. Another great Jewish lawyer, teacher, and judge of the International Court of Justice, Sir Hersch Lauterpacht—whose family had perished in Europe in the years of the Holocaust—was among the chief protagonists of the international protection of human rights. And yet another great son of the Jewish people—René Cassin—was one of the principal draftsmen of the Universal Declaration itself, and received the Nobel Peace Prize for his efforts.

Much remains to be done to translate the noble ideals and principles of the declaration into practice. On this anniversary let us rededicate ourselves to the task of making the Universal Declaration—this common standard of achievement—a living reality throughout the world.

It is in this spirit of rededication that I take great pleasure to announce that the Government of Israel—in its meeting of 10 December 1978, the thirtieth anniversary of the declaration—decided to ratify the Convention on the Elimination of All Forms of Racial Discrimination. This decision is a fitting tribute to the memory of a great woman and fighter for human rights, Mrs.

Golda Meir, former prime minister of Israel. An outstanding and courageous leader of the State of Israel and of the Jewish people, Mrs. Meir, in her capacity as foreign minister of Israel, led my country's delegation to the United Nations General Assembly for many years. On this day let me pay tribute here to the memory of a brave woman who in her lifetime did so much for the rights of the weak, the poor and the down-trodden not only in her country but also throughout the world. With her passing last week, the world has lost one of the towering personalities of our time.

13

The Plight of Oppressed Jewish Communities

A

Soviet Jewry

I. 1978–1982

Consolidated passages of statements made in the Third Committee of the UN General Assembly in the years 1978–1982.

Human rights have at long last attained general recognition as a subject which transcends national boundaries.

No longer may a state hold its nationals and other residents captive and when challenged at the United Nations on their behalf, seek refuge behind a claim of "interference in its internal affairs."

There is even a Commission on Human Rights of the UN, but unfortunately, its interest in the subject of human rights is selective, and it rarely, if ever, adopts resolutions concerning human rights problems in certain countries where serious probes would appear justified.

It is a sad fact that one of the worst violators of human rights in the world today is also one of the most powerful countries in this Organization. For years, we have drawn the attention of the United Nations to the Soviet Union's ongoing violations of the human rights of its Jewish community. And year after year, the Soviet Union has claimed that such violations and denials of human freedoms are solely its own internal affair. Undoubtedly the Soviet representative will make the same response again although such a claim affords no defense.

The documentation on Soviet human rights violations is now so overwhelming that no impartial observer can deny their existence. The rights to free emigration and to freedom of thought, conscience and religion are expressed without ambiguity in the Universal Declaration of Human Rights. Yet the Soviet Union continues to oppress and persecute its Jewish minority and to deny it even the most elemental rights existing for other minorities in that country. Though officially defined by the Soviet Union as a national minority, Jews are forbidden to teach and study their own language. Hebrew books have been confiscated and Hebrew teachers have been intimidated and arrested, as in the case of Yosif Begun who is still incarcerated in a Soviet prison. Jewish religion and culture have been systematically suppressed and dozens of synagogues have been closed. On the eve of the Jewish festival of Shavuot this year, Moscow's one remaining synagogue, which is expected to serve half a million Jews, was abruptly prevented from conducting a prayer service on the amazing grounds that young people were among those who wanted to pray. As if only old people are supposed to pray!

Not a single Jewish school exists in the entire U.S.S.R., in open breach not only of the Soviet constitution, but also of the UNESCO Convention against Discrimination in Education adopted on 4 December 1960 and ratified by the U.S.S.R. on 1 August 1962, which recognizes in Article 5 (c):

> the right of members of national minorities to carry on educational activities, including the maintenance of schools and. . . . the use and the teaching of their own language.

But an even more disturbing aspect of Soviet discrimination and persecution of Jews goes beyond a violation of basic human rights and embodies one of the most virulent forms of racism known to man. I refer here to the officially sponsored campaign of anti-Semitism which has intensified in recent times to a point where it recalls the darkest days of Stalinist oppression.

Millions of copies of anti-Semitic books, pamphlets and magazines circulate under official auspices in the U.S.S.R. In 1979, the Soviet Academy of Sciences published forty-five thousand copies of a book called *The Ideology and Practice of International Zionism*, which attacked Judaism as a religion and alleged that "Zionist Centers" controlled the western media and were spearheading an attempt to attack the U.S.S.R. (*The Washington Post*, 14 July 1979). An official "white paper" on Zionism, published in May 1979, warned readers that foreign Zionist spies were blackmailing and victimizing innocent Soviet citizens.

Some of that propaganda has reached such a level of crudity that it can only be interpreted as a deliberate attempt to incite the Soviet population against the Jews. According to *The New York Times* of 27 June 1979:

The official campaign against Zionism in the press, in books and in propaganda has been particularly intense this year. . . .

The unofficial echo is a swell of deep xenophobia that combines historical Russian anti-Semitism and paranoia. . . .

The "unofficial" anti-Semitism and the official campaigns directed against "Zionism" appear, however, to feed on each other. . . .

Soviet sources, both dissidents and intellectuals in good standing with the Government, say the are disturbed by parallels with the Stalinist "anticosmopolitan" secret police repressions that began in the late 1940s and continued until the dictator's death in 1953.

Some of the worst examples of anti-Semitism are clearly being tolerated by elements within the bureaucracy.

It is a frightening and puzzling phenomenon that a state that suffered so terribly at the hands of the Nazi invaders is today the greatest purveyor of anti-Semitic incitement since the days of the Nazi régime. There was a time when governments and peoples admitted that anti-Semitism existed in their countries. As the events of the last few years, and even of the last few months show, the scourge of anti-Semitism has not been eliminated. It is still very much with us, even in so-called "enlightened countries."

The difference is that today it is no longer fashionable to talk about anti-Semitism. Instead of attacking Jews or the Jewish people as such, anti-Semites now attack Zionism or Zionists. In this Organization, as elsewhere, a new code-word—"anti-Zionism"—has gained currency. But anti-Semites throughout the world understand its meaning full well, and the attempt in this Organization to bestow respectability upon "anti-Zionism" has, in practice, only encouraged anti-Semitism in various parts of the world.

Nowhere has this sad fact been more obvious than in the Soviet-bloc countries of Eastern Europe and in the Arab world.

The Soviet Union, which has a long history of official anti-Semitism, stretching back to Tsarist days, is still fanning the flames of anti-Jewish hatred. For example, there is Tzecar Solodar's infamous book, *The Dark Curtain*, which propounds a viciously anti-Semitic doctrine under the cloak of an attack on Zionism. Or the work of another well-known anti-Semite, Lev Korneyev, entitled *Israel: The Reality behind the Myths*, which the Soviet authorities pick out for distribution (in English) in such places as the international airport at Moscow. On 8 August 1980, the youth magazine *Pionirskaya Pravda* published an article by Korneyev asserting that Jewish bankers dominate the world. On 10 October 1980, the same magazine published another article typical of many appearing in the Soviet Union, attacking Zionism as "modern-day fascism" and "the main enemy of peace on earth." And the rabid Ukranian anti-Semite, Trofim Kitchko, is having another book published under the title *Judaism and Zionism—The Followers of Racism.* Slanderous works of this kind have a poisonous effect on attitudes and practices, both official and private, toward the Jews in the Soviet Union, as the experience of decades, indeed generations, in that country has shown.

For all the sensitivity toward anti-Semitic propaganda in some countries, no such sensitivity is displayed in the Soviet Union. The attacks come from all quarters. In February 1980, the official magazine, *Nauka i Religia* (Science and Religion), published a crude diatribe against Judaism, under the guise of scientific analysis. And in the same month, a magazine dealing with industry, *Sotsialisticheskaya Industria*, blamed Jews for international tension.

It should also be noted that, aside from the overt and crude anti-Semitism that appears in official literature, the Soviet Union also engages in other more subtle forms of racial discrimination which are no less dangerous in the long run. Jewish academicians, for example, are forbidden to publish articles and attend international conferences abroad. There has also been a marked decline, confirmed by published Soviet figures, in the number of Jewish students at institutes of higher learning as part of an apparent design to close the academic and professional avenues to Jews. In many institutions, Jews are systematically excluded from responsible top-level positions for no reason other than the fact that they are Jews.

The Soviet Union is no longer content with ignoring its international obligations, with preventing Jewish emigration, with victimizing its Jewish citizens, with interfering maliciously in the observance of the Jewish religion, with its virulent anti-Semitism. The Soviet Union renewed its efforts to strike at the very existence of a living Jewish community within its borders. The Soviet authorities have taken direct and deliberate steps to bring about the extinction of Jewish culture from Soviet territory. Today they shrink from no means or methods to achieve, once and for all, the complete elimination of Jewish culture, its values, its languages, its literature, its traditions and history from the consciousness of nearly three million Jews—roughly a fifth of all Jews living throughout the world.

The cultural policies of the Soviet Government are aimed at severing Soviet Jews from their heritage, at obliterating their historical memory and, in fact, at the destruction of their cultural identity and their forcible assimilation. They represent not only flagrant, massive breaches of the Soviet Union's obligations under virtually all the human rights conventions it has signed, but also a breach of the Soviet Union's own laws and constitution which purport to ensure equality of rights in all respects for all Soviet nationalities. The lamentable reality is that while all of the more than one hundred recognized Soviet nationalities—including those who are less numerous and more widely dispersed than the Jews—enjoy the full panoply of cultural rights, this does not apply to Jews. The violation of the collective rights of the Jews in the cultural field parallels the violation of the individual rights of Jews through anti-Semitic discrimination that I have earlier referred

ten different occasions, with seminars and scientific meetings on Jewish culture and history. Some of the participants were arrested; all of them were warned against indulging in such "dangerous" subjects again.

Those who follow the plight of Jews in the Soviet Union have recorded ample evidence of the violation of their rights through harassment, threat and arrest. I will not weary the Committee by listing all the instances known to us, save to say that they are numerous, and that the trend is on the rise.

This pattern of repressive acts can only be interpreted as an orchestrated effort on the part of the Soviet authorities to bring about the spiritual extinction of the Jewish people in their midst, to destroy the national identity of the three million strong Jewish minority, by forbidding the transmission of its spiritual heritage from father to son and from one Jew to another. From the inglorious days when Jewish books were burnt by the Nazis of the German Reich, we have not seen the like in efforts to put an end to a people. The Jewish people, in Russia as in other lands of its exile through two thousand years, has lived through such efforts, and has outlived them! The Jews of the Soviet Union will outlive them too, because these methods, painful and grotesque as they are, have never been of any avail.

This Committee is aware of the difficulties that the Soviet Union had in joining the consensus on the Declaration on the Elimination of All Forms of Religious Intolerance. These difficulties may have surprised delegates familiar with the laws and the constitution of the Soviet Union, which nominally guarantee religious freedom, both of belief and observance, to every individual and to every denomination. The surprise of those delegates will perhaps not be so great when I point out that, within the efforts of that superpower to suppress the spiritual existence of the Jewish minority, the Soviet authorities have recently also begun to confiscate Jewish ritual objects. Sacred Sabbath candlesticks, those simple symbols of the unity of the Jewish family, the traditional expression of the Jewish woman's religious commitment, have become, in the eyes of the heirs of the Tsar, subversive instruments, that must be assailed with the full rigor of the police and the KGB.

One may well wonder what value the Soviet Union attaches to the Declaration on the Elimination of All Forms Religious Intolerance. Agreeing to bare texts, joining consensuses is not enough! We must demand that the Soviet Union implement, and give concrete expression to, its obligations under this declaration, to its obligations under the Universal Declaration of Human Rights and, above all, to its obligations under its own constitution! The Jews in the Soviet Union have a right to observe their religion and to preserve their culture, as do Jews in other parts of the world! Denial of that right, the right to freedom of religion, belief and culture, is a denial of a basic human right.

Over the years, Israeli representatives have alerted members of the United Nations to the fact that the Soviet authorities have denied their Jews another basic human right—that of emigration, to Israel or elsewhere. The Soviet authorities have subjected the exercise of this right to an extraordinary maze of restrictive regulations, fines, victimization and punishment, all designed to impede the exit of those yearning to reunite with their families or to live amongst their own people in Israel. Yet, in spite of all this untold harassment, many thousands of Jews every year have been prepared to run the risk, and apply for exit permits.

In 1981, the harassment of Jews applying to leave the Soviet Union was stepped up and the number of permits issued severely reduced, so that tens of thousands of exit applications piled up at the "Ovir," the Soviet department dealing with such applications. To put things into perspective, I should point out that, while in 1979 an average of 4000 Jews a month were permitted to leave, the number in 1981 went down to a tenth of that, i.e. roughly 400 a month. The Soviet Union, that claims to be one of the most enlightened and progressive nations in the world, is violating, methodically and systematically, one of the most fundamental of human rights—the right to freedom of movement, by denying that right to hundreds of thousands of its Jewish citizens. Given the mere trickle being allowed to depart, one can say that for all practical purposes the gates of the Soviet Union have been closed to Jews seeking to emigrate. These policies are in flagrant violation of the international obligations of the Soviet Union, including the Helsinki Accords of 1975.

The right of Jews to emigrate from the Soviet Union was drastically curtailed in 1980. The Soviet authorities curbed Jewish emigration by severely restricting the eligibility of the applicants. Criteria for emigration, that had been in effect for ten years, were arbitrarily set aside, and invitational affidavits from only first-degree relatives living in Israel are being accepted. Other applications from cousins, nephews, nieces, grandparents and grandchildren are rejected.

The Soviet authorities are also using other ploys to restrict Jewish emigration. In many cities, especially in the Ukraine, emigration officials refuse to distribute the forms needed to apply to emigrate. The office hours of the Visa and Registration Department of the Ministry of the Interior have been limited to a few hours a week. In Kishinev, for instance, over two thousand Jewish families are waiting to apply for emigration. The Visa Department, however, accepts only five applications a week. Recently, in Kharkov, emigration officials began issuing "final refusals" to prospective emigrants, denying the applicant his right to reapply every six months.

Jews seeking to emigrate from the Soviet Union have always been required to run a gauntlet of bureaucratic procedures and requirements that in and of itself is a model system of administrative harassment. In recent years these procedures have been rendered even more oppressive than in the past. In contravention of the Universal Postal Convention, invitations from relatives in Israel are often illegally confiscated from the mails by the Soviet authorities and thus do not reach their intended recipients. Many of those who do receive their invitations are even barred from submitting requests for exit visas through the application of wholly arbitrary criteria. Those who succeed in applying are condemned to indefinite periods of waiting—often as long as two or three years—before receiving any reply. The reply, when finally received, is more often than not a refusal, that the authorities seek to justify by some absurd pretext or simply with the remark that the applicant's emigration would be "inexpedient."

In their despair at such arbitrary behavior, groups of Jews in Kharkov and Kishinev decided to go on a symbolic three-day fast on 11 November 1980, the day fixed for the opening in Madrid of the conference called to review the 1975 Helsinki accords on détente and human rights. Two potential participants were arrested by the KGB and, as a warning to others, were sentenced to fifteen days in prison, charged with "hooliganism." A third group of twenty-seven applicants in Riga signed a similar appeal to the participants in the Madrid Conference.

On 13 November 1980, two days after a press conference was held in his Moscow apartment to mark the start of a hunger strike, the prominent scientist and Jewish activist, Victor Brailovsky, was arrested on the charge of "defaming the Soviet State and public order." Dr. Brailovsky has been struggling since 1972 for his right to emigrate to Israel, and he is one of those many Soviet Jews who are called "refuseniks," because of the refusal of the Soviet authorities to grant them exit visas. His arrest provoked an international outcry, and a press conference was held in New York on his behalf, attended by leading public figures from all walks of life, including Dr. Arno Penzias, the winner of the 1978 Nobel Prize for Physics. Israel urges the Soviet Government to put a quick end to Dr. Brailovsky's detention.

The idea frequently voiced by Soviet representatives, that respect for humanitarian principles governing family reunification should be subject to the fluctuating state of great-power relations, and that Jewish families should be held hostage to international tensions, is as devoid of any moral or legal basis as it is unworthy of a great power. Equally reprehensible and illegal are the means employed by the Soviet authorities to restrict Jewish emigration.

While denied the prospect of living as equals, and with the backlog of unprocessed applications to emigrate steadily increasing, Jews in the Soviet Union face severe hardship in connection with their attempts to leave that country. Upon applying for emigration, they are usually dismissed from their jobs. Throughout the long and uncertain period of refusal they are either prevented from obtaining all but the most menial employment or charged with "parasitism" for being out of work. They are subjected to all manner of harassment and humiliation. Their children are frequently expelled from educational institutions and are subjected to selective and punitive conscription into the armed forces. Military service is then used as additional justification for indefinite refusal to grant an exit visa on the basis of the applicant's alleged possession of secret information. While treated as outcasts from Soviet society, where their requests to leave are regarded as akin to confessions of treason, the refuseniks are at the same time compelled to continue living in the society which has rejected them. Some refusenik families have been waiting for permission to leave for ten years or more in these intolerable conditions, their artificially maintained distress obviously designed by the authorities to intimidate other potential applicants.

For similar reasons, other Jews, active in the struggle to secure their right to leave for Israel, have been arrested and sentenced on trumped-up charges. These prisoners of Zion include Victor Brailovsky, Boris Chernobilsky, Vladimir Kislik, Osip Lokshin, Alexander Paritsky, Anatoly Shcharansky, Vladimir Slepak, Vladimir Tsukerman and Stanislav Zubko.

Yet another name on this list—a list of shame for the Soviet authorities—is Felix Kochubievsky of Novosibirsk who, in the eyes of the Soviet authorities, has aggravated his "offense" of seeking to join his two sons in Israel by committing an even more heinous crime—he has attempted to promote friendship between the Soviet and Israeli peoples by establishing a Soviet-Israel friendship society in the U.S.S.R., to complement the Israel-Soviet Friendship Society that has long been in existence in Israel. There are scores of friendship societies in the Soviet Union and they involve people in many states with which the Soviet Union's governmental relations are not free from problems. Apparently, however, it is impermissible in the U.S.S.R. for such a society to exist where the Israeli people are concerned. As a result, Mr. Kochubievsky, because of his efforts to promote international friendship and understanding, is now in detention and under criminal investigation.

Not content with unjustly imprisoning Jews actively struggling for their right to leave, the Soviet authorities have sought even in prison conditions to harden the lot of the Prisoners of Zion. Thus, Anatoly Shcharansky, currently serving a thirteen-year sentence, has been transferred from labor camp to an isolation cell in prison and denied even the minimal rights of correspondence normally permitted in such circumstances. His mail has been confiscated for more than ten months and no relative has been permitted to see him. Mr. Shcharansky has protested this harsh treatment by declaring a hunger strike that he has now adhered to since the eve of Yom Kippur, the Day of Atonement, on 17 September 1982. The Soviet authorities have been force-feeding him intravenously and Mr. Shcharansky is now in danger of dying as a result of his continued ill-treatment.

Alexander Paritsky of Kharkov has also been subjected to unwarranted ill-treatment in detention. He has been placed in a camp with common criminals who steal his food and, despite failing health, has been isolated in a punishment cell.

Nor does the ordeal of the Prisoners of Zion end with their release from prison. Relentless hounding by the authorities continues as the former prisoners continue to be denied their right to leave for Israel. The example of Ida Nudel is typical. Upon returning from a four-year term of exile in Siberia (for publicly displaying a poster demanding an exit visa) she was promptly forced out of her home in Moscow and is now forbidden even to visit that city. In failing health and with no relatives in the Soviet Union, Ida Nudel has again been denied the right to join her relatives in Israel on the ludicrous ground that she possesses secret information—from her employment in 1971 as a cost accountant in a food processing plant.

The most recent addition to the list of Soviet shame is Yosif Begun. Mr. Begun applied to emigrate in April 1971, more than a decade ago, and has been waiting for all that time to reach his homeland, Israel. A radio engineer and mathematician by profession, Yosif Begun taught himself Hebrew and became a teacher. He fought for the legalization of the Hebrew language.

Yosif Begun has already served two terms as a Jewish prisoner of conscience. In March 1977 he was arrested and charged with "parasitism" and sentenced to exile. Upon returning to his family in Moscow, in March 1978, he was refused a renewed residence permit, was arrested in May 1978 on charges of violating internal passport regulations, and again sentenced to exile. He was released in August 1980 and went to Strunino, about one hundred fifty kilometers from Moscow, since he was again denied permission to live in the capital.

Yosif Begun was again arrested on 7 November 1982, in Leningrad while en route to Moscow. The Soviet authorities are charging him with "anti-Soviet agitation and propaganda."

There has been no indication of any change for the better in the situation of the Jewish minority in the U.S.S.R. It appears, therefore, that the professed support in November 1981 by the Soviet Union in this Assembly for the Declaration on the Elimination of all Forms of Intolerance and of Discrimination based on Religion or Belief was intended merely as yet another cynical attempt to mislead the world regarding the bitter realities of Jewish life in the U.S.S.R.

My delegation protests in the strongest terms the denial by the Soviet authorities of the right of Soviet Jews to join their relatives in Israel and of their right to live free from discrimination as Jews in the U.S.S.R. We call upon the Soviet Government to fulfill its legal obligations by ceasing its harassment of Jews seeking to leave the Soviet Union for Israel, by allowing all Jews who wish to do so to proceed on their way unhindered, and by allowing those Jews who choose to remain in the U.S.S.R. to live as equals among their non-Jewish neighbors, free of anti-Semitic discrimination, and to enjoy and propagate their national culture and religion free from discrimination and on a basis of equality with all Soviet nationalities.

II. 1983

Excerpt from statement made in the Third Committee of the UN General Assembly on 29 November 1983.

Despite all the risks, uncertainties and hardships with which the Soviet authorities have burdened the emigration process, more than a quarter of a million Jews have succeeded in leaving the Soviet Union since the early 1970s. Now, however, the Soviet authorities have all but closed the exit gates. Compared to 51,000 Jews allowed to leave for Israel in 1979, only 21,500 were permitted to do so in 1980. The number was further reduced to 9,500 in 1981 and to 2,700 in 1982. In the current year, as of 30 September 1983, fewer than 1,100 Jews have been granted permission to leave.

In no way do these numbers reflect a reduction in the number of Jews desiring to leave; rather, they reflect an arbitrary and illegal halting of the exodus by the Soviet authorities. The Soviet bureaucrats resort to all kinds of intricate complexities and harassment in their attempts to deprive Soviet Jews en masse of their elementary right to leave the U.S.S.R. and join their families in Israel.

It is superfluous to add that these practices constitute flagrant violations of the freedom of emigration provisions in numerous human rights conventions to which the Soviet Union is a party. The consequences of these violations are, in the first instance, acute suffering for the thousands of Jews in the U.S.S.R. and in Israel who are arbitrarily denied the possibility of reuniting with their relatives. Callously indifferent to the human suffering caused by this cruel division of families and contemptuous of its international legal obligations regarding human rights, the Soviet Government cynically mocks the hopes of long-separated families with its false claim that reunification of families has essentially ended and the desire to leave the U.S.S.R. for Israel no longer exists. In fact, over 382,000 Soviet Jews now hold in their hands invitations from relatives in Israel to enable them to at least begin the process of applying to leave.

Those denied permission to leave, the refuseniks, live in conditions of excruciating uncertainty regarding their future; some have been waiting for ten years or more for permission to emigrate to Israel. In the meantime, they are forced to live as outcasts of Soviet society for an indeterminate period, prey to the vengeful whims of the authorities and subject to all manner of harassment and persecution with no effective means of redress. Dismissed from their jobs, and denied employment in their fields of expertise, they live in great economic hardship under permanent threat of criminal prosecution for what the authorities in the U.S.S.R. label as "parasitism"—the Soviet "crime" of being unemployed. Such harassment is a glaring violation of conventions of the International Labor Organization to which the U.S.S.R.

is a party. The children of the refuseniks are often expelled from Soviet higher educational institutions where increasingly severe anti-Semitic discrimination has already reduced the percentage of Jewish students—and that even according to published Soviet statistics—by approximately 40 percent over the past decade. Increasingly, they are subject to the selective, punitive use of military conscription as still another means of denying them exit permits.

For those "refuseniks" who persist in struggling for their rights, police repression remains the tried weapon of the authorities. Since this Committee's meetings of last year, four new names have been added to the list of Prisoners of Zion—those who have been imprisoned solely because they have struggled for their legitimate right to leave for Israel or to live as Jews free from anti-Jewish discrimination in the U.S.S.R. To the names of those we have had occasion to speak of previously in this forum and elsewhere—Yosif Begun, Victor Brailovsky, Boris Kanevsky, Vladimir Kislik, Felix Kochubievsky, Osip Lokshin, Alexander Paritsky, Anatoly Shcharansky, Vladimir Tsukerman and Stanislav Zubko—must now be added those of Simon Shnirman of Kerch, Dr. Yury Tarnopolsky of Kharkov, Lev Elbert of Kiev and Alexander Panariev of Sukhumi.

Tarnopolsky was sentenced at the end of June to three years of imprisonment for allegedly "defaming the Soviet State and social system" whereas his real "crime" in the eyes of the authorities was his participation in the effort to teach and further the education of children in Kharkov, who, because their parents are refuseniks were being denied the opportunity to study in Soviet universities. Another factor which led to his sentencing was his publicizing the plight of the refuseniks.

Shnirman, Elbert and Panariev are the latest victims of the cynical use by the Soviet authorities of military conscription as a means of denying the right of emigration. All three knew that the Soviet authorities use prior military service, in any case where application for emigration has been made, as justification for refusing that applicant an exit permit for at least five years, and often for far longer periods, on the grounds that the applicant had acquired secret information during his period of service.

Elbert, thirty-five years old, has been denied an exit permit for seven years on the basis of his military service nine years ago. Consequently, when subjected to a special call-up this year, he requested assurances that his service would not be used as a pretext to delay even further his emigration. When these assurances were refused, Elbert chose prison rather than an indefinitely long denial of his right to leave the U.S.S.R. for Israel.

Similar considerations guided Alexander Panariev, aged nineteen, of Sukhumi, whose widowed mother has been seeking to leave with him for Israel for the past ten years. Both Elbert and Panariev were recently sentenced to one year of imprisonment. Shnirman, who had previously served a sentence of one year in prison, was reconvicted of the same offense and is now serving an additional three-year term. Lev Elbert was placed in a cell with common criminals and then threatened, while in prison, with prosecution on a completely new trumped-up charge based on fabricated evidence.

After their release from prison, Prisoners of Zion are still regularly denied exit visas. Former Prisoners of Zion—Boris Chernobilsky, Kim Fridman, Grigory Geishis, Grigory Goldshtein, Boris Kalendarev, Evgenii Lein, Mark Wapshitz, Ida Nudel, Dimitri Shchiglik, Isaak Shkolnik, Victor Shtilbans, Vladimir Slepak and Alexander Vilig—continue to wait indefinitely for their exit visas.

The recent trial of Dr. Yosif Begun illustrates the fate of Jews who refuse to be intimidated. Begun has been denied an exit visa for Israel since 1971 and, having previously served two terms of Siberian exile on trumped-up charges of "parasitism" and "malicious violation of passport regulations," was convicted just last month, on 15 October 1983, of anti-Soviet agitation and propaganda, that in the Soviet criminal code is categorized as an "especially dangerous crime against the state." Begun's trial was conducted illegally behind closed doors so that even his closest relatives were excluded, and he received the maximum sentence of seven years of imprisonment to be followed by five years of exile. Dr. Begun, who is fifty-one years of age, is not a political person; he is concerned solely with the perpetuation of the Jewish heritage and the teaching of Hebrew among Soviet Jews. The cruel and vindictive punishment inflicted upon him demonstrates that the Soviet authorities, in the style of medieval inquisitors, consider Jewish cultural activity anti-Soviet in its very essence.

The halting of Jewish emigration by the Soviet authorities has by no means meant a relaxation of the pressures upon Soviet Jews that helped generate the exodus of the 1970s. Those pressures have, on the contrary, been intensified.

It is, however, the increasing volume and ferocity of the anti-Semitic incitement in the government-controlled media, masquerading as anti-Zionism, which has recently introduced an ominous new element into the plight of Soviet Jewry.

Symptomatic of this heightened threatening atmosphere was the establishment in April 1983 of a so-called Anti-Zionist Committee of the Soviet Public, a puppet body whose leadership is comprised mainly of Jews thoroughly alienated from their own people, long employed as apologists for discriminatory and oppressive policies toward the Jews of the Soviet Union. With branches in many Soviet cities, this committee has become notorious for its scurrilous attacks on Israel and for its preposterous claim that Jewish emigration has stopped because the re-unification of families "has essentially been completed" and that Soviet Jews "have ceased to succumb to the Zionist temptation."

That committee has also acted as the spearhead of a vicious campaign in the Soviet media which, replete with Stürmer-like cartoons, presented standard Soviet propaganda themes with growing intensity and virulence: the obscene equation of Zionism with nazism and the State of Israel with Nazi Germany; the grotesque attempts to depict Judaism and its sacred texts as the inspiration for the alleged racism, chauvinism, aggressive militarism and atrocities libelously attributed to Israel; and the description of Zionism, as given in *Leningradskaya Pravda* in April 1983, as the shock troops "of the aggressive forces of imperialism against the U.S.S.R., the socialist bloc and the cause of peace." A recent book, *The Class Essence of Zionism* by Lev Korneyev, one of the professional anti-Semitic publicists in the U.S.S.R., has reached proportions that would be truly comical if they were not so tragic. It propounds nothing else than the preposterous thesis that the Jews were responsible for anti-Jewish pogroms and excesses in Tsarist Russia. Korneyev further advances the calumnious assertion that Zionist leaders and Jewish bankers "helped Hitler prepare for the seizure of power, even though they knew of Hitler's intention to exterminate the Jews" and that the Jews collaborated with the Nazis in implementing "the Final Solution." He also claims that wherever Jews live outside the State of Israel they constitute a potential fifth column. Echoing that infamous Tsarist anti-Semitic forgery, *The Protocols of the Elders of Zion*, Korneev postulates the existence of a vast Jewish conspiracy aiming at world domination.

We do not intend to dignify these outrageous lies with detailed refutations; they are as obscene as they are absurd and their falsity is patently obvious to every literate person. Knowing, however, that everything that appears in print in the Soviet Union is subjected to rigorous prior censorship; knowing moreover, that Korneyev's book bears the *imprimatur* of the notorious Trofim Kichko, whose anti-Semitic writings in the 1960s were in such bad taste that even his Soviet sponsors were embarrassed; and knowing further that it was favorably reviewed in *Izvestia*, the organ of the Soviet Government, we are bound to ask ourselves: What is the meaning of this venomous anti-Semitic campaign? For anti-Semitic it is, despite the disclaimers of its sponsors. The term "Zionist" and "Jew" have long been used interchangeably by Soviet propagandists, and the fact that only a Jew can be a Zionist in Soviet society ensures that the code word will be universally understood.

Recently a sinister new aspect of this policy has appeared. A series of press articles in various Soviet republics has attacked Jewish culture—including the study of Hebrew—and Jewish activities as being of a subversive and treasonous character. In a manner redolent of the infamous "Doctors' Plot" of Stalin's last days, a recent article in *Sovietskaya Rossiya*, the organ of the government of the Russian republic, accused Soviet Jewish activists of acting in concert with intelligence services of foreign states to commit espionage, subversion and treason against the Soviet Union. The authorities obviously hope that by signaling to the Soviet public at large that anti-Semitic behavior will not be regarded unfavorably, an atmosphere of fear will be created to supplement the police measures invoked to deny Jews their legitimate rights under international and Soviet law. The purpose of the Soviet authorities in conducting this campaign is to sever Soviet Jews from the Jewish people as a whole and deter them from expressing any interest in emigration to Israel or, indeed, in preserving their own Jewish heritage and identity.

In the name of decency and common sense, we call upon the Soviet Government to put an immediate end to this ominous campaign of anti-Semitic incitement. We call upon the Soviet authorities to conform their policies and practices regarding Soviet Jews to the international obligations of the Soviet Union as well as to Soviet law and, in particular, to end their discrimination against the Jewish minority. We call on them to release those Jews who have been unjustly imprisoned—their only real "crime" having been their persistent effort to secure their exit visas for Israel and their legitimate rights as Jews—and to allow all Jews seeking to leave the U.S.S.R. for Israel to do so freely.

On behalf of the State of Israel, I wish to reiterate our determination to persist in and intensify our efforts to arouse the conscience of the civilized world so long as Soviet Jews are denied their legitimate right to leave the U.S.S.R. and reunite with their families in Israel without hindrance, or, if they so choose, to live in the Soviet Union as Jews free from discrimination and fear.

B

Jews in Moslem Lands

Excerpt from statement made in the Third Committee of the United Nations General Assembly on 29 November 1983.

I have spoken at some length about the situation of the Jews in the Soviet Union, because the largest Jewish community in the world whose fundamental rights are being violated is to be found there. But let us not lose sight of what is happening in the Middle East to the tiny remnants of what were once large and glorious communities, with histories going back thousands of years.

We are bound to express our anxiety about the condition of the tortured Jewish community of Syria, whose human rights are severely curtailed. The members of this tiny community—consisting of just over one thousand families of forty-five hundred souls—are still denied their right to emigrate, in violation of Syria's international commitments. They continue to live as second-class citizens in the ghettoes of Damascus, Aleppo and Kamishli, and are under constant surveillance by the Muhabarat, the Syrian secret police. Travel, even within the country, is restricted. Jewish men, suspected of helping Jewish families flee the country, have been brutally beaten by the Muhabarat, young Jewish women in Aleppo were raped. In grave violation of the Helsinki Accords, to which Syria is a signatory, the régime of that country has, as a rule, denied Syrian Jews the right to emigrate. Those few Jews who are granted an exit permit to visit their relatives abroad, have been forced to deposit huge sums of money—the equivalent of US $5,000—as well as to leave their families behind in Syria as guarantees for their return.

The Jewish community of Syria has been made a virtual hostage of the régime that has rejected even humanitarian appeals, such as requests to allow a few hundred young Jewish women to leave Syria so that they could marry within their faith; these young women are thus being denied even the right to establish families.

Israel appeals to the Government of Syria to respect the basic human rights of its Jewish community, which it holds as hostages and which it prevents from leaving. We also hope that humanitarian pleas by distinguished European leaders will no longer go unheeded. We appeal to the Syrian Government to set aside political considerations, and allow this small community of Jews to emigrate, in accordance with its obligations under the International Covenant on Civil and Political Rights, to which it adhered in 1969, and the UN Declaration of Human Rights, which it too has accepted.

In another part of the Middle East, the dramatic events in the Persian Gulf should not be allowed to obscure the fact that the Jews of Iran have suffered painfully in recent months, and their situation is deteriorating from day to day. Many Jews have been thrown in jail; others have been executed, in most cases on "charges" of contact with Israel. We know, of course, of the difficulties in dealing with the present régime in Iran, to whom fundamental concepts of human rights and the norms of international relations seem foreign. But we hope that sight will not be lost of the situation of the Jews there, who are perhaps among the most vulnerable of the minorities in that troubled land. We appeal to the Government of Iran to respect their human rights, including their right to emigrate if they should so wish.

We must voice our deep concern also regarding Yemen's persecution of the remnants of its ancient Jewish community, whose human rights are being gravely violated. The Jews of Yemen have been completely cut off from all external contacts. They have been forbidden any postal communications with relatives and Jewish communities outside Yemen. They are not permitted to leave Yemen, whether temporarily or permanently. Moreover, the authorities have denied entry visas to Jews of other countries who wish to visit relatives in Yemen.

We demand that the Government of Yemen fulfill its obligations under Article 13(2) of the Universal Declaration of Human Rights by allowing the emigration of those Jews who wish to leave. Moreover, the Jewish community of Yemen must be permitted to receive religious articles that Jewish organizations abroad wish to donate so that their brethren will be able to preserve their Jewish heritage.

14

The Apartheid Policies of South Africa

Consolidated version of excerpts from statements made in the UN General Assembly in the years 1978–83, in the course of the annual debates on South Africa's apartheid policies, with particular reference to the accusations against Israel made in that context.

The position of Israel with regard to all forms of racism and racial discrimination, including *apartheid*, has been stated and reaffirmed annually in this forum. The Jewish people's concept of mankind has always been that of a unity, deriving its character from a common origin and a common destiny. This doctrine was enunciated at the very beginning of our civilization over three thousand years ago, in the Holy Bible, where the origins of all mankind are traced to a single person, formed by God in His own image (Genesis 1:27), while the Book of Exodus unambiguously rejects a system whose legal code does not apply equally to all citizens:

> One law shall be to him that is home-born and unto the stranger that sojourneth among you. (Exodus 12:49)

And the Book of Leviticus states clearly that freedom is a universal principle:

> And thou shalt proclaim liberty throughout the land, unto all the inhabitants thereof. (Leviticus 25:10)

The same universalistic message is developed later by the prophets of Israel. The prophet Malachi, for example, proclaimed:

> Have we not all one father?
> Has not one God created us?

Why then do we deal treacherously
every man against his brother?

(Malachi 2:10)

This doctrine is further expounded in the writings of the Jewish sages, where it reaches its clearest expression.

"Why did the Creator form all life from a single ancestor?" they ask; and the reply is, "that the families of mankind shall not lord one over the other with the claim of being sprung from superior stock. . . . that all men . . . may recognize their common kinship in the collective human family." (Tosefta Sanhedrin 8:4)

This belief, this deep conviction, is reflected in the Jewish legal code from the earliest times.

But the traditional Jewish support for the struggle against racism stems not merely from a deep-rooted abhorrence of the very notion of discrimination based on race, color or creed, but also from the fact that more than any other nation, the people of Israel have, throughout their long history, been the classic victims of discrimination. Jewish nationhood was born in captivity and in the longing of enslaved masses for freedom. In the Middle Ages, Jews lived for hundreds of years fenced off in ghettoes, a nation apart, victims of ruthless persecution and oppression in an unending succession of pogroms and expulsions. Only a generation ago the Jewish people suffered the loss of one-third of its numbers, including a million and a half children, murdered by the most brutal, racist régime in the history of man. That historical heritage, along with the ancient teachings of the prophets of Israel, has led our people throughout the world, and the State of Israel, to fight racism whenever and wherever it rears its ugly head.

Indeed, it has been forgotten that it was an anti-Semitic assault that led the United Nations itself to become involved in combating racism. In the wake of a worldwide swastika-daubing epidemic in 1959, the UN-affiliated Jewish non-governmental organizations brought the question of racial discrimination to the United Nations for the first time, an initiative that was vigorously supported by the newly emerging African nations that were then entering the world organization. Moreover, the direct link between the Jewish experience of racial persecution and the determination of Jews to end racial discrimination had been manifested in the United Nations during its very first session. After the adoption of resolution 96(I) in 1946, declaring genocide a crime under international law, it was a Jewish lawyer, Raphael Lemkin [whose family had been wiped out in Poland during the war] who was instrumental in writing the Convention on the Prevention and Punishment of the Crime of Genocide, adopted by the United Nations on 9 December 1948. Since that time, Jewish organizations in more than forty countries have campaigned actively for ratification of that convention, that outlaws the most extreme and brutal form of racism known to man—the attempt to liquidate an entire race or ethnic group. Israel was among the first states to ratify the genocide convention.

It is saddening to realize that the lessons of the past have yet to be learned, and that the evil of discrimination against the Jewish people has found its way even into the latest in the series of reports of the Special Committee against Apartheid. For what have we here but another attempt to single out the people of Israel and to subject them to scurrilous and false accusations, as in the past.

By selecting Israel as a special target of attack, on the basis of its miniscule trade with South Africa, the report has tried to divert attention from the real issue at hand and to divert this world forum in a cynical display of transparent hypocrisy from what should have been its proper task. Seldom does one encounter a more one-sided and selective document than the Report of the Special Committee against Apartheid. Once again, we have before us a document inspired by motives of discrimination and bias, motives that we are supposed to be collectively attempting to eradicate.

Indeed, it is preposterous to single out Israel for special treatment because of her trade with South Africa, when the volume of that trade amounts to less than two-fifths of one percent of South Africa's foreign trade. The only thing special about Israel's trade with South Africa is its insignificance by contrast to the latter country's other trading partners, who account for the remaining 99.6 percent, but who were deemed unworthy of a special report.

If the aim of the debate on *apartheid* is to compile a compendium of trade transactions with South Africa, few countries here would be absent from the list, and Israel would take a minor place even by comparison with those states who are most vocal in their condemnation of *apartheid*, including the countries represented on the special committee. Indeed, if a fair account of economic interests were presented in the report, we would find that South Africa continues to import oil in the same quantities as before, and that the two-way traffic of oil and gold between South Africa and the oil-producing Arab states goes on unabated. The figures relating to trade can be learned from official international publications (including those of the International Monetary Fund) that reveal, as already indicated, that Israel's trade with South Africa still constitutes no more than 0.4 percent of the latter's total foreign trade. Now, we are quite prepared for those economic links to be discussed here with the simple proviso that precisely the same standards be applied to every state represented here. If it is economic ties to South Africa that are at issue, let us receive a full account of all trade, investment, tourism, gold purchases, oil supplies and visits, both overt and covert, and let us then vote on a separate resolution for every country found to maintain such links.

We have already received evidence (in the Third and Fourth Committees) that indicates that such links are maintained by the very countries who have made such a point of singling out Israel. And we have yet to receive in this forum a full accounting of the millions of petro-dollars spent annually by Arab states in the purchase of South African gold. Of even greater interest is the article published in *The New York Times* of 17 November 1978, which stated that "ammunition for the (Rhodesian) Security Forces—once in short supply—is reported to come in by a circuitous route from Middle Eastern Arab states."

According to South Africa's own official records of June 1980, exports from South Africa to black Africa in 1979 increased by 39 percent over the previous year. Moreover, South Africa had commercial relations with 46 of the 52 member states of the Organization of African Unity. Consistent press reports also reveal that despite their pious disclaimers in this hall, the Arab petro-hegemonist powers continue to trade billions of dollars' worth of their oil for gold, for foodstuffs and for building materials from South Africa.

How thus can anyone be expected to take seriously a report that in one paragraph describes Israel's infinitesimal trade with South Africa as "an alliance with *apartheid*," while confining itself in the paragraph preceding it to a routine call to "the major trading partners" of South Africa to desist from their commercial activities. This blatant imbalance only goes to prove that the vilification of Israel continues to be the main concern of those who are responsible for drafting the report.

The sections of the report of the Special Committee on Apartheid dealing with nuclear and military collaboration with South Africa refer again to the groundless and false allegations of military ties between Israel and South Africa. The committee preferred to rely on concoctions based on the wildest journalistic speculation and sheer imagination, and never troubled to peruse the relevant UN documentation. The lack of fairness in the committee's report can best be seen in its decision to omit all mention of Israel's letters to the Security Council on the subject in question. This omission of relevant official documentation not only constitutes an affront to the intelligence of member states of the United Nations. but also demonstrates the total lack of integrity characteristic of the special committee's approach to its work. I will, therefore, refer members to an official communication, dated 14 September 1979, in which Israel reconfirmed its undertakings of 7 December 1977 and 3 April 1978,

> that it will comply with Security Council resolution 418 (1977), and accordingly, Israel will not provide South Africa with arms or related materiel of all types, including the sale or transfer of weapons and ammunition, military vehicles and equipment.

The same note also reiterates Israel's commitment of 1 December 1978 that with regard to licences granted in the past relating to the manufacture and maintenance of arms and ammunition, the Government of Israel has called on industry to take measures to terminate such licences, and the Government will not approve any application for renewal or extension of such a license.

Section III of the report is entitled "Military and Nuclear Collaboration." I confess that I read that section no less than four times searching for some mention of nuclear collaboration. There is not a word about it, for the simple reason that such collaboration does not exist. It exists only in the title and in the table of contents of the committee's report, presumably because the committee no longer expects anyone to read the report or take it seriously. The special committee clearly sets no store by official government statements, contained also in official United Nations documents, and proceeds, as in past years, to tabulate false allegations of military ties between Israel and South Africa, thus completely ignoring those government statements. In even greater desperation, the committee has snatched at one or two second- or third-hand reports, gleaned from the realm of newspaper speculation, in an attempt to prove its wholly untenable thesis of nuclear collaboration between Israel and South Africa.

To be sure, had this ridiculous thesis been presented to any impartial forum for an independent verification of the patchwork of fabrications adduced as "hard evidence" and of the logic behind its conclusions, then, clearly, any self-respecting panel of judges would have dismissed it *in limine*.

I therefore wish to reject, categorically, the baseless and unsubstantiated allegations in the report of nuclear and military collaboration between Israel and South Africa.

The committee's special report reaches its ludicrous crescendo by reporting in its last paragraph that "the Directors of the South African Board of Jewish Education were honored by the President of Israel at a special ceremony in Jerusalem in May 1980." Let me inform this Assembly that the event mentioned there is indeed accurately reported. But by what twisted logic can the committee find fault with encouraging education for any sector of the population in South Africa? The whole Jewish people and the people of Israel have nothing to be ashamed about. We are proud to honor an institution that contributes, often under difficult conditions, to the education of our people in the eternal values of Judaism, one of the most humane traditions in history; a tradition that has contributed significantly to the evolution of such sacred concepts as the dignity and equality of man, inalienable human rights, social justice and peace among nations. In this context the Assembly may be interested to know that on 10 November 1980, B'nai Brith, the well-known Jewish service organization, accorded its Janusz Korczak Award for Children's Poetry to Miss Zindzi Mandela, the sixteen-year-old daughter of Mr. Nelson Mandela.

Most regrettably, many of the countries represented here today, although
pretending to be among the most outspoken critics of racism, have cynically
exploited that issue to serve their own nefarious partisan objectives, that have
nothing whatsoever to do with the eradication of racism. On the contrary,
these pretentious critics represent régimes that, themselves, have come to
exemplify the worst evils of discrimination, intolerance and oppression. We
must never lose sight of the fact that many, if not most, of the states that
orchestrate and lead the verbal offensive against Israel, while ostensibly
addressing the problem of *apartheid,* have ruthlessly trampled underfoot
their own minorities and have enslaved their peoples under cruel dictatorships. Widespread imprisonment without trial, disappearances of alleged political opponents, degradation and torture, summary executions and
wholesale butchery have become their hallmarks.

Among the countries represented on the Special Committee Against
Apartheid we note, for example, Syria. The brutal policies of Syria's ruling
Alawite minority have claimed thousands of victims and in 1982 culminated
in the horrifying massacre of between 10,000 and 25,000 people and the
annihilation of whole families at Hama; the orphaning of an estimated 20,000
of that town's children, and the widespread devastation of the town's historic
quarter. The savage character of the Syrian régime was also pointed out
recently in a special report of Amnesty International, that described not only
the atrocities committed by Syrian forces in Hama, but also cited overwhelming evidence showing that over the years thousands of people have
been harassed, arbitrarily arrested, horribly tortured and even summarily
executed by Syrian security forces.

Algeria, another member of the special committee, is noted for its oppression of the native Berbers, who are denied the right to separate cultural
expression.

The Eastern-bloc states and some others as well have persisted in denying
their citizens the most basic freedoms, and have thus violated various international treaties to which they are signatories; indeed they have violated the
United Nations Charter itself.

Outside the special committee, but very outspoken nevertheless, are such
countries as Libya and Iraq. The fanaticism and extremely oppressive
character of Libya's régime has become notorious. Indeed, the hysteria that
marks the religious intolerance of Libya's dictator has recently reached a
higher pitch as Colonel Khaddafi has increasingly taken to openly inciting
against people of other faiths, particularly Christians—as, for example, in his
speech of 1 September 1983 on the anniversary of his coup. Iraq, too, has
become infamous for its own brand of bloody suppression of human liberties
and the cruel persecution of its Kurdish and Assyrian minorities.

In conducting their cynical campaign against Israel in the context of
apartheid, Arab states and their allies conveniently manoeuvre attention

away from their own central role in the history of racism against black Africans. For centuries, the slave trade in Africa was dominated by Arab traders and in certain Arab countries today slavery still exists. Arab brutalization of black Africans was recalled in the 17 February 1973 issue of Ghana's *Weekly Spectator*, which wrote that, during Ghana's struggle for independence, Arab merchants "constituted themselves into a volunteer force and with batons cudgelled down freedom fighters in the streets of Accra in open daylight." Khaddafi's calls for a *jihad*—a holy war—against Christianity in Africa led the black African Archbishop of Abidjan to raise the question in the Milan newspaper *Avenire* (19 June 1974) whether this might mean a return to the days when eighty thousand Africans a year were enslaved by the "Arab colonialists." Arab economic domination led Joseph Nyerere, the brother of Tanzania's president, to write that

> . . . Arabs, our former slave masters, are not prepared to abandon the rider-and-horse relationship. We have not forgotten that they used to drive us like herds of cattle and sell us as slaves. (Zambia *Daily Mail*, 21 June 1974)

Most regrettably, the apparatus of the United Nations has been harnessed to the campaign to defame Israel. The United Nations Special Committee Against Apartheid has been at the forefront of this campaign with its annual mendacious reports alleging that Israel has been "collaborating" with South Africa. It has also organized an "international conference" in Vienna between 11 and 13 July 1983 for the purpose of perpetuating that falsehood. By its involvement in this unsavory exercise, the Special Committee Against Apartheid gave official United Nations backing to a partisan conference. Thus, the United Nations once again squandered and misused international funds to finance a nefarious partisan venture rather than worthy projects that would have been in true keeping with the purposes of the United Nations Charter.

Another ominous development has been manifested in the related activities of the United Nations Center Against Apartheid. Forces extraneous to the United Nations system have turned the Center Against Apartheid into a tool to serve their own interests that, more often than not, have nothing in common with the purposes of the United Nations. Indeed, one of the most blatant examples of such partisanship was evident in the role fulfilled by the Center Against Apartheid in connection with the conference held in Vienna in July 1983. The initiative for that gathering came from organizations outside the United Nations system. I do not need to elaborate on the character and orientation of the three well-known Soviet front organizations which sponsored the conference—the Afro-Asian People's Solidarity Organization, the Organization of African Trade Union Unity, and the World

Peace Council. Obviously, they sought to manipulate the Center Against Apartheid and the said conference for their own political objectives, that have no bearing whatsoever on the genuine struggle against *apartheid*.

The democratic nations would be deluding themselves and making a very serious mistake if they were to assume that the position adopted by the Center Against Apartheid and the Vienna conference constitutes solely an attack upon Israel's reputation and legitimacy. While the reputation of a member state of the United Nations is certainly a matter that should not be taken lightly, what is at stake here transcends that question; there are ramifications here involving many other arenas as well.

These ramifications must be of vital concern to all democratic nations in this Organization. In any event, we must not become silent partners to the constant undermining and discreditation by the Center Against Apartheid of the United Nations system in general, and of the Secretariat in particular.

Those who exploit the *apartheid* issue for their own ends belittle the injustices suffered by those subjected to the scourge of racism and play upon the misery of the victims of bigotry. Indeed, the countries arrayed against us view the victims of *apartheid* as mere pawns to be used in the pursuit of other objectives.

It is, indeed, disheartening that the effort needed to eradicate racism is thus diverted to vitriolic attacks upon my country, and that the United Nations' scarce funds are squandered in the financing of that vituperative hate campaign. Moreover, the attempt to paint Israel as a proponent of racism is a vile manoeuvre worthy only of contempt. We urge all those who sincerely aspire to rid our world, once and for all, of the evils of racism, intolerance and fanaticism to turn their backs on such cynical and devious policies.

Israel's position concerning *apartheid* and other manifestations of racial discrimination is clear: we oppose bigotry completely and unreservedly, wherever and whenever it emerges. We have made this position known to the Government of South Africa on numerous occasions. By this direct approach, rather than through acrimonious rhetoric, we believe that the cause of eliminating racial discrimination is better served.

Our position on *apartheid* remains unchanged. It is the same today as it was in the 1950s and the 1960s. Those were the years when few nations enjoyed the respect of African states as did Israel. It was not only sympathy for the modern-day victims of racism that motivated us to seek out the friendship of the newly emerging and independent African states, but also a strong sense of identification born of our own historical experience. Indeed, it is no wonder that almost eighty years ago Theodore Herzl, the founding father of modern Zionism, compared the oppression of blacks in Africa to that which the Jews themselves had suffered, and he vowed that when he had witnessed the redemption of his own people, Israel, he would work for freedom in Africa. Israel remained faithful to this noble legacy, placing at the disposal of the African nations its own experience in making the transition from an underdeveloped to a progressive economy and by devising methods to share that experience with the emergent African countries. Israel's contribution to the African continent was acknowledged as recently as 20 October 1979 by the Reverend Charles Kenyatta, who wrote in the *Amsterdam News* of Harlem:

> One tiny nation has contributed more in foreign technical aid to Black African nations than any or all of the oil-rich Arab bloc. That nation is Israel.

Those who persist, then, in confounding and confusing the issues before us today by seeking to exploit the world's justified abhorrence of *apartheid* and by turning this forum into yet another Middle East debate in which they can pursue their relentless campaign of hatred, do not merely diminish the gravity of the injustices perpetrated in the name of racism and racial discrimination, but sow division in a place where consensus is necessary and vital to remove discrimination and restore human dignity. The specious singling out of Israel for its alleged relations with South Africa, therefore, serves no useful purpose, aside from the fruitless campaign of political warfare to which some states here are clearly addicted.

As far as Israel's position is concerned, it could not have been summed up better than by our former Prime Minister, Golda Meir. In her autobiography, she wrote:

> We share with the Africans not only the challenge posed by the need for rapid development, but also the memory of centuries of suffering. Oppression, discrimination, slavery—these are not just catchwords for Jews or for Africans. They refer not to experiences undergone hundreds of years ago by half-forgotten ancestors, but to torment and degradation experienced only yesterday.

"The bond of real brotherhood and of shared aspirations" between Africans and Jews, to which she so often referred, will outlive the dead wood of lies and slander accumulated by the special committee and by this Assembly.

Israel's Jewish heritage and the multiracial background of its citizens strengthen our opposition to any policy or system that seeks to humiliate others and deprive them of their basic rights due to race, religion, creed or color. Those states which sincerely seek to rid our world of racism must address the problem directly. Those who sincerely oppose racism in all its forms must release themselves from the spell cast by the cynics, bigots and opportunists. Only through such an approach can the victims of bigotry expect a better future. Those countries that genuinely stand against racism and racial discrimination will find in Israel an active ally, ever ready—in spirit, thought and deed—to join in the common effort for the eradication of these evils.

Because Israel has been singled out as the only country in the world for specific condemnation on its own in a special resolution, my delegation will not participate in the voting on the issues before us. We take this stand to express our abhorrence at the cynical debasement of this entire discussion. However, in order to leave no doubt as to our position on *apartheid* and our irrevocable opposition to racism in any form, we shall vote in favor of the resolution that offers tribute to the memory of leaders and outstanding personalities who have made significant contributions to the struggle of the oppressed peoples.

15

On Soviet Hypocrisy

A

The Soviet Invasion of Afghanistan

Statement made in the UN General Assembly on 14 January 1980.

Israel joins all those nations from every corner of the globe who have condemned unambiguously the Soviet invasion and occupation of Afghanistan. We cannot accept the explanations offered by the Soviet Union for its actions, for they violate common sense, not to speak of the fundamental norms of international law, as reflected also in the Charter of the United Nations.

Israel shares the apprehensions expressed by the majority of the member states of this Organization at the military intervention by the Soviet Union in Afghanistan. This massive and naked aggression has far-reaching implications that threaten the fundamental balance of the international system. Beyond that, Israel's concerns are even more immediate, specific and concrete. For we are part of the geographical region into which the Soviet Union has marched so rudely and brutally.

We are part of a region that has been vulnerable for decades to the expansionist designs of the Soviet Union. Our region has witnessed the brutality and callousness of the Soviet Union as it seeks to further its expansionist aims. Experience shows that, when it suits the Soviet Union, it does not hesitate to violate the most elementary norms of conduct among nations or to place twisted and arbitrary constructions on the Charter of the United Nations, and its purposes and principles. When the Soviet Union's imperialistic and hegemonistic ambitions are concerned, it is prepared to ride shamelessly roughshod over any state which is in its way.

The Soviet invasion of Afghanistan gives particular grounds for international concern because we are confronted here with an act of blatant aggression by a super-power. The security of the Soviet Union and its military might are based on a vast army and on a gigantic arsenal of ultra-sophisticated weapons, backed up by extraordinary strategic depth.

Many states here would be content if they had a small fraction of the security enjoyed by the Soviet Union. But the Soviet Union, after decades of expansionism and consolidation, is still not satisfied with its power, and is apparently still bent on buttressing itself with a ring of satellites and puppets. It seems to matter little to the Soviet Union if, in the process, it crushes the independence of states, the freedom of nations and the human rights of their peoples. Similarly it seems to matter little if it undermines the very basis of the international system which has been built up so laboriously and at such great cost in terms of human and other resources since the end of World War II.

Certain states among us have very concrete reasons to fear external threats of a military nature. For these states the problems of self-defense and security are real and grave. By comparison, who and what has the Soviet Union to fear? Who would challenge the security, the sovereignty, the territorial integrity of a global power such as the Soviet Union? It has at its disposal not only a military deterrent capacity of huge dimensions but also a vast array of political and diplomatic means to make its weight felt. The Soviet Union has been accorded within this Organization a special responsibility for the preservation of international peace and security. A corollary of that responsibility is found in the special rights conferred on the Soviet Union as a permanent member of the Security Council. But these privileges surely do not entitle the Soviet Union to trample underfoot the rights of other states.

As we have been reminded by various speakers, it is the Soviet Union that has over the years launched numerous initiatives in this Organization against intervention in the internal affairs of other states and against the use of force in international relations. The sheer hypocrisy and cynicism of the Soviet Union's pontificating and posturing has again been exposed by its naked aggression against Afghanistan. The principles it has so piously preached at others count for nothing when the leaders of the Kremlin decide to impose their will and grip on other states.

Mention has been made here of Soviet actions in Hungary and in Czechoslovakia in 1956 and 1968, respectively. The analogy is not complete. Until recently Afghanistan was an independent, non-aligned nation. It first fell victim to Soviet subversion and was then overrun by tens of thousands of Soviet forces, laden with tanks and guns, and backed up by airborne support units and logistics. This most recent manifestation of Soviet aggression and expansionism coupled with the arrogance flaunted by the Soviet Union in the face of the international community necessarily raises the question of what country is next on the Soviet Union's list.

In this day and age, independence and liberty are indivisible. Every state that cherishes its sovereignty must speak out. Each country must raise its voice in protest.

In the 1930s the world stood idly by when the aggressors of another age swallowed up one small state after another.

The entire world paid a heavy price for its complacency, its passivity and its acquiescence in the acts of the aggressors.

We must not repeat that mistake. The nations of the world must act to check aggression and to ensure that that terrible price is not paid again.

B

The Soviet-Nazi Pact of 23 August 1939

Statement made in the UN General Assembly on 2 February 1982 in response to a Soviet statement of the previous day in which Israel was likened to Nazi Germany.

A flood of invective against Israel has been let loose again in this hall, and for many of the speakers this kind of speech is apparently in the nature of a ritualistic incantation. The fact that this kind of verbal pogrom is severely damaging what little is left of the badly battered prestige of the United Nations is apparently of no consequence to the slanderers. Nor are they impressed by the fact that even within this hall representatives have massively "voted with their feet"—to use a Leninist expression—by absenting themselves from this charade as much as possible.

All this, however, cannot exempt the participants in these proceedings from observing a modicum of decency that is obligatory even in exchanges of this kind. To our regret, the representative of the Soviet Union, in his statement yesterday, saw fit to overstep the bounds of elementary decency in drawing an obscene comparison between the accursed régime of Hitler's Germany and Israel—the homeland of the people that was the foremost target of Nazi lunacy, both before and during World War II.

This is not the first time that a Soviet representative indulges in such despicable desecration of the memory of 6 million Jewish martyrs—the victims of Nazi tyranny. Soviet representatives apparently believe—like the Nazi Goebbels before them—that the mere repetition of a big lie makes it stick eventually, however absurd and however sacrilegious. There is no redeeming feature to the repetition of lies and obscenities. Their repetition merely heightens the obscenities.

Let me tell the representative of the Soviet Union that my people never compromised with Nazi tyranny and never signed a pact with Hitler's Germany as did the Soviet Union when it concluded with it its infamous Non-Aggression Treaty on 23 August 1939. That treaty not only precipitated World War II, with all the resultant misery and destruction, but more specifically, it provided for the joint dismemberment by Nazi Germany and the Soviet Union of Poland, the disappearance of which was hailed by the then Foreign Minister of the Soviet Union, Mr. Molotov, in his address to the Supreme Soviet of the U.S.S.R. on 31 October 1939, when he termed Poland "that monster child of the Treaty of Versailles."

In view of the events of recent weeks in Poland, it is particularly pertinent to draw this Assembly's attention to the Secret Additional Protocol appended to the Pact on Non-Aggression of 23 August 1939. It reads as follows:

> On the occasion of the signature of the Non-Aggression Pact between the German Reich and the Union of Socialist Soviet Republics, the undersigned plenipotentiaries of each of the two parties discussed in strictly confidential conversations the question of the boundary of their respective spheres of influence in Eastern Europe. These conversations led to the following conclusions:

> Article 1. In the event of a territorial and political rearrangement in the areas belonging to the Baltic States (Finland, Estonia, Latvia, Lithuania), the northern boundary of Lithuania shall represent the boundary of the spheres of influence of Germany and the U.S.S.R. In this connection the interest of Lithuania in the Vilna area is recognized by each party.

> Article 2. In the event of a territorial and political rearrangement of the areas belonging to the Polish State the spheres of influence of Germany and the U.S.S.R. shall be bounded approximately by the line of the rivers Narew, Vistula and San.
> The question of whether the interests of both parties make desirable the maintenance of an independent Polish State and how such a State should be bounded can only be definitely determined in the course of further political developments.
> In any event both Governments will resolve this question by means of a friendly agreement.

> Article 3. With regard to south-eastern Europe, attention is called by the Soviet side to its interest in Bessarabia. The German side declares its complete political disinterestedness in these areas.

Article 4. This Protocol shall be treated by both parties as strictly secret.

Moscow, August 23, 1939
For the Government of the German Reich:
V. Ribbentrop
Plenipotentiary of the Government of the U.S.S.R.:
V. Molotov.
(Whiteman's *Digest of International Law*, 3:179)

It should be noted that in this protocol Nazi Germany and the Soviet Union speak of their respective spheres of interest. This term of course has a well-known colonialist and imperialist ring, thus revealing the true character of Soviet foreign policy.

In compliance with the said protocol, the Soviet Union, in September 1939, joined Nazi Germany in overrunning and dismembering Poland. On 28 September 1939 it concluded with Nazi Germany a Frontier and Friendship Treaty to which was appended the following declaration:

After the Government of the German Reich and the Government of U.S.S.R. have, by means of the Treaty signed today, definitively settled the problems arising from the collapse of the Polish state and have thereby created a sure foundation for a lasting peace in Eastern Europe, they mutually express their conviction that it would serve the true interests of all peoples to put an end to the state of war existing at present between Germany on the one side, and England and France on the other. Both Governments will therefore direct their common efforts, jointly with other friendly powers if occasion arises, toward attaining this goal as soon as possible.

Should, however, the efforts of the two Governments remain fruitless, this would demonstrate the fact that England and France are responsible for the continuation of the war, whereupon, in case of the continuation of the war, the Governments of Germany and of U.S.S.R. will engage in mutual consultations with regard to necessary measures.
(Whiteman's *Digest of International Law*, 3:184–85)

The representative of the Soviet Union should be among the last to invoke the memories of the 1930s or to draw comparisons based on them. But since he chose to speak of the catastrophe that culminated in World War II, he would do well to ponder who abetted the Nazi policy of aggression and expansion, accompanied by claims of living space, who acted as its accomplice, and who supplied Germany with strategic materials, including foodstuffs, raw materials, minerals and oil, until June 1941.

C

Soviet Concern for Holy Places

Statement made in the UN Security Council on 19 April 1982.

We have been treated here to a statement by the representative of the Soviet Union, who has joined the list of bigots who profess to show concern for the sanctity of Jerusalem. I welcome his participation because it puts this entire exercise in its proper perspective. One could not fail to be moved by the display of concern of the representative of the Soviet Union for the sanctity of the holy places. After all, his country has an enviable record in preserving holy places all over the Soviet Union. I know, of course, that the Soviet constitution guarantees freedom of religion, but then it also guarantees freedom of expression, freedom of association, freedom of movement and virtually all basic freedoms. The Soviet constitution also introduces the right to conduct atheistic propaganda while prohibiting the right to reply, or even to conduct religious education for children and young people. In effect, this means that there is a constant bombardment of anti-religious propaganda to which no redress is even available.

How does this work out in practice? Over the years the Soviet Union has closed tens of thousands of churches, synagogues and mosques. At best they are used as barns or stables; at worst, as museums of atheism. Those who, for instance, have been to the former Cathedral of Saint Isaac in Leningrad know what has happened to that Christian holy place. Those who have been to the former Kazan Cathedral in Leningrad know what has happened there: it is now a museum of atheism.

The Moslems of the Soviet Union have not fared any better. There are about fifty million of them—one of the largest Moslem communities in the world. But the number of trained ulema—Moslem religious clergy—is derisively low. There are only two medreses—two theological colleges—one of which provides the equivalent of secondary school education where boys can enter only after completing their military service, and the other, supposedly higher Moslem theological education. Students are not accepted every year and the total student population of these medreses for the six-year course is about seventy young men in each. The essential qualification for entry is a good knowledge of Arabic, something that is extremely difficult to acquire outside the medrese since there are very few people who now know this language in central Asia, and, religious education being banned, none of the ulema dare risk teaching it.

Now what has happened to the mosques in the Soviet Union? There were about twenty-five thousand mosques in the Soviet Union sixty years ago. There are 398 left—so called working mosques—despite the fact that the

Moslem population has increased considerably over the past sixty years. Religious publications are almost nonexistent and copies of the Koran are in very short supply. If the representative of the Soviet Union wants to check on my figures, I have the honor to refer him to an article published in 1979 in a book entitled *Religion in Communist Lands,* and the article from which I am quoting is by A. Benningsen and Chantal Lemercier-Quelquejay, "Official Islam in the Soviet Union."

Thus we have been treated here again to a manifestation of the well-known Soviet cynicism. I know, it is much more convenient for the representative of the Soviet Union to keep this Council busy with alleged desecrations of holy places in other parts of the world than to discuss the situation in Kampuchea or the activities of Soviet-Cuban mercenaries in various parts of Africa, or the situation in Poland, or for that matter, in Afghanistan. How many mosques, Ambassador Ovinnikov, has the Soviet army of occupation destroyed in Afghanistan over the past two years? Perhaps you could oblige the Council by enlightening us on these and other relevant facts before leaping into this debate as the protector of holy places.

16

The Holocaust Remembered

Address delivered at Yeshiva University, New York, on 23 April 1979, at the annual memorial observance of Remembrance Day for Jewish Martyrdom and Heroism.

It is difficult for me to speak of the Holocaust in the abstract. The Holocaust wiped out most of my mother's family. My grandfather, all eight of my mother's brothers and sisters, their spouses, twenty-two of their children, some of them married with children of their own—all perished at the hands of Nazi Germany and its Fascist collaborators in other European countries. Likewise, most of my father's uncles and aunts and many of his cousins and their children became the victims of what Sir Winston Churchill called "a monstrous tyranny never surpassed in the dark lamentable catalogue of human crime." Fate also willed it that I should celebrate my own bar mitzvah in the Bergen-Belsen concentration camp, and that experience remains an integral part of my life today in my role as Israel's ambassador to the United Nations. Indeed, these two events in my life symbolize the road traversed collectively by the Jewish people over the past three decades. From the depths of persecution, anguish, misery, death and destruction, the Jewish people has defiantly risen again—as it has on so many occasions in the past—and has miraculously staged a national renaissance of which few of us would have dreamed at the end of World War II. What is more, our generation has been granted a privilege denied to eighty successive generations of Jews: in the aftermath of the greatest tragedy that befell our people in the course of its long history of martyrdom, we, of all Jewish generations, were permitted to witness the reemergence of Jewish statehood and Jewish sovereignty in Eretz Yisrael, the Land of Israel.

Nothing better demonstrates the immense difficulty we have today in discussing and understanding the Holocaust than the recent controversy over the television series by that name. On the one hand, many of us felt that a soap opera package interspersed with commercials served only to diminish the enormity of the tragedy that befell our people. On the other hand, we all had to admit that millions throughout the world who had never heard of the Holocaust became aware of it for the first time through this series, and that perhaps they *could* only have grasped it in such a watered-down form.

Therein lies the dilemma. How, with the passage of time, do we remember the Holocaust without ever diminishing its magnitude or losing sight of its profound significance? The issue is not simple "remembering." That, perhaps, we may finally be learning to do. The question, rather, is *how* we remember. To tackle that question honestly is no easy task, for it requires not only overcoming deep psychological resistance but also a willingness to face squarely the issue of *responsibility*, for actions both then and now. I feel duty-bound to address the question I have posed as directly and straightforwardly as I possibly can.

I speak here tonight as a survivor of the Holocaust, as well as a Jew and as an Israeli, rather than as Israel's envoy to the United Nations.

In the years immediately following World War II, it was extraordinarily difficult for the Jewish people as a whole, and for the survivors in particular, to talk about the Holocaust at all. A certain sense of shame remained attached to every memory of the event. In an almost unspoken way, the survivors were given to feel that they should somehow apologize for their own survival; that they themselves were somehow to blame; that they should have resisted; that the victims of the greatest crime in human history somehow contributed to their own doom. The Jewish world bore a different burden of shame—that they had not responded as they should have during the war to the plight of their brethren in Europe. With such feelings, often unconscious, rarely openly discussed, we entered a conspiracy of silence following the war. We lived in a world of denial.

That denial was not confined to the Jewish people. It took years of pressure and persuasion to add Hebrew and Yiddish inscriptions to the already existing memorials in German, French, English and other languages at the sites of the former death camps. To this day, at the sites of many of the most infamous extermination camps, especially in Eastern Europe, the victims are described as Polish nationals, French nationals, Russian nationals and others, but never as Jews. Many countries still implicitly deny that the overwhelming majority of victims came to these sites as Jews, and died there *because* they were Jews. But to refer to them in any other way is a desecration of their memory. Indeed, it amounts to an attempt to destroy even their memory, following the destruction of their physical existence.

However, the major problem today is perhaps not primarily one of forgetfulness or an attempt to deny the Holocaust for anti-Semitic reasons, although forgetfulness and anti-Semitic attitudes certainly still exist, as evidenced in recent years by the flood of publications that either deny the very fact of the Holocaust or are bent on reducing the numbers of its victims; as if the murder of "merely" 1 or 2 million Jews were morally different from the murder of 6 million. Rather, the problem lies in the quality of the memory itself. There has undoubtedly been a real growth of consciousness among both Jews and non-Jews that has taken us a long way from the period of denial and silence that followed the war. Looking back over the last three decades, I see a major turning point in this regard, one agonizing and wrenching experience that forced us to come to terms with our history and to look reality squarely in the face: the trial of Adolf Eichmann in Jerusalem in 1961.

The significance of that event was not only the capture and execution of one of the chief Nazi criminals, although that in itself was important. That the murderer could be brought to justice by and in the State of Israel demonstrated decisively that Jewish blood could no longer be shed with impunity. It was a most poignant manifestation of the dramatic change that had occurred in the destiny of the Jewish people. But, significant as it was, that was not, I believe, Prime Minister Ben-Gurion's primary motive in ordering the capture of one of the most infamous architects of the "Final Solution." If Eichmann's life had been the issue, he could more easily have been killed in Argentina.

The trial itself was a catharsis; the horrors were described, aloud, in excruciating detail, and in their true dimensions, by the survivors. The facts emerged, agonizingly, from the closet, and were presented to the youth of Israel, to the Jews of the Diaspora and to the world, as *their* history and *their* reality. It could no longer be hidden. For the first time, before an international audience, the truth had been told, and it became possible to speak of the unspeakable. We had awakened from the nightmare and we demanded of ourselves and of the world—to remember, to learn, to analyze, and, if possible, to understand the Holocaust.

The degree of misunderstanding that, in fact, existed, as well as the agonizing process of re-awakening, could not be better demonstrated than by the story of a young Israeli girl, twelve years old, who asked her parents during the Eichmann trial whether they had voted for Ben-Gurion in the recent parliamentary elections. Yes, they told her, they had indeed. In that case, she asked solemnly, I request that you *not* do so in the future. Why, her parents inquired? Because, she said, Ben-Gurion did not send our paratroopers to Europe during the war to rescue the Jews of Europe.

The process of education, in which the Eichmann trial proved such a landmark, has not been an easy one. With the passage of time, as we have become more removed from the event, it is sometimes difficult even for those of us who went through the horrors to comprehend the depth to which man's inhumanity to man can descend. The cruelty was such that the psychological defense mechanisms of most sound and healthy people reject a full comprehension of the barbarities. So incredible do they seem in retrospect they must surely be figments of sick people's imaginations, inventions, horror stories, not real human behavior. I myself am often incredulous at the brutality I witnessed as a child. Did it really happen? I ask myself. Is it not, perhaps, some horrible nightmare that exists only in the darkest recesses of my own imagination? How do I grasp the reality?

Indeed, as the facts emerged, the reality seemed often stranger than fiction. Could it be that the commandant of an extermination camp could spend the day supervising the ghastly mass murder of thousands of individuals, including women and small children, and then return home to *his* wife and children to relax and enjoy a Brahms symphony? Shortly after the Eichmann trial, and indeed as one of the results of that trial, a series of trials against Nazi criminals was started in western Germany. At one of these, in 1963, the top executioners of Auschwitz were put on trial at Frankfurt. The judge ordered psychiatric examination for all the defendants. Everyone was pronounced "normal." Is psychiatry at fault? Or does the Holocaust simply reveal in its most extreme form an indescribably ugly component of "normal" human nature? The playwright Peter Weiss clearly took the latter view in his play *The Investigation*, based entirely on transcripts of the Auschwitz trial, in which he arranged the chairs of the defendants in such a way that it was unclear where the stage ended and where the first row of the audience began. His message was clear: are we merely spectators? Or were we all and are we still, in some way, participants?

One of the primary effects of the newly awakened consciousness was highly salutary. As the survivors learned of the hostile environment within which they had suffered, when they saw their own situation in a wider context, they reassessed, for the first time, their own self-image. They noted that as a rule the male population had been called up by the Germans for forced labor so that the first victims of deportations were usually women, children, the old and the disabled. In these circumstances resistance was well-nigh impossible, especially since the victims had been weakened through constant starvation and humiliation, and since the Germans employed the subtlest techniques of deception to create an atmosphere of total dependence, in which the victims fluctuated wildly between renewed hope and abject despair.

This is not all that the survivors learned. They saw that other peoples, in a much better position to resist, succumbed totally to the German onslaught. The entire people of Poland, living in their own communities and on their own land, not in the midst of an often hostile population, nevertheless crumbled in a shorter period of time than the fighters of the Warsaw Ghetto. France, with a modern and well-equipped army, was overrun in a matter of days. In Russia, millions were slaughtered by the invading Germans. Tens of thousands of Red Army officers captured by the Germans were murdered by their captors without resistance, after having been starved and humiliated by them, in a manner virtually identical to the extermination policies practiced by them against defenseless Jewish women and children. Indeed, far from being ashamed of any supposed Jewish passivity, the survivors learned that the extent of Jewish resistance was remarkable, in the circumstances. The survivors gradually shed their shame, and learned to take pride in the Jewish uprisings at Warsaw, at Treblinka, at Vilna, at Bialystok, at Cracow and at Czestochowa, and they learned to understand the true dynamics of their own painful experience. Moreover, they learned to take pride in an even greater act of collective heroism: their ability to preserve their human dignity and their Jewish identity and heritage under the most adverse of circumstances.

And herein, I believe, lies the answer to the question with which I began: *How* should we recall the Holocaust? Not, I submit, in the abstract. Not in purely philosophical terms. But in terms of people and their actual experiences and responsibility. Human history is made by human beings. And if we are truly to remember and at least attempt an understanding of the Holocaust, it is not enough to ask *"What* happened." We must also ask: *Who?*—Who made it happen? Who were the murderers? Who were the victims? Who were the bystanders? And who are we, the spectators, looking back to the event from a distance?

It is a difficult approach, for it entails the deepest soul-searching. Above all, it cannot avoid the question of responsibility. If those who make history are to be held responsible for their own actions, it is the duty of historians to subject that responsibility to the closest scrutiny. The survivors, I believe, are the only participants who have, through an agonizing reappraisal of their own experiences, begun to come to terms with their responsibility. More and more of them, having shed the false burden of shame, have emerged with a new burden, and perhaps a greater one. It is a sense of responsibility. If I, belonging as I do to a generation of Jewish youth in Europe few of whom were privileged to witness the end of World War II, survived Bergen-Belsen, when so many of my relatives, friends and classmates perished, then I surely have a responsibility to represent *them* before posterity. I owe them more than I can ever give—the responsibility of bringing their message to the next generation, of telling their story, and of calling their persecutors to account.

But what then is the responsibility of others? What, for example, is the responsibility of the German people? In referring here to the German people I mean, of course, the people that lived within the boundaries of the German Reich after 1938. In that territory there are now three states—the Federal Republic of Germany, East Germany, and Austria. For the German people to plead ignorance is to deny responsibility and to abstain from human history. It is no answer to the question we are asking. For the plain fact is that the German people, even if they did not know the exact details of Auschwitz, knew enough to determine the course of their own history. They knew about the Nuremberg Laws of 1935, that imposed an array of discriminatory legislation against German citizens of Jewish ancestry. They knew about the opening of the Dachau concentration camp as early as March 1933. And they both knew and witnessed the brutalities of the Kristallnacht in November 1938. They knew enough, in short, for people with any kind of normal, moral sensitivity to raise searching questions about their own behavior.

Even the gassing was known. On our way to Bergen-Belsen in 1944, we were taken off the train at Linz, in Austria, for a bath and disinfection. Linz, incidentally, was the town where Hitler grew up. As my mother and my nine-year-old sister were standing in line for the women's bath-house, my sister became hysterical and began shouting in German:

Mutti du wirst sehen, man wird uns vergasen.
[Mummy, you'll see—they're going to gas us.]

If a nine-year-old girl knew that Jews were being gassed by the Germans and even associated bath-houses with this process, many German adults knew it, too. Not only did many who lived in towns near the camps smell the stench of burning human bodies and see tens of thousands shipped into the camps, never to return; tens of thousands of Germans were directly engaged in the entire operation, employed in the railroad stations, managing the slave factories, working in the camps themselves. These people talked of what they saw to their relatives and to their friends. Only if we were to assume that machines, not men, perpetrated these crimes could we avoid the question of responsibility.

If ignorance is no plea, then the claim that a totalitarian régime prevented dissent, that others in similar circumstances would have responded similarly, is equally an evasion of responsibility. The existential fact remains that nazism arose in Germany, and that Hitler had mass popular support for his anti-Jewish policies and measures. This is not to say that such horrors *could not* happen elsewhere. But the fact is that millions of Germans went along with—and even enthusiastically supported—the myriad discriminatory steps against Jews that led inexorably to Auschwitz. And throughout the twelve years of Nazi rule over Germany there was not one single popular uprising against the Hitlerite tyranny. From the Nuremberg Laws to the yellow armbands, the same question must be asked: What was the responsibility of the German people?

And what is it today? What of the thousands of criminals directly involved in the murders who have been able, under all kinds of pretexts, to evade justice? What of the procrastination and evasion tactics not uncommon even within the judiciary itself, evidenced in the Maidanek trial in Düsseldorf that last week brought about worldwide criticism of the German judicial system? What about the interminable delays in bringing criminals to trial? And what about the attempts to apply to the crimes perpetrated by the Nazi criminals the common statutes of limitations, in utter disregard of the enormity of those crimes? Has German society yet taken real responsibility for its own history or is it missing an historical opportunity to do so? If it waits for the Holocaust generation to die out, this opportunity will have been missed forever.

But not only the Germans participated in the Holocaust. A heavy responsibility lies with the other peoples of Europe, too. Most, today, disclaim any responsibility, and are only too pleased to see the entire burden of guilt shifted to the Germans. The fact is that very few acted to save their Jewish populations. Some did nothing. Others had created enough of an anti-Semitic climate in their own lands for the Nazi message to fall on fertile ground. Many of them helped create conditions which made an effective Jewish resistance and Jewish rescue operation virtually impossible. Some actively collaborated, assisted in the deportations and even participated in the massacres.

It need not have been so. Those peoples who were determined to save Jewish lives succeeded in doing so. The Danes saved almost their entire Jewish population by smuggling them to Sweden. Only one hundred fifty Danish Jews were deported to Theresienstadt. Even then, the Danes pestered the Germans so long that a Danish commission of investigation was finally allowed to visit Theresienstadt to ascertain the living conditions of the Danish nationals there. The fact that the Germans deceived that commission is beside the point here. The Tsar of Bulgaria actively opposed the German deportation of Jews and saved tens of thousands of Jewish lives. The Finns resisted every anti-Jewish measure demanded by the Nazis, refusing, for example, even a German demand to dismiss Jewish officers from the Finnish army. Indeed, the Finnish commander-in-chief, General Gustav Mannerheim, became so furious at the German demand that he immediately appointed a Jew as liaison officer with the Germans.

Those who wanted to resist the persecution of the Jews did so even if they happened to be, like Bulgaria and Finland, the allies of Germany. I shall not mention by name those peoples that behaved differently. I only ask—what was their responsibility in the murder of six million Jews?

And what of the free world—those countries that were not under the yoke of Nazi occupation, countries that were either neutral in the war or actively participated in the struggle against the Nazi-Fascist scourge? How did they react to the systematic persecution of German Jews before the war, and to the news of mass killings in the death camps, news that had been verified by the middle of 1942? In most cases the public reacted with righteous outrage and indignation. But none of those countries was willing to relax its stringent immigration regulations. Great Britain even blocked immigration into Palestine, the "Jewish national home" that the League of Nations mandate had entrusted to it. The Evian Conference of July 1938, attended by thirty-two countries, convened by the President of the United States for the purpose of assisting the emigration of refugees from Germany and Austria, ended in complete failure, with no country committing itself to any practical measures. As Evian convened, Hitler jeered that he could

> only hope and expect that the other world which is so sympathetic towards these criminals would at least be generous enough to turn this sympathy into actual aid.

When Evian failed, the Germans drew the obvious conclusion—nobody wanted the Jews. A similar conference in Bermuda, in April 1943, at the very time of the Warsaw Ghetto uprising, also convened to consider the refugee problem and ended just as inconclusively.

As for Allied military action during the war, recently released information raises the question of responsibility to a new level. Undoubtedly, many of you recently read the dramatic report revealing the existence of Allied aerial reconnaissance photographs of the Auschwitz death camp. The photos, taken by American and British reconnaissance planes more than a year before the end of the war, according to *The Washington Post* report of 23 February 1979,

> clearly show the camp's chambers and crematoria where victims' bodies were burned. Several photos show prisoners undergoing disinfection and standing in line to be tattooed. . . .

It is not too late to ask the question again: Why did the Allies never bomb the camps? Why did they never bomb the rail line that took victims to the camps? Five miles from Auschwitz, an I. G. Farben synthetic fuels plant was repeatedly bombed by American and British planes in the last year of the war. Yet Auschwitz was spared, on the sanctimonious pretext that the bombing might kill some of the inmates. By mid-1944, the Allies knew that twelve thousand Jews were being murdered every day at Auschwitz, and that one million Hungarian Jews were at that time being transported to their deaths along an undamaged railway line. But the line to Auschwitz was not a "military" or a "strategic" objective.

There are even more sinister questions that must be probed before we come to terms with the responsibility of the free world. There were, it is now alleged, strong undercurrents of relief in certain chancelleries, that what was happening to the Jews of Europe might have a beneficial effect after the war with regard to the question of Palestine.

But if such questions remain to be asked, we cannot avoid the issue of responsibility when it hits closest to home. The Jewish communities of the free world remained largely incapable either of grasping what was happening in Europe or of responding adequately to it. As news of the horrors gradually unfolded, Jewish life outside Europe went on normally—weddings and bar mitzvahs were celebrated, families took their weekend vacations, concern and outrage were frequently voiced, but in practical terms, caused little disruption to the daily lives of the vast majority of Jews.

Not long ago my attention was drawn to one of the New York Yiddish newspapers, published just a few days after Kristallnacht in November 1938. On one side of the page, framed in a large black border, was a vivid description of the terror that had been unleashed against German Jews the previous week. Right next to that article, literally adjoining the black border, were advertisements inviting people to Lakewood and Atlantic City for Thanksgiving celebrations, as well as an advertisement for the Breakers Hotel in Atlantic City, with a picture of streamers and noise-makers, inviting readers to make advance party reservations for New Year's Eve.

I am not suggesting that the insensitivity of that layout editor reflected the overall attitude of American Jewry. But I *am* insisting that individually and collectively, Jews cannot shirk the question of responsibility that we have posed for others. What did the Jewish communities do? Was it enough? Could they have done more? Did they repress the reality rather than look it squarely in the face? These questions require a degree of soul-searching no less intense than that which the survivors have had to undergo. Indeed, the difficulty and intensity of this process is magnified according to the area of autonomy available to the actor. The more free we are to determine our own actions, the greater is the responsibility which we have for those actions. (And I need not add that inaction is itself a form of action, for it produces no lesser consequences for history than active involvement.)

Finally, if we are to question Jewish responsibility, one must also question that of Christianity, both ideologically and institutionally. There can be little doubt that, over a period of hundreds of years, Christianity laid the ideological basis for the persecutions of the twentieth century. The eternal responsibility of the Jews for the death of Jesus, preached for centuries by Christian priests throughout Europe, had demonized and dehumanized the Jewish people in Christian eyes, an essential prerequisite for the creation of the climate within which Nazi anti-Semitism and persecution could flourish.

Without going into the question at great length, it remains a fact that Christianity, both Catholic and Protestant, did not speak out forcefully and unequivocally against the persecutions, and that thousands of individual priests in the various countries under German occupation actively abetted and assisted the anti-Jewish measures. In my native Slovakia, a Catholic priest, Josef Tiso, presided over the deportation of the Jews in his capacity as president of Slovakia. His ideological mentor had been another Catholic priest, Andrei Hlinka, a leader of the virulently anti-Semitic Slovak Fascist party. In Budapest, a Protestant pastor, Father Kun, was one of the most notorious butchers in charge of one of the firing squads. He daily led Jews in 1944 to the banks of the River Danube and prefaced their execution with the command: "In the Holy Name of Jesus Christ, fire!" There were, of course, many individual priests who acted very differently and who will always hold a special place in our memories for their noble efforts to save Jewish lives. But this cannot blind us to the actual role of institutional Christianity. Let us therefore ask in all candor and sincerity: Is Christianity truly aware of its responsibility for the tragedy that befell the Jewish people and has it done its best to face up to that responsibility?

I certainly do not intend to suggest that my remarks constitute any kind of definitive answer to the question of responsibility. For a start, I have undoubtedly hurt some, though that is certainly not my intention. Secondly, I have spoken in generalities that cannot do justice to the millions of individual deeds, both good and evil, that constitute the history of the Holocaust. I can only hope that I have suggested the vastness of the task that lies ahead if we are to do justice to the memory of the Holocaust victims. Incidentally, if the task is to be accomplished, at least in part, I cannot overemphasize the vital importance of documentation in order to maintain the living reality of the events as time diminishes their immediate impact.

I do not wish to conclude this address with recriminations. There *are* vital lessons that we have already begun to learn from the Holocaust, and it is well at least to mention them, in conclusion.

First, at the root of the Holocaust lay the reality of Jewish homelessness. In that sense at least, the young girl who complained to her parents that Ben-Gurion had not ordered the rescue of the European Jews was correct. Though her historical sense was a little askew, she understood what the rest of the world sometimes has difficulty in understanding—why we take our security so seriously. For Israel, in addition to being the natural expression of Jewish history and national identity, is today vital for the very existence and security of the Jewish people. It is the manifestation of our collective Jewish vow that Jewish blood will no longer be spilled with impunity and that the days of Jewish homelessness and defenselessness are forever over.

Second, we have learned the necessity of Jewish solidarity. Whatever happens to a Jew in one part of the world directly affects every other Jew in the world. The Holocaust experience has undoubtedly lent urgency to the fight to save Soviet Jewry, and it has taught us to stand alongside our persecuted brethren in Arab lands.

Third, we have learned to rely on ourselves. In 1948 and in 1967 we learned again that when the chips are down we stand as alone as we were in the face of the Nazi onslaught. Lest this be misinterpreted as a paranoid reaction to anti-Semitism, I must emphasize that it is not the Jews alone who understand that the outside world will not necessarily extend itself when innocents are in need. Genocide and international barbarism did not cease with Auschwitz and Bergen-Belsen. Who remembers Biafra, Burundi, Bangladesh, Uganda and Cambodia? What help did those innocents receive from the world outside, and with whom does responsibility for those massacres lie? Only with the perpetrators of the crime? Or also with the bystanders, those who trade with the criminals, and those who remain silent? Who can look at the boatloads of Vietnamese refugees floating helplessly from shore to shore, begging for refuge at the doorstep of a world with deaf ears, and not recall the boatloads of Jewish refugees who were the unwanted baggage of a previous generation?

Finally, what happened to the Jewish people contains a powerful lesson for all humanity. For the cruelty perpetrated against one portion of humanity can no sooner be divorced from the rest than can a limb be separated from the human body without severely impairing the function of the whole. Persecution degrades and dehumanizes the persecutor even more than it does the victim.

In the Passover Haggada we read:

בכל דור ודור חייב אדם לראות את עצמו כאילו הוא יצא ממצרים

In each and every generation, it is a man's duty to regard himself as though he went forth out of Egypt.

In the same sense it is the duty of every Jew to regard himself as a survivor of the Holocaust. We are all its survivors. If the parents or grandparents of American Jews had not emigrated to this country before World War II, their children and grandchildren might have been among the victims of the Nazi-Fascist beast. And in a more profound sense, the entire Jewish people is a people of survivors for an additional reason: we are all the descendants of generations of persecuted Jews who miraculously, and through the grace of God, preserved the continuity of our people and ensured its immortality.

Let us therefore remember, and let us bear in mind the wonderful words of the Baal Shem Tov: "Forgetfulness," he said, "leads to exile, while remembrance is the secret of redemption."